Mini Dictionary of Punctuation & Hyphenation

William Gould

MEDWAY

First Published in Great Britain 2004
By MEDWAY Publishing Ltd
152a Park Street Lane, Park Street
St Albans AL2 2AU

© Medway Publishing Ltd 2004

All rights reserved. No part of this
Publication may be reproduced in
any form or by any means without
the prior permission of
Medway Publishing Ltd

ISBN: 1-902712-10-2

Printed in India by Replika Press

Preface

This book has been conceived and produced to meet a dual need. For users and learners of English, the 19 chapters on Punctuation deal with all but the most technical applications of punctuation marks and their accessories, such as spacing and use of boldface and italic letters. The Punctuation section concludes with a chapter on Hyphenation, with advice on how to solve the knotty problem of where to split a word that is too long to fit at the end of a line of text. This is followed by a Hyphenation Dictionary, which lists 12,000 words of more than one syllable with indications of where they can be hyphenated if necessary. Finally there is a glossary of grammatical terms.

The production of this book has required two specialist skills, and the publishers wish gratefully to acknowledge the people who supplied them. The knowledge of grammar and working practice of modern English usage – essential for the creation of the chapters on Punctuation – was contributed by William Gould. His in-depth experience gained while writing and editing various dictionaries and encyclopaedias has enabled him to provide a comprehensive and definitive account of the latest views on English punctuation.

Correct hyphenation practice is also an editorial skill, but one that has now become the province of the experienced proofreader. For many years, Fred Gill has fulfilled this role for publishers, typesetters and printers, and has used his extensive experience in compiling the Hyphenation Dictionary.

J.O.E.C. London, 2003

Contents

Introduction 1
The Purpose of Punctuation 1
A Brief History of Punctuation 2
A History of the Full Point ....

1. **Full Point** 9
   Full Point at the End of a Sentence 9
   Full Point and Quotation Marks 11
   Non-Punctuational Uses 12
   History of the Comma 17

2. **Comma** 18
   Commas between Clauses 18
   Commas and Relative Clauses 23
   Parenthetical Commas 24
   Commas in Quotations 28
   Commas in Lists 29
   Commas between Adjectives 30
   Non-Punctuational Uses 31
   History of the Semicolon 35

3. **Semicolon** 36
   Semicolons between Clauses 36
   Semicolons in Lists 39
   Non-Punctuational Uses 40

4. **Colon** 41
   Colon in a Sentence 41
   History of the Colon 42
   Non-Punctuational Uses 46

5. **Parentheses** 50
   Symbols of Parenthesis 50
   Parentheses 51
   Punctuation and Parentheses 54
   Square Brackets 55
   Other Types of Brackets 57
   Brackets within Brackets 57
   Non-Punctuational Uses 57
   Braces 58

6. **Dash** 60
   Parenthetical Dashes 60

Contents

	The Single Dash	62
	En Rule	63
	Em Rule	65
7.	**Ellipsis**	**66**
	Ellipsis in Quotations	66
	Other Uses of Ellipsis	68
8.	**Quotation Marks**	**70**
	Quotation Marks in a Sentence	70
	Direct and Reported Speech	73
	Other Uses of Quotation Marks	74
	Quotation Marks and Other Punctuation Marks	75
	General Use of Quotation Marks	77
9.	**Apostrophe**	**78**
	The Possessive Use	78
	History of the Apostrophe	79
	Use in Marking Omissions	82
	The Plural Use	85
	Possessive and Plural Abbreviations	85
	General	86
10.	**Question Mark and Exclamation Mark**	**87**
	Question Mark in a Sentence	87
	History of the Question Mark	87
	Question Marks and Quotation Marks	90
	Non-Punctuational Uses	91
	Exclamation Mark	92
	Exclamation Marks and Quotation Marks	95
	Non-Punctuational Uses	95
11.	**Capital Letters**	**97**
	Uses of Capital Letters	97
	History of Capital Letters	97
	Capitals and Small Capitals	102
	Capitals and Alphabetical Order	102
	Modes of Address within the Family	102
12.	**Boldface**	**104**
	Uses of Boldface	104
	Punctuation and Boldface	105
13.	**Italics**	**106**
	Uses of Italics	106
14.	**Numbers in Text**	**110**

Contents

Arabic Numerals	110
Roman Numerals	115

15. Accents, Diacritics and Textual Symbols **116**
- Acute Accent 116
- Ampersand 117
- Asterisk 117
- Breathings 117
- Breve 117
- Cedilla 118
- Circumflex 118
- Currency Symbols 118
- Dagger 118
- Diaeresis 119
- Foreign Language Symbols 119
- Grave Accent 120
- Hacek 120
- Inferior Numerals 120
- Macron 120
- Mathematics and Science 120
- Paragraph Marker 120
- Per Cent Sign 121
- Section Marker 121
- Superior Numerals 121
- Superior Ring 121
- Tilde 122

16. Paragraphs, Indention and Headings **123**
- Layout of Paragraphs 124
- Other Forms of Indention 125
- Quotation Marks and Paragraphs 126
- Headings and Subheadings 126

17. Space **128**
- Ems, Ens and Thins 129
- Points and Picas 129
- White Space 129
- Spaces between Words 130
- One Word or Two 130

18. Slash, Solidus, Oblique or Virgule **132**
- History of the Slash 132
- Ordinary Uses 132
- Technical Uses 134

19. Hyphen **135**

Contents

History of the Hyphen 135
Punctuational Uses 135
Joining Uses 136
End-of-Line Hyphenation 143

Hyphenation Dictionary **145**

Glossary **229**

Introduction

For truly, I say to you, till heaven and earth pass away, not an iota, not a dot, will pass from the law until all is accomplished.

– Matthew 5:18

Punctuation and hyphenation are not all-powerful, but they are both a good deal more important than some people think. In relation to punctuation, the late Eric Partridge, whose book *You Have a Point There* is one of the few classic studies of the pure art of using punctuation marks, was not far wide of the target when he wrote:

The ability to write a letter is extremely important; and if you think that you can write an even passable letter without knowing how to use [apart from the full point] one and preferably two other stops (comma and semicolon), you are making a grave mistake. To go further: if you think you can write a good business report or an essay or an article, without also knowing how to employ at least two of the remaining stops – the colon, the dash, and the parenthesis – then you are probably overestimating your own abilities as a writer and the intelligence of your readers.

Partridge was writing in 1953, when punctuation was rather more in evidence than it often appears to be today. Even though throughout the twentieth century writers have been scaling down their use of punctuation marks, particularly commas, the general trend of Partridge's argument is not invalidated. But we have not yet reached a time when we can do without stops altogether, and probably we never shall.

The Purpose of Punctuation

Punctuation is an essential part of good writing that we all have a duty to master: without it, we cannot make our meaning fully clear; with it, we can enhance the elegance and abtlety of our use of language.

Hyphenation is a branch of punctuation, but it is almost a object in itself. It is idiosyncratic in operation, but its underlying principles can be learned. The term means not only the insertion of a hyphen into a word or the joining up of two or more words with a hyphen or hyphens, but also the breaking of a word at the end of a line of text, whether handwritten, typed or typeset. Such a break is signalled with hyphen, and end-of-line hyphenation is an essential ingredient that gives a piece of typed or printed copy that professional look. It is not, therefore, something to be taken for granted or ignored. If you produce justified text (that is, text that has an even appearance on both the left- and the right-hand margins) on your typewriter, word processor or typesetting machine, then familiarity with hyphenation is a skill that you really ought to acquire.

The computer software that runs sophisticated word processors and typesetting equipment these days almost always contains a hyphenation and justification (H & J) program. This is a computer routine that automatically breaks words at the end of a line when necessary in accordance with preset instructions. But often these instructions are geared to American demands and solutions to end-of-line hyphenation problems. What happens if you want to hyphenate according to a different set of rules? What happens when the H & J program breaks down?

The purpose of the second part of this book is to explain the recommended principles of end-of-line hyphenation and to provide a comprehensive word list showing how words should be broken according to the most widely held practices.

It is preceded by a guide to all the other marks of punctuation taken in logical order from the indispensable (the full point) to the arcane (accents, reference symbols and the like). Each topic is explained as clearly as possible, and the uses of every punctuation mark and other sign are illustrated with examples. We also discuss such matters as capitalization, typographical emphasis, and numbers in text. We end our survey with sections on paragraphing, spaces and the hyphen, which serves as an introduction to the extensive word list.

This book is designed for everybody who writes or is connected, however remotely, with the business of putting words on paper – somebody writing a letter to a friend or to the bank manager; an author tapping out a novel or technical manual; an executive responsible for producing a cogent report; a busy secretary who might have to type that report or generate one of his or her own; and a student with an essay or term paper to hand in. We hope that the book will appeal particularly to those with only a sketchy knowledge of the guidelines of punctuation and hyphenation. But we also hope that it will be of value to a busy editor or typesetter who may need a reminder of some of the less common aspects of the subject.

Whether you belong to any of these categories or to none of them, we sincerely hope that you will find this book both instructive and enjoyable. Everbody should be able to punctuate and hyphenate adequately. We trust that this book will provide a way of discovering the principles involved.

Brief History of Punctuation

Punctuation (or pointing, as it was once called) is the use in handwritten, typed or printed matter of a standard set of signs, symbols and typographical devices (such as capital letters, bold or italic type, etc.) by which meaning is clarified and sentences are split into their grammatical or structural elements. The system of conventional punctuation marks that we now use has evolved since the sixteenth century to divide off words, phrases and clauses from each other within the sentence and to indicate where one sentence ends and the next begins. But those same punctuation marks also serve to indicate pauses in reading, both silently and aloud, and some of them, notably the exclamation mark and the question mark, are tones of voice written down.

Introduction

Punctuation Before the Age of Printing

Punctuation in its modern form is a by-product of the birth of printing, when the characters and symbols that we use to represent our language first began to achieve their mass-produced, standardized forms. But the use of special signs to indicate pauses in writing is far older than the fifteenth and sixteenth centuries, the era of the earliest printers. Our notions about punctuation were borrowed, along with terms such as colon, comma, and period, from the Greeks. Their punctuation was in practice quite different from ours. But even the Greeks were not the first to break up their written texts with what we might call punctuation marks.

The most ancient instance of a 'punctuated' text so far known is an inscription in the Canaanite language (a Semitic tongue related to Hebrew) dating from the ninth century BC. The 34-line inscription, preserved on the so-called Moabite Stone, is written in an alphabetic script from right to left and tells of the wars fought by King Mesha of Moab against the Israelites and Edomites. The words of the inscription are separated by dots, and what we might call sentences are marked off from each other by vertical lines. The Moabite Stone was discovered at Diban, east of the Dead Sea, in 1868 and is now in the Louvre, Paris.

Greek alphabetic inscriptions that survive from the sixth century BC and later were mostly carved as continuous lines of capital letters with no separation of words and no punctuation marks. The lines of text often ran in alternate directions, first right to left, then left to right. If the Greeks had been writing modern English, the opening of the American Constitution might have looked like this:

```
REDRONISETATSDETINUEHTFOELPOEPEHTEW
TOFORMAMOREPERFECTUNIONESTABLISH
YTILIUQNARTCITSEMODERUSNIECITSUJ
PROVIDEFORTHECOMMONDEFENSEPROMOTE
EHTERUCESDNAERAFLEWLARENEGEHT
BLESSINGSOFLIBERTYTOOURSELVESAND
SIHTHSILBATSEDNANIADROODYTIRETSOPRUO
CONSTITUTIONFORTHEUNITEDSTATESOF ACIREMA
```

The modern version is of course this:

> We the people of the United States, in order to form a more perfect union, establish justice, insure domestic tranquillity, provide for the common defense, promote the general welfare, and secure the blessings of liberty to ourselves and our posterity, do ordain and establish this Constitution for the United States of America.

This example demonstrates why punctuation is so necessary to us. But for the Greeks, unseparated words posed less of a problem than they do for us because the Greek language, being inflected, had more regular word endings than an uninflected language such as English does. The *-os*, *-a*, *-on*, etc., of Greek nouns, for instance

Introduction

functioned almost like word spaces. Nevertheless, in a few inscriptions dating from before the fifth century, groups of words were separated by a vertical row of two or three dots. In the famous Law Code of Gortyn, found on a site in Crete, a single sign consisting of two triangles placed horizontally with their apexes touching is used once to separate a pair of clauses in the code.

The earliest surviving Greek texts written on papyrus date from the fourth century BC. They too are written in undivided capitals. A horizontal line was drawn under the beginning of a line of text in which a new topic was brought in. This mark was called the *papagraphos* and is the origin of our English word *paragraph*.

The Greeks were far more interested in splitting, not words, but whole sections of text that formed discrete units of thought or argument in a piece of writing as defined by the rules of rhetoric. The shortest such unit was a *komma*, the next a *kolon*, and the longest a *periodos*. This approach opened the way for the development of a coherent punctuation system and ultimately led to the one that we know today.

The credit for the invention of the Greek punctuation system is usually assigned to Aristophanes of Byzantium, a scholar who became head of the great library at Alexandria in about 190 BC. He invented a three-point system, in which a point or dot placed high in relation to the letter that it followed signalled the preceding rhetorical unit as being a periodos (period), a centrally placed point indicated a komma (comma), and a point written after the bottom of a letter signalled a kolon (colon). Aristophanes was also said to have invented the system of accents, breathings, and other signs still used in the printing of classical Greek today. His set of symbols included one for a hyphen, which was a curve joining the bottom of the last letter of a word with the bottom of the first letter of the next word. Sadly, the three-point system of Aristophanes was rarely employed, except in a debased form using only two points.

Roman inscriptions, from the earliest to the latest, separated words with points or dots. They also used a large number of abbreviations, a fact which may account for the presence of full points in abbreviations today. Latin manuscripts surviving from the period between the first century BC and the second century AD also show the use of dots to separate words, although this practice was subsequently abandoned in favour of unseparated capitals. The introduction of a new topic was sometimes signalled by a new paragraph, the first letter of which was enlarged and sometimes decorated and projected into the margin. The use of enlarged letters in this, way reached artistic heights in the illuminated manuscripts of the Middle Ages and survives today in the use of an enlarged capital to introduce a chapter or lead off a magazine or newspaper article.

From the third century BC, a tally was kept of the number of lines in a manuscript, probably as a way of working out the copyist's fee. A standard line was counted as being about 15 or 16 syllables long. In the course of time, manuscripts began to be written in 'sense lines', with each line representing a coherent thought or complete step in the argument of a piece of writing. St. Jerome, who supervised the Vulgate (the Latin translation of the Bible) between 382 and 405 AD, arranged the manuscript into cola (lines of 8 to 17 syllables) and commata (lines of less than 8 syllables). This arrangement was like that found in the speeches of the great classical orators Demosthenes and Cicero, and was specifically designed to help someone reading the text aloud. Cola and commata (what we might call clauses and phrases) were the origin of the division of each chapter of the Bible into verses. The first letter of each clause or phrase projected into the margin, and the reader was expected to take a breath before each one. Successive editions of the Vulgate preserved this careful punctuation.

In the seventh and eighth centuries, the form and style of lettering changed in manuscripts. Until then, scribes had broadly used undivided capitals known as majuscules. Now copyists introduced minuscule letters, which had parts that projected above or below the average vertical extent of a line of text. We now call these parts ascenders and descenders. Minuscule letters resembled modern lower-case letters.

Now also, for the first time, words were divided from each other by spaces. Anglo-Saxon, German and Irish scribes, to whom Latin was a foreign language, were chief among those who introduced this practice. Spaces were always left at the end of a sentence, and an enlarged letter, usually a majuscule, was used to start a new sentence as well as a new paragraph. A point, placed high or low, was written inside or following a sentence, and a compound point (two or three points written together) might signal the end of a sentence.

Towards the end of the eighth century, Charlemagne, King of the Franks and Holy Roman Emperor, presided over an educational revival led by his Anglo-Saxon adviser Alcuin. The revival laid stress on improvements in spelling and punctuation in Biblical and liturgical manuscripts. Over the next century, new marks appeared: the primitive comma (in fact just a plain point), the question mark and the punctus elevatus (a kind of inverted semicolon). An arrow-head was commonly used to signal a quotation.

The end-of-line hyphen (often doubled) appeared towards the end of the tenth century. By the twelfth century, a mark resembling a figure 7 (known as a punctus circumflexus) came into use to indicate a pause and a rise in the pitch of the voice at the end of certain clauses. In the thirteenth and fourteenth centuries, the virgule or solidus (/) came into use as a pause mark. It proved to be the forerunner of the modern comma. The simple point was finally emerging as the end-of-sentence marker.

During the fifteenth century books appeared in a new form of script known as the Italian humanist style. After 1450 the punctus elevatus and punctus circumflexus fell out of use, and the virgule was widely used along with what we now think of as the colon (:) to mark slight pauses. Parentheses (round brackets) appeared in 1500, and the earlier printers, notably those in Italy, borrowed the Greek question mark for use as a pause mark between the comma and the colon. This eventually became known as the semicolon (;).

By the time printing had got under way, most of the elements of our punctuation system had been finalized. In 1566 Aldus Manutius the Younger (1547 – 1597), grandson of the famous printer of Venice whose name he shared, published *Orthographiae Ratio*, a Latin spelling system in which he described, under different names, the modern comma, semicolon, colon and full point. By the end of the seventeenth century all the punctuation marks now in use had acquired their modern names, and the apostrophe, dash, exclamation mark and quotation marks had been added to the punctuation 'pantheon'.

The Approaches to Punctuation

The Greeks and Romans punctuated their writing in accordance with rhetoric and oratory. Initially, texts were broken up in a way that helped to get the argument across in manageable 'chunks' of clear and consistent thought. Later the punctuation was designed to mark off breathing points to aid the reading out loud of a speech or other public utterance. In the Middle Ages, the most accurate punctuation was reserved for Biblical, liturgical and other religious texts that might have to be read out loud as part of Christian ritual. The punctuation marks signalled pauses of differing lengths, for breath or for dramatic or oratorical effect.

Punctuation up to the beginning of the age of printing was haphazard. The symbols used were rarely consistent: often a simple point meant a short pause, such as that signalled by a comma, as well as a long pause, indicating the end of a sentence. Moreover, the virgule and the simple point might mean the same thing – i.e. a short breath mark.

The confusion did not end with standardization of the system in the sixteenth and seventeenth centuries. Although widely accepted relative values were assigned to the main punctuation marks or stops (so that one full point was considered equal to two colons, three semicolons or four commas), the use of punctuation marks in written texts veered between two extremes – the elocutionary or rhetorical, in which the marks, employed quite freely, stood for the different lengths of pauses observed by someone reading aloud to an audience or congregation, and the syntactical, in which the marks were used more systematically to separate out from each other the grammatical building blocks that made up the structure of a sentence or paragraph.

In regard to English punctuation, the syntactical approach had won the day by the end of the seventeenth century. Among its proponents had been the dramatist Ben Jonson, whose *English Grammar*, written in about 1617, was published posthumously in 1640. From about 1660 onwards, syntactical punctuation was the norm. But rhetorical or elocutionary pauses often coincide with breaks required by syntax, and modern punctuation, although basically syntactical, also takes note of the subtleties of rhetoric.

Heavy and Light: Close or Open Punctuation

During the eighteenth century, excessive, or 'close' punctuation became endemic. Alexander Pope wrote in the Prologue to his Satires:

> Commas and points they set exactly right,
>
> And 'twere a sin to rob them of their mite.

The worst offenders in this respect used a comma to introduce every subordinate clause or separable phrase. Pedantic writers on grammar made up rules for correct punctuation. One author gave 40 rules governing the use of the comma.

It was not until 1906 that the brothers H.W. and F.G. Fowler, in their book *The King's English*, outlined a rational punctuation system in which the light, or 'open', use of stops was recommended. Since then the trend has continued in the direction of 'open' punctuation, reducing the use of punctuation marks to a minimum. As G.V. Carey put it in his short guide to punctuation *Mind the Stop*: 'At its best modern punctuation uses no more stops than are needed to give immediate clarity and force to the sense; and beyond that point it can hardly go.'

1

Full Point

The symbol. (⊙ in a proof correction or typescript amendment) represents the full point, full stop, or period. This is the one punctuation mark whose presence is obligatory in every sentence that is not a question or an exclamation. Obligatory, that is, unless you happen to be James Joyce, for example. Joyce wrote the last 46 pages of his epic *Ulysses* without using any punctuation at all. However, not everybody is an experimental writer like Joyce, and most people work on the principle that all non-interrogative, non-exclamatory sentences end in a full point. The sentence that you are reading now ends in one. So does this one. In the United Kingdom, the full point is generally known as the full stop, except among printers and typographers. In the United States, it is called a period.

Full Point at the End of a Sentence

Three main types of sentences end in full points. They are direct statements, indirect questions, and polite or formal requests.

1. Direct Statements. The full point is the mark that rounds off a sentence, pure and simple. These examples illustrate its use:

Anne arrived at the office early.

She took off her raincoat and sat down at her desk.

Tom will be in town again on Thursday.

The defective sentence. Certain utterances that lack a finite verb or obvious subject, and therefore not strictly allowable as sentences, nevertheless end in a full point as if they were sentences. The second "sentence" in each of these examples is typical of what we might call the defective sentence.

Angela did not dislike her job. Far from it.

Tom would never say such a thing. Of course not.

Defective sentences such as these almost always have a strong connection with what has gone before, either as answers to questions or as contradictions or reinforcements of a previous statement. Generally they are elliptical expressions, and a main subject or finite verb is readily understood in working out their meaning. For example:

Where's the car? In the garage.

I believe he's gone to China. Quite right.

Full Point

Here we could have written "It is in the garage" or "That is quite right".

Defective sentences can be as short as one word and still take a full point. For example:

> What's for breakfast? Toast.
>
> Was he willing to be chairman? Certainly.
>
> Is there life on the Moon? No.
>
> We'll have to dismiss him. Agreed.

Greetings or salutations, such as "Hello", "Cheers", etc., although strictly exclamations, may be written with a full point, especially when no emotional or dramatic connotation is involved.

Defective sentences lacking a subject are illustrated by the following examples. In each case the missing subject of the second sentence is understood to be the same as that of the first.

> She enjoyed her work. Loved it, in fact.
>
> His patriotism was not in doubt. Was not even to be suspected, since he had performed many deeds of heroism for his country.

Full points used in this way provide a clear break that lends weight to an emphatic or rhetorical effect. Such a mode of expression is likely to be used by journalists or political speech-writers. In ordinary writing, however, a different kind of punctuation is to be preferred, as in:

> She enjoyed her work – loved it, in fact.
>
> His patriotism was not in doubt: was not even to be suspected, since he had performed … etc.

A few writers indulge in defective sentences in writing descriptive or racy passages. For instance, a string of noun phrases might be separated by full points, as in:

> The beach was crowded with every example of the British holidaymaker. Little girls with buckets making sandcastles. Horrid little boys knocking the sandcastles down or playing French cricket with reluctant fathers. Young bikini-clad beauties worshipping the sun. Old men snoozing in deck chairs. Homely women eating candy floss.

The sequence could easily be extended.

Conservative authors and editors frown on this kind of writing. In the United States it is known as the period fault. Careful writers would probably prefer to punctuate the above example as one sentence using commas or semicolons, yet full points in such passages are great attention-getters, purely because their use is unorthodox.

2. *Indirect Questions.* An indirect question is a statement with a question embedded in it. So the correct punctuation for an indirect question is a full point, not a question mark. Note the difference between these two examples:

> What time is the train due to leave?
>
> She asked what time the train was due to leave.

The first is a direct question and takes a question mark. The second, being an indirect question, takes a full point.

As we shall see in a later section on quotation marks, thought can be represented verbatim, as it were, without the quotation marks being present. So sentences like this are not uncommon:

> What would he be like? she wondered.

This is a sentence containing a quoted question, but there are no quotation marks round the question itself. However, the position and even the presence of the question mark is open to some controversy. Omission of the question mark and its replacement by a comma is probably the most usual form of punctuation in this kind of sentence:

> What would he be like, she wondered.

We shall discuss this aspect of the question in detail in the sections on the question mark and exclamation mark.

3. *Polite or Formal Requests.* These are logically not questions but very weak commands. They therefore end with a full point.

> Could you please send me a copy of your latest catalogue.
>
> May I draw your attention to the mistake on page four.

Full Point and Quotation Marks

Writers and editors in the United States generally place a full point inside quotation marks regardless of whether the full point belongs to the quoted material or not. British writers and editors place the full point inside the quotation marks if it ends the quotation and outside if not. These examples illustrate the idea:

American usage:

> "Sheila," said John, "I love you."

Tom's ideas were not crazy. He liked to think of them as "modern."

British usage:

> "Sheila," said John, "I love you."

Full Point

Tom's ideas were not crazy. He liked to think of them as "modern".

Note that the only difference between these pairs of examples is the placing of the full point in the last one.

An important principle to bear in mind is that when the end of a quotation coincides with the end of the whole sentence, the full point ending the quotation goes inside the quotation marks and the full point ending the whole sentence is suppressed. For a full discussion of all punctuation in relation to quotation marks, see the chapter on Quotation marks later in this guide.

Non-punctuational uses

Three categories of the non-punctuational use of the full point are discussed here: its employment in abbreviations, with initials and with numerals.

1. Abbreviations. Some publishers continue to follow H.W. Fowler, who in his book *Modern English Usage* suggested that if an abbreviated word consists of the first and last letters of that word, then the full point ought to be omitted after the abbreviation; otherwise it should be included. First-and-last-letter abbreviations are sometimes called contractions. Following Fowler, we are supposed to write, for example, Capt. (with a full point) for Captain, but Cpl (with no full point) for Corporal. Another recommendation is that of the compilers of *The Oxford Dictionary for Writers and Editors*, who say that single-letter abbreviations and abbreviations consisting of a mixture of upper- and lower-case letters should (with certain exceptions) take a full point. Thus we should write Jan. for January and Yorks. for Yorkshire, but Hants (no full point) for Hampshire.

Whatever the established authorities say, however, the modern trend in the United Kingdom is now towards an "open" style for abbreviations, in which there are few full points. A more conservative approach predominates in the United States, where full points are still required in many abbreviations.

It is impossible to make hard and fast rules on the use or omission of a full point in a given abbreviation. The best recommendation is to follow the house style if you are writing for publication, avoid ambiguity and be consistent. The following brief selective lists of common abbreviations are based as far as possible on present-day usage. Remember too that if you are writing for publication, some abbreviations derived from foreign words ought to be set in italic.

Use a full point in the following:

anon. (for anonymous)

approx.

c., ca. (for *circa* - prefer *c.*)

Co.

et al.

etc. (prefer this form to the now old-fashioned &c.)

ibid.

in. (for inch)

mi. (for mile)

No. or no. (for number – plural Nos., nos.)

op. cit.

p. (page)

pp. (pages)

viz.

In the United States the symbol # is commonly used for number. The abbreviation No. or no. ought, however, to be substituted in what you write in order to prevent readers outside the United States being puzzled and to avoid confusion with the proof-reader's symbol still regularly used in Britain to mark a space.

For abbreviations of the names of states in the United States, follow American traditional practice and use a full point, e.g. Pa. for Pennsylvania, and Mo. for Missouri. For addresses the US postal service uses capital letters and no full points – PA and MO.

Do not use full points in the following:

C (Celsius or centigrade, used in quoting temperatures)

Dr (Doctor)

E (east)

f or ff (following)

K (kelvin temperature)

Ltd (limited)

M

Mlle (modes of address in French)

Mme

Mr

Mrs (modes of address in English)

Ms

N (north)

Full Point

> NE (north-east)
>
> NW (north-west)
>
> p (pence)
>
> per cent
>
> Rev or Revd (Reverend)
>
> Rd (Road)
>
> S (south)
>
> SE (south-east)
>
> St (Saint, Street)
>
> SW (south-west)
>
> W (west)

Do not use a full point with scientific units or weights and measures, except for in. (inch) and l. (litre), where ambiguity might arise (see the section on numbers in text).

Do not use a full point with chemical symbols or formulae: Au, C, Ca, H, N, O, Pb, H_2O.

For a note on the plurals of abbreviations, *see* the section on the Apostrophe.

2. Initials. The coining of initials, in particular those that stand for organizations, is one of the biggest growth industries of our generation, and a selective list is hardly likely to scratch the surface. Suffice it to say that for initials involving capitals the full point is now very much the exception rather than the rule. B.B.C. is old hat and BBC is now widely accepted, even by the BBC.

When it comes to company names, the conscientious writer and editor will find out the preferred abbreviation from the firm concerned. Thus British Petroleum itself prefers BP, not B.P., and AT&T is what the American Telephone and Telegraph Company likes to be called.

"Euro-abbreviations" such as CAP, EEC, EFTA, MEP and so on, do not take full points. With regard to other organizations, write, for example, PLO, KGB, not P.L.O., K.G.B.

Capital initials can, if the typography allows it, be rendered by small capitals. The forms AD and BC, rarely seen with full points these days, regularly appear in small capitals. So too do academic qualifications, such as BA or DD, and the designations MP or PC (Privy Councillor), when written after somebody's name.

Lower-case initials tend to cling to their full points, notably i.e., e.g., a.m., p.m., q.v. and the like. But the form emf (for electromotive force) is replacing e.m.f. The abbreviations ecu (European currency unit) and plc (public limited company – also written PLC) have never had full points.

Initials that form pronounceable words are known as acronyms, and some well-known examples are ACAS, ANZUS, GATT, NATO, NATSOPA, SOGAT, UCCA, UNESCO and VAT. Some of these forms can be written as words with an upper-case initial, e.g. Nato, Unesco and Sogat. Full points are still the norm when quoting the initials of a person's name. H.G. Wells (not HG Wells, although some publishers do like H G Wells). How the initials in a name should be spaced is a matter of debate. H. G. Wells (with a space after each point) is still the general custom, but the closing up of initials with full points has become common practice with the introduction of word processors.

If an abbreviation or set of initials closing with a full point comes at the end of a sentence, do not put in another full point to finish the sentence off. All the other stops, however, follow a full point when it closes an abbreviation or set of initials.

> For forty years Henry had been employed by the firm of Trotter & Co. (not "Trotter & Co..")
>
> Come to my office at 5 p.m., Jones.

3. *Numerals.* A full point may be used after Arabic or Roman numerals in a list.

The agenda is as follows:

> Minutes of the last meeting
>
> Matters arising
>
> Secretary's report
>
> Any other business

or:

The four states of matter encountered in nature are:

> I. Solid
>
> II. Liquid
>
> III. Gas
>
> IV. Plasma

Alternatively, the numerals can be enclosed in parentheses or followed by a half-bracket, in which case they should not take a full point: (5) or 5); (v) or v).

Decimal Point. A full point is commonly used in printed text to precede a decimal fraction. It is also used in quoting sums of money:

> 2.5   0.428571   A330.62 $120.79

Full Point

Mathematical texts may use a centred point for a decimal point:

    2·75   0·7428571   A330·762 $120·779

In Britain a full point is often used when quoting the time in the hours-and-minutes format.

    10.25   6.05 p.m.   8.00 a.m. (or 8.0 a.m) 19.45

In North America a colon is commonly used instead of a full point in quoting the time in the above form.

All-figure formats for dates usually take full points or slashes (solidi), but remember that the British and American formats differ. See the chapter on Numbers in text.

    29.5.89 or 29/5/89 (UK)

    5.29.89 or 5/29/89 (USA)

In both of the above examples, the date rendered is 29 May, 1989.

4. Leaders. Widely spaced groups of two or three full points used in tables to guide the eye when reading related items are called leaders. They can be useful in helping to make a complex table more readable, but care should be taken to avoid a cluttered effect. Leaders should be used only when absolutely necessary. They should also be carefully positioned, one group of dots lying directly above the other:

    Table of Contents

1. Introduction	7
2. The Land and its People	12
3. The Archaeological Record	25

For the use of three and four full points to denote missing text or faltering dialogue, see the section on the ellipsis. *See also* the chapter on the Paragraph for full points in headings.

History of the Comma

A mark looking more or less like a comma or a modern figure 7 was in use in medieval times, but its function as a stop was not consistent. Often a single point served to mark a pause that would now be rendered by a comma.

The modern comma symbol dates from the fifteenth century. It was descended from the virgule or solidus (/), which up until then had been used to denote a brief pause in text. Scribes placed the virgule next to the upper part of a preceding letter. In the course of time, however, it sank to the baseline and became curved, thereby giving rise to the comma as we know it today. The virgule persisted as a stop into the age of printing: it can be found in a number of early sixteenth-century books. (It is perhaps worth noting that the modern French word for comma is indeed virgule.)

The word comma itself comes through Latin from the Greek word komma, a noun formed from the verb koptein, 'to cut'. Komma meant, in effect, 'a part cut off'. The ancient Greek grammarians used this word to denote the shortest section of a piece of rhetorical text and, by transference, the symbol signalling the end of such a section. Thinking of the present-day comma as a mark that 'cuts off' sections of text is still a valid guide to its modern punctuational usage.

2
Comma

From the full point, the most emphatic of stops, we turn to the comma, the least emphatic but the next in importance. The sign for this punctuation mark is , (<?> or <?> in corrections to proofs or handwritten amendments to typescripts).

The comma is the most ubiquitous and, it would seem, the most misused of all punctuation marks in English. G.V. Carey, in *Mind the Stop*, called it 'Punctuational Enemy No. 1'. Putting a comma in the wrong place or not putting it in the right one certainly accounts for a lot of the mistakes in its use. But peppering one's text with commas is a far worse error; as one writer has succinctly put it: 'Commas are for sense not decoration.'

In line with a modern tendency to reduce all punctuation to a minimum, experienced writers today use far fewer commas than their predecessors ever did. Their practice is governed by a desire not to slow down the pace of the text and a belief that the reader will be distracted – even irritated – by being brought up short too many times by too many commas. They emphasize the role of the comma as a way of marking out the syntax or grammatical structure of a sentence rather than as a pure stop. This grammatical approach to the comma is especially important in writing non-fiction. But all careful writers are sensitive not only to the comma's purely grammatical applications but also to its rhetorical or elocutionary use in marking a short but often crucial pause. For example, the sentence

> She walked into the room and found her husband there

is a matter of fact statement, but

> She walked into the room, and found her husband there.

conjures up a *double entendre* or a layer of meaning that could be rather sinister. Using the comma properly needs a feeling for both good grammar and good taste – backed up with common sense and a little observational skill.

Commas between Clauses

A comma marks off discrete sections of a sentence, or to put it another way, a comma helps to parcel up the bits of a sentence that belong together and keeps them apart from the bits to which they do not belong. The most significant components of a sentence are clauses.

1. Between Independent Clauses. Independent clauses are clauses that can stand alone as separate sentences without any grammatical connectives (such as conjunctions) but are nevertheless linked by sense or logic. Independent clauses can be treated as separate sentences, being separated by full points, as in:

> I came. I saw. I conquered.

The cumulative effect of these statements is better seen, however, if they can be put into a single sentence. But how should we punctuate this sentence? The answer is to use commas:

> I came, I saw, I conquered.

In choosing this well-worn example, we have probably lighted upon the only general instance when commas between independent clauses are regarded as permissible – that is, the situation in which three or more independent clauses are linked together. We can justify it mainly on the ground that words or short phrases in a list are separated by commas. We shall come back to lists later.

The placing of a comma between two independent clauses in a sentence is a practice frowned on by most writers, especially in the United States, where it is considered a 'comma fault'. So there is a ban on such sentences as:

> They could not go on, the road was blocked by a fallen tree.

The explanation for the prohibition is that a comma, being the weakest stop available, is too brief a pause between two stand-alone statements that would in the normal course of events be separated by a full point but are in this case too closely connected for a full point to be used. The connection between them ought to be signalled by a conjunction or, failing that, another stronger stop – namely, a semicolon. The sentence should therefore be punctuated:

> They could not go on; the road was blocked by a fallen tree.

(Incidentally, we could have written earlier 'I came; I saw; I conquered'. Such a form is allowable but rather literary. *See* the chapter on Semicolon.)

2. Between Co-ordinate Clauses. The use of a comma between co-ordinate clauses in a sentence – i.e., clauses of equal status connected to each other by co-ordinating conjunctions such as *and, but, for, neither, nor, or,* etc. – depends (in British English, at least) on the length of the clauses, the closeness of the link between the clauses, and the writer's overriding duty to eliminate all ambiguity from the mind of the reader, however fleeting that may be.

On purely syntactical grounds, no commas are needed in the following plain statements:

> John has bought a computer and is using it for work.
>
> John has bought a computer but can only use it for work.

In these two sentences, both clauses share the same subject, and because the clauses are short, there is no need to repeat the subject or commute it to the corresponding pronoun.

Comma

Even if we had made the sentences read:

> John has bought a computer and he is using it for work.
>
> John has bought a computer but he can only use it for work.

there would clearly still be no need for a comma between the two clauses, mainly because the links between them are so close.

When the subject is different, however, notions of contrast arise. Many writers under these circumstances, especially those in the United States, feel that a comma before the conjunction is required, as in:

> John has bought a computer, and Jane has bought a typewriter.
>
> John has bought a computer, but Jane is using it all the time for her word processing tasks.

Some British writers might balk at using a comma in sentences such as these, but a comma before a clause in which the matter is significantly different is usually essential:

> Helen thought of herself as photogenic, but the camera doesn't lie.
>
> He was dying to go out to the pub for a drink, and the dog obliged him by asking to be taken for a walk.

If you are seeking guidelines, the tag 'Change the subject; chuck in a comma' might not be a bad rule of thumb. Although not expressed in the most refined terms, it does have the important merit of being clear and consistent – something punctuation rarely is but always should be.

In the next, more complicated, sentence we insert our first comma mainly in order to clear up doubt – in this case, to stop the reader from momentarily thinking that John and David want to develop a brewery as well as the site. But what we said earlier about changing subjects reinforces our need for both commas here.

> John and David want to develop the site, and a brewery is backing their challenge, but the owners of the land are trying to put off making a decision until next year.

Commas between co-ordinate clauses where subjects change are, however, not necessarily obligatory. At the risk of taking back our rule of thumb, we must concede that in the next examples, even though the subjects change, adding a comma is superfluous:

> The band played and everyone danced.
>
> Tessa sings quite well but Caroline is tone-deaf.
>
> She agreed with them but I did not.

No commas are needed here for three very good reasons:

All the clauses are short

They are closely linked with each other

None of the sentences is likely to be misleading or ambiguous for readers

In the light of all this we have to restate our rule of thumb relating to commas between clauses linked by a co-ordinate conjunctions: 'Change the subject, chuck in a comma, but check for linkage, brevity and clarity first'.

3. Between Main and Subordinate Clauses. Every normal sentence must have a subject and a main finite verb, a verb whose special distinguishing features – tense, mood, person, etc. – tie it to that subject. The clause containing the subject and the main verb, together a predicate that may or may not be present (depending on the nature of the verb), is known as the main clause. Other clauses may be dependent on the main clause or some of its components: these are known as subordinate clauses and are introduced by subordinating conjunctions, such as *after, before, that, who, which, when,* etc.

In the golden age of the over-punctuator, back in the eighteenth century, a comma was virtually obligatory between a main clause and a subordinate clause. Noun clauses introduced by 'that' were always preceded by commas. These days the best writers generally avoid commas – they never use them before 'that' clauses at all. Any commas that are used are there for rhetorical purposes or for making vital grammatical distinctions and eliminating doubt. The latter, non-rhetorical, uses of the comma are in fact mandatory.

Each of the following examples consists of a main clause followed by one subordinate clause. All are plain statements. None of them contains ambiguities, none of them poses a grammatical problem, so none of them requires any commas.

> She left the office early that day because she was going out to the theatre in the evening.
>
> I'd love to read that book when you've finished with it.
>
> He said that he would come.

No commas are needed when two subordinate clauses follow the main clause, provided that each clause is dependent on the one before:

> He said that he would come when he could.
>
> John said that Jane could use his computer whenever she liked.

When more than two subordinate clauses follow a main clause, however, a comma is usually advisable:

> John said that Jane could use his computer whenever she liked, as long as she was careful with it.

Comma

A comma may separate a main clause from a subordinate clause for various reasons, mostly to do with the comma's rhetorical uses. However, a comma is valuable in denoting certain shifts of meaning that may be rather subtle. Compare these pairs of examples:

(a) I am doing this job because I need the money.

Don't lecture me, because I won't stand for it.

(b) He would be able to have some coffee when the milk arrived.

He had just resigned himself to having black coffee, when the milk arrived.

Since. A significant use of the comma in this connection is encountered in distinguishing between the two senses of *since:* the causal sense, in which since equals 'because' or 'for', and the temporal sense, in which since means 'during the period following the time when'. A comma is regularly used to signal the causal since; the absence of a comma usually indicates the temporal since. Thus the comma is essential in sorting out these two sentences:

I haven't seen her in London, since she got married last year. (causal)

I haven't seen her in London since she got married last year. (temporal)

Using a comma between a main clause and a following subordinate clause is generally restricted to the instances we have already described. When a subordinate clause precedes a main clause, a comma is much more likely to be used. But such a comma can be left out if the subject of both clauses is the same and especially if the subordinate clause is short. No commas are needed in these two sentences:

When he moved to Berlin he bought a flat.

Before I go I must tell you this joke.

But commas are needed in these:

Whether you like it or not, she will have to go.

As I told you yesterday, we have asked Smith to accept the position of chairman.

When John left, the house was all locked up securely.

If he dies, there will have to be a post mortem examination.

In the last two examples, the comma is essential in stopping the reader from assuming at first sight that (a) *the house* is the object of the verb *left*, and (b) *there* functions as an adverb modifying the verb *dies*.

If you are in doubt about using a comma between a subordinate clause and a following main clause, you should feel free to use one. Such commas are not wrong, always provided of course that they do not cause confusion in the reader's mind. Using commas between a main and a following subordinate clause, however, needs careful thought. Ideally, the comma should be reserved for clarifying doubt, marking distinctions in sense, and only rarely for achieving subtle rhetorical effects.

Commas and Relative Clauses

Relative clauses are adjectival subordinate clauses that qualify a noun. There are two types: specifying relative clauses define or specify the noun, picking it out, as it were, from a host of others of its kind; non-specifying relative clauses add extra information about a noun that has already been implicitly or explicitly specified or identified.

One of the few but also one of the most important genuine rules of punctuation is that a comma must never be used with a specifying clause but must always be used with a non-specifying clause. Here are some examples:

> He is the man who came looking for you yesterday. (specifying)
>
> The car that I bought from the garage up the road has broken down three times in the past month. (specifying)
>
> The statement that she made to the police turned out to be false. (specifying)
>
> America's third man in space was John Glenn, who made three orbits of the Earth in February 1962. (non-specifying)
>
> The postman, who had lived in the village all his life, greatly resented the newcomers. (non-specifying)
>
> The mole, which spends nearly all its life underground, has very poor vision. (non-specifying)

It is hard to overstress the importance of the job that the comma performs in distinguishing between specifying and non-specifying clauses. If a writer fails to use the comma properly in this respect, he or she is likely to be misunderstood. A wrongly placed comma, or the absence of a comma when it should be there, can change the meaning of a sentence completely, often with results that are at best embarrassing, at worst insulting or insensitive:

> This exacting career requires intelligence and is unlikely to appeal to women, who feel that their place is in the home. (Remove the comma to remove the insult.)
>
> The pope who is Bishop of Rome is the head of the Roman Catholic Church. (How many popes are there? Insert a comma after *pope* to show that there is only one and we are adding extra information about him.)

We have so far skated over the fact that in a couple of our examples the relative clause has been 'embedded' in the main clause. When the relative clause is a non-specifying one, we need not one but two commas to mark it off from the surrounding main clause. Remember what we said earlier about cutting off or 'parcelling up' the parts of a sentence that should be taken together. In our next example, correctly comma'd, we note the two commas that mark off the non-specifying clause from the rest of the sentence:

> The pope, who is Bishop of Rome, is head of the Roman Catholic Church.

The fact that the pope is Bishop of Rome is a piece of extra information about him that can, grammatically at least, be dispensed with. The words:

> The pope is head of the Roman Catholic Church.

still make a coherent sentence. There is a loss of information but not a change in meaning. The clause 'who is Bishop of Rome' stands outside the main sentence structure in terms of grammar and is also peripheral to the meaning of the sentence. It is a parenthetical phrase and as such is marked off by commas.

These comments provide a useful test for whether one is dealing with a specifying or non-specifying relative clause. In the example just discussed, a non-specifying clause, comma'd off from the rest of the sentence, can be removed without losing the basic meaning of the sentence because it adds extra detail that is marginal to the issue. In the case of a specifying relative clause, however, the detail contained in the clause is anything but marginal. Consider an earlier example:

> The car that I bought in the garage up the road has broken down three times in a month.

If we take out the relative clause, we are left with 'The car has broken down three times in a month.' This immediately begs the question 'Which car?' Something material has been lost: namely, the information identifying or specifying the car. The missing clause is therefore a specifying relative clause and should not have commas around it.

Parenthetical Commas

Any word or group of words that naturally stands outside the main framework of the sentence is parenthetical. In practice, this means an adverb or adverbial phrase that modifies a clause or part of a clause; a certain type of subordinate clause that lies within a main clause upon which it depends (a non-specifying relative clause, for example); and even an independent clause or sentence introduced into another sentence as an aside.

Punctuation provides a number of different ways of signalling the breaks between the parenthetical and the main material, ranging from nothing at all to the abrupt interruption of the dash.

The comma is, next to the use of no punctuation at all, the lightest and least disruptive way of signalling parenthetical material. For example:

> Mr Harrington, the owner of the painting, was surprised that it had fetched such a high price at the auction.

> Everyone remarked that Thomson, not usually given to expressions of emotion, had cried like a baby on the night of his mother's death.
>
> He was, poor fellow, completely distraught.

When the parenthetical material comes in the middle of a sentence, it must be both introduced and followed by a comma, as in these examples. Writers sometimes forget this and use only one comma:

> The mole, which spends most of its life underground has very poor vision. (Insert a second comma after *underground*.)
>
> The day when it finally came, dawned like any other. (Insert a comma after *day*.)

A parenthetical phrase at the start of a sentence takes only one comma – that is, the one that follows it and cuts it off from the main sentence:

> In an open letter to the prime minister, the leader of the opposition accused her of being anti-European.
>
> Apart from a childhood interest in stamp collecting, he had had few hobbies in his life.

A modern tendency is to use no commas after short introductory phrases or one-word sentence modifiers, except to avoid any ambiguity. Thus no comma is now normally needed in the following:

> Normally I do not write sentences like this, but my editor insists upon them. (No need for comma after *normally*.)
>
> As far as I know he doesn't live in London any more.

But commas in the following examples help the reader to avoid comprehending the adverbs in the opening phrases as prepositions or conjunctions.

> Inside, the house had been decorated in the most modern style.
>
> A few weeks before, the event had already been advertised in the local newspapers.
>
> On the morning of 30 January 1649 King Charles I walked and talked; half an hour after, his head was cut off.

The last example, rather an old chestnut, also serves to illustrate the modern practice of no longer following dates with commas. The same is true of simple year dates used in introductory parenthetic phrases. Thus we now write:

> In 1989 Konrad Lorenz, the famous behavioural scientist, died.

A comma after 'In 1989' would now be considered unacceptably fussy or old-fashioned, except when another number follows it, as in this example:

> On 8 January 1989, 47 people died when a Boeing 737 airliner crashed onto the

M1 motorway near Kegworth, Leicestershire.

Parenthetic words or phrases at the end of a sentence take only the introductory comma. The second comma coincides with and is absorbed by the final full point of the sentence. Note the last word in the above example. Note also the following:

> He was met at the door by Jarvis, a tall handsome man in his early 40s.

A parenthetical phrase at the end of a clause separated from the next clause by a semicolon or colon also loses its second comma by the same rule, as in these examples:

> The report is concise, as we have already explained: it presents its case in only 32 pages.

> She was overburdened with worries, poor girl; yet she bore them all with uncomplaining fortitude.

Conjunctive adverbs – words such as *moreover, however,* etc., that connect sentences or clauses to previous sentences or clauses in the manner of conjunctions – are traditionally set off by commas from the rest of the clause or sentence that they modify. We shall have more to say about conjunctive adverbs when we discuss the semicolon. Meanwhile, we shall provide just two examples here:

> Moreover, there is little doubt that this man is a scoundrel.

> Much can be said, however, for his inspirational qualities as a writer.

or:

> However, much can be said for his inspirational qualities as a writer. (Note that a comma after 'However' is obligatory here because of the confusion with 'However much'.)

1. Commas with Participal Phrases. A parenthetical adjectival phrase containing a participle – a verbal adjective – is generally set off from the rest of a sentence by commas:

> Walking into town the other day, I was stopped by a man driving a large black car, who asked me for directions to the nearest garage.

> John, seeing Helen unconscious on the floor, immediately phoned for a doctor.

Not all participial phrases are parenthetical, however. No commas are needed in the following examples, where the participal phrase is integral to the sentence and not peripheral to it.

> John saw Helen lying unconscious on the floor and immediately phoned for a doctor.

> He saw the men tearing down the poster.

Note the comma-ing in this sentence:

> John, seeing Helen lying unconscious on the floor, immediately phoned for a doctor.

Using participial phrases can hold traps for the unwary. Do please avoid absurdities like these:

> Driving through the desert, the sun beat down relentlessly.

> Hurrying down the street, her handbag fell into a puddle.

2. Absolute Constructions. One of the trickiest aspects of using the comma in parenthetical phrases concerns the so-called absolute construction. An absolute construction is a phrase containing a present participle and a subject and/or predicate that stands outside the grammatical framework of a sentence. It is very easy to get the commas wrong in a sentence containing such a construction. The following example is incorrect:

> Liverpool, having won the FA Cup, their match against Arsenal assumed great importance because a win would give them the League championship as well.

The first comma is wrong because the absolute construction in this sentence is the phrase 'Liverpool having won the FA Cup'. The sentence, correctly punctuated, reads:

> Liverpool having won the FA Cup, their match against Arsenal assumed great importance because a win would give them the League championship as well.

Here is one more example of an absolute construction, with the commas placed correctly:

> The protesting students having taken over the main square of the city, the authorities retaliated by sending in troops against them.

3. Appositional and Restrictive Uses. Parenthetical phrases that stand in apposition to a noun or serve to restrict its meaning or application are regularly marked off from the rest of a sentence by commas. This example illustrates both apposition ('a grocer's daughter from Grantham, Lincolnshire') and restriction ('Grantham, Lincolnshire', not any other Grantham):

> Margaret Roberts, a grocer's daughter from Grantham, Lincolnshire, dreamed of someday becoming prime minister of Great Britain. (Note that the second comma required for the whole appositional phrase and the second comma needed after the restrictive phrase coalesce into one.)

Whether one uses commas to mark appositional nouns and phrases these days is increasingly a matter of taste. Eric Partridge claimed to see a difference in meaning between 'This is my cousin, John Smith.' (= this is my only cousin, and his name is John Smith) and 'This is my cousin John Smith' (= I have several cousins, and this

Comma

particular one is named John Smith). Few people now subscribe to this distinction, and one can use a comma or not. On the whole, journalists not wishing to have too many commas slowing down their snappy prose will go for 'My cousin John Smith', just as they write of 'Prime minister Margaret Thatcher'. However, no journalist or any other writer is likely to omit the commas in this example:

> Margaret Thatcher, Britain's prime minister, visited Paris on the 200th anniversary of the French Revolution.

The purely restrictive use of commas, especially in place names and identifications, is retained by today's writers; the forms 'Kegworth, Leicestershire', 'Paris, France', and 'London, Ontario' are still the norm. But beware the omission of that all-important second comma in the middle of a sentence. These examples are correct and should be followed:

> He was born in Paris, Texas.
>
> After moving to Shaftesbury, Dorset, in the 1950s, Mr Jones became a well-respected member of the community.
>
> She attended school at Cheltenham, Gloucestershire.

This example is wrong but amazingly prevalent among all writers:

> She was born at Grantham, Lincolnshire and educated at Somerville College, Oxford during the 1940s. (We need commas after both 'Lincolnshire' and 'Oxford'.)

The Vocative Comma, or Comma of Address. One final parenthetical use of commas needs to be mentioned. The name of a person or thing addressed or apostrophized in a speech, piece of dialogue, poem, etc., is set off with commas:

> Come on, Jones. Get a move on.
>
> You, sir, are a scoundrel.
>
> Where do you think you're going, dog?
>
> 'Lord, thou hast been our refuge in every generation.'

Commas in Quotations

The entire question of where one places other punctuation marks in relation to quotation marks is dealt with in the chapter on Quotation marks later. Here all we need do is say that, among British writers, commas are included inside quotation marks if they form part of the original quotation or if they mark a significant pause within it. We shall elaborate on this in the later chapter just mentioned. Meanwhile, a few examples will suffice. (Note that United States usage requires that the comma be placed inside the quotation marks as a matter of course. Here we shall illustrate non-US practice only.)

'Well, Jane,' said Tom, 'here we are.' (Tom's actual words were 'Well, Jane, here we are.')

'Come in', said Dick, 'and have a drink.' (What Dick said was 'Come in and have a drink.' Because there is no pause in the original quotation, the comma is placed outside it.)

Lennon and McCartney's most famous songs include 'Please please me', 'Can't buy me love', 'Eleanor Rigby' and 'Yesterday'.

Commas in Lists

Three or more items in a list or nouns and phrases in a series are normally separated by commas.

A musical sound is defined in terms of its pitch, duration, tone colour and volume.

Among the stalwarts in the tenor section of the choir were Martin Miller, Tom Taylor, Michael Wright and Martin Hart.

Old boots, tin cans, cigarette packets, non-biodegradable sweet wrappers were all deposited in the entrance to the building.

The vexed question here is whether, in a cumulative list in which the last item is introduced by 'and' or 'or', a comma should be included or omitted before the 'and' or 'or'. The habit among British writers has generally been to omit, as in the first two examples just given. American writers, on the other hand, have tended to include the comma before 'and' or 'or', and it is hard to see why one should not do this. Where phrasal items in a list themselves contain conjunctions such as 'and' or 'or', a comma before the final 'and' or 'or' in the list is a mandatory aid to clarity. These examples show the recommended use of the comma in such lists:

Dostoevsky's greatest books include *The Idiot, Crime and Punishment*, and *The Brothers Karamazov*.

My favourite meals include bacon and eggs, fish and chips, steak, cheese on toast, and sausage and mash. Lovely!

I do not like peanut butter, chicken and ham paste, or mustard and cress in my sandwiches

Putting a comma before 'and' or 'or' in a simple list is not wrong. Sentences such as this are quite acceptable:

The car park contained three Toyotas, a Nissan Cherry, a Ford Fiesta, and a Mercedes.

If, however, you write for publication, you should first find out your editor's preference before putting commas in front of all your 'ands' and 'ors'.

Comma

Comma with 'etc.' Some editors have a liking for a comma both before and after etc., when it precedes another part of the sentence. The word etc., like 'and so on', is properly thought of as a parenthetical element in a sentence and can therefore be legitimately 'comma'd off':

> Lions, tigers, jaguars, etc., all belong to the cat family.

> Each child brought his or her books, pencils, erasers, compasses, etc., into the classroom.

Commas between Adjectives

When two or more adjectives modify the same noun, are they or are they not separated by commas? This is a difficult problem that does not allow of an easy solution. Rules have been suggested covering this question. G.V. Carey, for instance, recommended that commas should be included if the adjectives 'are, so to speak, cumulative, but not otherwise'. Thus he was able to distinguish between 'a dazzling, luxurious limousine' and 'a large grey sports car'. In *You Have a Point There*, Eric Partridge gave an example that used a list of adjectives with the last preceded by *and*; so, presumably, he supported the use of commas: 'An odd, strange, curious and queer creature.' Other authorities say that if *and* can be placed 'meaningfully' between each adjective and the next, commas should be used, but not otherwise. But what do they mean by 'meaningfully'? Unfortunately, we are dealing here with one of the most subjective aspects of punctuation. Nevertheless, it is our duty to make some recommendations, so here goes.

1. Absence of Commas. We do not use commas in these sentences:

> He wore a pale blue shirt and a dark red tie and light green socks.

> Outside the graceful Georgian house stood a large black Mercedes.

In the first sentence the colour names are in fact nouns used as modifiers. We can prove this by turning the sentence to read: 'He wore a shirt of pale blue 85' or 'The colour of the shirt he wore was a pale blue 85' The adjectives 'pale', 'dark', etc., go with the colour names and not the nouns that the colour names modify.

In the second sentence, 'Georgian house' can be thought of as a linguistic unit that is modified by 'graceful'. Other similar linguistic units might be 'old man' or 'young woman', as in 'a kind old man' or 'a beautiful young woman'. The two adjectives 'large' and 'black' both say something about the physical appearance of the Mercedes. We can signal this fact by not using commas between them.

2. Presence of Commas. We use commas in these sentences:

> Our Galaxy contains dwarf, giant(,) and supergiant stars.

> He lived in a large, comfortable house on the outskirts of the city.

In the first sentence, the adjectives amount to a straightforward list, and the recommendations already made under 'Commas in Lists' apply here. The comma in parentheses is optional.

In the second sentence, the two adjectives, 'large' and 'comfortable' describe different aspects of the noun 'house'. One says something about its physical appearance; the other refers to its qualities as a place of residence. Because the adjectives describe different aspects of the noun, we separate them with commas. Further examples of this use of the comma might be given by the phrases 'a tall, kind old man', 'a large, smoke-filled room' or 'her long, slinky dress'.

Before we leave the punctuational uses of the comma, it is worth making two general points.

First, never let a comma come between the subject of a sentence and its verb, or the verb and its object, except when you are introducing a parenthetical phrase. The most careful writers have done this in the past, but it is a fault. These sentences are wrong:

> The debate over whether the modern teaching of English should or should not stress the need for good punctuation, has barely got off the ground.

> The answer to the question of whether punctuation should be formally taught in our schools today must surely be, yes.

No comma is necessary in either of the above sentences. However, commas are rightly inserted in this sentence:

> The second largest party in the House of Commons, which during the 1980s was the Labour Party, forms Her Majesty's Opposition.

Second, if you find yourself having to use too many commas and the commas are all justifiable on any of the above grounds, you should still avoid an excess of commas by changing some of the parenthetical ones to parentheses or dashes or by rewording your sentence. Commas have a duty to clarify not clutter the text. When they do clutter it, they cause a barrier to communication and ought to go. If that means recasting your thoughts, so be it.

Non-Punctuational Uses

The most frequently encountered non-punctuational use of the comma is in alphabetically arranged lists of personal names using the surname-first system, such as those found in biographical dictionaries or encyclopaedias. Other uses of the comma are those found in simple bibliographies, in personal and business letters, and in the writing of numbers.

1. Alphabetical Lists of Personal Names. In most lists of this kind, the surname is followed by a comma and then by the forenames or initials. Any additional information is also preceded by a comma, although other punctuation may also be used. For example:

Bach, Johann Sebastian, German composer: b. Eisenach, 21 March 1685; d. Leipzig, 28 July 1750 . 85

2. Simple Bibliographies. The simplest way of presenting a bibliography, especially a brief reading list attached to an article in a book or magazine, is to use a form where author, title, publisher and year are set off form each other by commas. This example will demonstrate:

Paul Johnson, *The National Trust Book of British Castles*, Weidenfeld & Nicolson, 1978.

An alternative way of presenting bibliographical information, but one which requires additional punctuation, is as follows:

Johnson, Paul. *The National Trust Book of British Castles.* Weidenfeld & Nicolson, 1978.

A way of presenting a brief book list continuously is illustrated as follows:

Johnson, Paul: *The National Trust Book of British Castles*, Weidenfeld & Nicolson, 1978; Warner, Philip: *Guide to Castles in Britain*, New English Library, 1981.

Other bibliographical formats are possible.

3. Personal and Business Letters. A comma is used in the following circumstances:

(a) In addresses. A comma is usually placed after each element of an address or name and address written at the top of a letter. The format of the name and address of the recipient on business letters is usually as follows:

Mr Thomas Smith,

'Sunnyview',

Elmers End Road,

Beckenham,

Kent BR3 4SZ.

A quoted name and address may be written out continuously in this form:

Mr Steve Mason, 106 Roslyn Hill, London N15.

Note that commas are no longer used to separate house numbers and street names and are not used to set off postcodes:

30 Eden Park Avenue, Beckenham, Kent BR3 3HN.

If the person identified in the name and address has a title or set of letters after his name, the use of a comma may be regarded by some people as unclear:

John Smith, MA, Esq., 75 Cornwall Gardens, London SW7.

An alternative way of representing this, noted by Eric Partridge, employs the use of colons:

John Smith, MA, Esq.: 75 Cornwall Gardens: London SW7

A more modern method might be to include extra spaces:

John Smith MA Esq. 75 Cornwall Gardens London SW7

This last style might work well for letterheads, but for general purposes the all-comma format is usually adopted.

Note that in informal letters on unheaded notepaper it is still the norm to write the sender's address in the top right-hand corner.

(b) In salutations. The style common in countries such as Britain is to begin letters with a salutation followed by a comma:

Dear Jane,

How lovely it was to go with you to the concert last week. I can't wait until we see each other again . 85

Dear Mr Smith,

Thank you for your recent enquiry about our hotel . 85

Dear Sir,

Further to our letter of 16 July, I am sorry to have to inform you . 85

Sir,

May I through your columns express my opinion that Prof. Ramsbotham's theory concerning the use of the letter v in Middle English is utter nonsense. 85

Note that in the case of formal and business letter-writing, the American practice is to follow the salutation 'Dear Mr Smith' or 'Dear Sir' with a colon:

Dear Sir:

Since you have not replied to our letter of 16 July, it is my duty to inform you. …

Informal private letters, however, follow British practice in using a comma. *See* the chapter on Colon.

At the end of a letter, before the signature or name of the writer, it is customary to write 'Yours sincerely' (for personal letters or business letters where the name of the recipient is stated in the salutation) or 'Yours faithfully' (where the recipient is addressed as 'Dear Sir', 'Dear Sirs' or 'Dear Madam'). Other variants, such as 'Yours truly', 'Best wishes' or 'With all my love', are also found. A comma usually immediately follows this closing tag.

Yours sincerely,

Jane

Note that some offices follow the practice of placing the closing tag, signature and name on the right of the page at the foot of a letter when the paragraphs of the letter are indented. When they all start flush left, the closing tag, name and signature are also placed flush left.

4. Numbers. Numbers of four or more digits are normally 'comma'd off' in groups of three digits moving leftwards from the implied or actual decimal point:

5,000 years ago. A327,642.50 population 12,865,370

However, if you are writing a technical report or an article for a science magazine, you may be asked to write four-figure numbers without a comma:

5000 metres   2361.75   8000BAC

In technical or scientific papers numbers containing more than five digits before the decimal point may be marked off not with commas but with spaces (in printed matter, these may be thin spaces):

22 584 631   50 000 km

Years consisting of four digits do not contain a comma:

1989   2000 BC   AD 1645 (not 1645 AD)

On the European continent, the comma is generally used as the decimal point, with the space used to group the digits in a number with five or more figures:

263,8   56 421,75

For further information, *see* the chapter on Numbers.

History of the Semicolon

We use the symbol ; to represent the semicolon, a sign derived not from the full point and comma, as one might expect, but from the Greek question mark. Anglo-Saxon manuscripts from the eighth and ninth centuries used a symbol known as the punctus elevatus, which, as a stop, had a value similar to our semicolon. Modern printed editions of Old English texts sometimes render this mark as a reverse semicolon (<?>), but early printers required something neater and tidier, and the Greek question mark filled the bill admirably.

Although it formed part of the hierarchy of stops in use during the sixteenth and seventeenth centuries, the semicolon was dominated by the colon until the 19th century. Now the roles have almost been reversed: the semicolon predominates over the colon, although both remain under-utilized.

3

Semicolon

Although the semicolon is now probably not as neglected as its more emphatic brother the colon, it is rare enough in ordinary writing to be considered something of a bogey. Most people who do not write for a living – and a few who do – hardly use it at all. Some people seem to be afraid of it; others are clearly prejudiced about it. It is certainly possible to overwork the semicolon, and some experts on English, notably H.W. Fowler, were perhaps overfond of it. But our stock of punctuation marks is not so rich that we can do without it. In fact, we ought to welcome the semicolon rather than distrust it; in the right place it can add freshness and subtlety to the most tired and pedestrian prose.

The semicolon is now no longer seen principally as a weak form of colon. In its strictly punctuational uses, it occasionally duplicates the duties of the colon, which has itself become much more important as a non-punctuational device. The fortuitous appearance of the semicolon as a combination of full point and comma advertises exactly what the semicolon now is – a cross between a comma and a full point, signifying a more significant break than the former but altogether lacking the finality of the latter.

Semicolons between Clauses

The semicolon's modern status as a strong comma or weak full stop is amply demonstrated in its chief use within the sentence, that of separating clauses. A semicolon may separate clauses with or without connecting conjunctions.

1. Without Connecting Conjunctions. We said earlier that one of the 'thou-shalt-nots' of using the comma was the placing of it between two independent clauses not linked by a co-ordinate conjunction. A comma in such a position is felt to be too weak a break. Normally, syntax would require a full point. But if the clauses are close to each other in sense – so that the second or subsequent clauses represent logical additions to, restatements of, or marked contrasts with the first – then a full point might be too disruptive a break. The mark that shows the connection in the absence of an appropriate conjunction is the semicolon. We therefore avoid this kind of sentence:

> The sky was black, the rain fell continuously.

From what has just been said, a comma is not allowable after 'black'. A full point is acceptable, but a semicolon is better because it establishes the logical link between the two clauses:

The sky was black; the rain fell continuously.

The following examples illustrate the types of independent clauses so far mentioned that can be linked by semicolons:

> He was born in the seaside town of Lowestoft; he died in Aldeburgh, another town by the sea. (Logical addition)
>
> He lived a life of debauchery; wine, women and gambling were his constant pursuits. (Restatement)
>
> He lived in London all week; he spent his weekends in the country. (Contrast.)

The use of semicolons between independent clauses gains maximum impact and effect when the clauses are short and employ parallel constructions:

> He lived in the town; she lived in the country.
>
> Describe it you may; explain it you cannot.

When the independent clauses share a main verb, that of the first does not have to be repeated in subsequent clauses. We may or may not signal its presence with the use of a comma:

> To err is human; to forgive, divine.
>
> The sun shines by its own light; the moon by reflected sunlight.

2. With Connecting Co-ordinate Conjunctions. Co-ordinate clauses linked by conjunctions, when they need to be punctuated, are normally marked off by commas. But we may need to strengthen the comma by replacing it with a semicolon to achieve a rhetorical effect, especially to emphasize a contrast:

> He was brave; but he feared the thought of entering the forest at night.
>
> He hated commuting; and he hated the office even more.
>
> His novels were much admired; yet his poetry attracted nothing but caustic criticism.
>
> Give me liberty; or give me death.
>
> He would do anything for her; for he loved her beyond all reason.

When co-ordinate clauses in a sentence each contain several internal commas, the break between them is signalled not by another comma but by a semicolon.

> The doctor took off his hat and coat, removed his gloves and went upstairs; but he could not find the room in which his patient lay.
>
> Time, we all know, is a great healer; and, despite all the anguish and suffering she had endured, it eventually worked its miracle for Jane.

3. Semicolons Before Conjunctive Adverbs. In the earlier section on commas, we touched on a group of linguistic forms called conjunctive adverbs. These are a group of adverbs and adverbial phrases that are used parenthetically in a clause and serve to mark some form of connection with a previous clause. Many of these conjunctives are not restricted to the beginning of the clause they modify and can appear some way into it. Typical conjunctives are the following:

accordingly	in addition
also	indeed
anyway, anyhow	in fact
as a result	likewise
at least	moreover
besides	nevertheless
consequently	still
even so	then
furthermore	therefore
hence	thus
however	yet (and yet, but yet)

A few examples will illustrate the use of the conjunctives:

He bought the car in Belgium; at least, that's what he said.

No one died or was hurt in the shooting incident; in fact, the only real damage was to a few panes of glass.

He considered himself a talented writer; the critics, however, did not agree with him.

A couple of important conjunctives are the phrases 'for example' and 'that is':

None of her relatives liked her; her aunt, for example, refused to communicate with her or mention her at all.

He was believed to have flown to Paris; that is, a ticket for a flight bound for Orly Airport had been booked in his name.

Note that the abbreviated forms of 'for example' and 'that is', e.g. and i.e., may also be preceded by semicolons:

The terrestrial planets have relatively slow axial rotation periods; e.g., Mercury completes one rotation every 59 days.

A fugue is a musical form that is based on imitative counterpoint; i.e., each part follows the one before, presenting broadly the same melodic theme.

4. Between Main and Subordinate Clauses. In general, it is wise to steer clear of using semicolons between main and subordinate clauses. However, subordinate clauses introduced by the word *because* occasionally benefit from being prefaced by a semicolon, which emphasizes the decisiveness of the clause:

> Davidson was certainly grateful to Dr Boone; because without that good doctor's skills as a healer he would surely have died.

> He rushed to carry out the captain's command; because he knew that disobedience meant certain death.

The conjunctions *because* and *for* are virtually interchangeable. Because *for* is a co-ordinate conjunction, it will take a semicolon, as in our earlier example:

> He would do anything for her; for he loved her beyond all reason.

Its counterpart *because* is traditionally regarded as a subordinate conjunction and should not normally be preceded by a semicolon – at least, so the pundits say. However, sensible writers who adhere to the spirit of written communication rather than the law of grammar see no reason why *because* and *for* should be treated differently from each other and use a semicolon with both when they feel it appropriate to do so. Apart from this one exception, though, do follow the pundits and keep semicolons for separating co-ordinate clauses only – unless you have some extremely subtle or dramatic effect in mind.

5. Between Complex Sentences. Semicolons can be placed between independent clauses, as we have seen; they can also be put between whole sentences that contain a main and subordinate clause, as in this sentence. The two sentences should stand in a logical or contrasting relationship to each other, and ideally they should employ the same grammatical construction for maximum effect. Here are just two further examples:

> When he arrived in Berlin, he bought a flat; when he left, he sold it again.

> Mr Wilson believed that the new extension would cut off a significant amount of daylight from the library; Mr Smith contended that, because it was not a very tall structure, it would do no such thing.

Semicolons in Lists

Semicolons may do the work of commas by marking off items in a list or phrases in a series that themselves contain commas. This is a case of promoting a few commas to semicolons to achieve clarity and avoid ambiguity. Notice how hopelessly confusing this sentence is when commas only are used:

> The people on the guest list included Sarah Wilson, a writer of biography, Andrew Stephenson, one of the country's most distinguished poets, Robert Bronson, an industrialist, art collector and motor racing enthusiast, and the Bishops of Bristol and Bath and Wells.

With semicolons separating the items, everything becomes clear:

> The people on the guest list included Sarah Wilson, a writer of biography; Andrew Stephenson, one of the country's most distinguished poets; Robert Bronson, an industrialist, art collector and motor racing enthusiast; and the Bishops of Bristol, and Bath and Wells.

Semicolons add to the literary quality of this accumulation of infinitives:

> To stand firm, even when the world is telling you that you are wrong; to face adversity with a calm spirit; to die for your country, if need be – such are the qualities that I would wish to see in you, my son.

Non-Punctuational Uses

The chief non-punctuational use of the semicolon is to separate items or categories of item in an inventory, string of bibliographical references, etc.:

> Ground Floor: three reception rooms, kitchen and onservatory; First Floor: four bedrooms, bathroom and WC; Outside: garage (with space for two family cars), spacious garden to rear.

> V.E. Nash-Williams, 'The Roman goldmines at Dolaucothi', *Bulletin of the Board of Celtic Studies*, xiv (1950), 79–81; G.D.B. Jones, I.J. Blakeley and E.C.F. Mcpherson, ibid. xix, 71–84.

In some dictionaries, the semicolon serves to separate two synonymous or almost synonymous words or phrases in a definition. For example, a definition of the word *doleful* might run:

> characterized by grief; sad or sorrowful.

4

Colon

Dr Samuel Johnson, in his famous *English Dictionary* of 1755, defines the word colon like this:

> A point used to mark a pause greater than that of a comma and less than that of a period. Its use is not very exactly fixed; nor is it very necessary, being confounded by most with the semicolon. It was used before punctuation was refined, to mark almost any sense less than a period. To apply it properly, we should place it, perhaps, only where the sense is continued without dependence of grammar or construction; 85

If Dr Johnson were alive today, he would probably find that not much has changed regarding the use of the colon, except perhaps that far fewer people employ it nowadays, and of those that do, most have trouble discriminating between it and the semicolon. Indeed, in sentences the two punctuation marks may be made to do substantially the same jobs. Yet there is still an important place for the colon in our punctuation system and an even more important one in the area of non-punctuational uses.

Colon in a Sentence

We can divide the use of the colon within a sentence into two main categories: the true stop or pause mark and the mark of introduction. Of these two categories the second is by far the more important, but in order to preserve some logic and clarity of approach, we shall deal first with the colon as a stop, mainly because this is exactly what it was originally.

1. Colon Between Clauses. This is the area in which confusion can most readily arise between the colon and the semicolon. In certain instances, the colon can function as a strong semicolon even in modern writing. But in general, today's authors have restricted their use of the colon quite severely: it is largely confined to signalling a narrow range of logical connections.

A couple of general points are worth stating. The first thing to note is that colons should generally be used to link only two independent or co- ordinate clauses. And secondly, the clauses may or may not be connected by conjunctions, such as 'and', 'but', 'or', etc.

(a) Balancing Clauses. A sentence that naturally falls into two equal parts contained within a pair of independent clauses may have the break between the clauses signalled by a colon:

Colon

The managing director has only just heard about Jones's report: he demands to see it straight away.

I'm thirsty: please give me a cup of tea.

(b) Contrasting Clauses. More often than not, balanced sentences contain contrasting or antithetical clauses, one of which is the opposite of the other, as in these well-worn proverbs:

To err is human: to forgive is divine.

Man proposes: God disposes.

More practical examples, perhaps, include the following:

Audiences and critics loved her: her fellow artists despised her.

He may be a good man: he is certainly a foolish one.

History of the Colon

The colon is another of our punctuation marks that has its beginnings in Greek oratory and rhetoric. It is interesting that there is an anatomical connection, although not the one you may be expecting: in ancient times the Greek word kolon, literally meaning 'limb' or 'member' (rather than 'part of the large intestine' – that sense comes from a different kolon), signified a passage of rhetorical discourse midway in extent between the periodos, or period (see the chapter on Full Point) and the komma (see the chapter on Comma). (A kolon also meant part of a strophe in a choric song or a division in Greek prosody or versification.) Naturally, the Greeks had a mark signalling the end of a kolon, and that mark, which was in fact a simple point placed high, became known as a kolon too. The Romans, who borrowed their rhetorical ideas from the Greeks, gave us our word colon.

The double point : now used for the punctuation mark that we call the colon has been part of the punctuation system since the eighth century. It was used to mark off sections of written text in medieval manuscripts, often in conjunction with a single point (:.), although its force as a pause mark was not always consistent. In the sixteenth century, soon after the age of printing began, the double point – that is, the colon – became part of the modern punctuational hierarchy, halfway between the full point, or period, and the semicolon. In practice, however, the colon usurped many of the duties of the semicolon, proving (as Dr Johnson implied) that English punctuation needed only one pause mark between the full point and the comma.

The semicolon made a comeback during the eighteenth century, and by the end of the nineteenth the colon had been all but restricted to the status of a mark used for introducing a quotation or list.

(c) The Colon of Promotion. In an involved sentence, in which semicolons have already been used, a colon may be introduced to mark a major break. For example:

> Time, as we all know, is a great healer; it worked its miracle for Jane: but who could have known how short-lived that miracle would be?

(d) Explanatory or Interpretive Clauses. In this usage, the colon separates two independent clauses, the second of which serves to explain, amplify, interpret or reveal something connected with the first.

> Getting hold of the explosive would be simple: the store room was full of it, and as security officer Evans had the key to the room.

> Haydn was a prolific composer: his output included more than 100 symphonies, about 80 string quartets, 50 sonatas, and more than 40 piano trios.

> Mission control was becoming anxious: there had been no radio contact with the astronauts for four hours.

> Our report is based on the most exhaustive investigations: we have made a detailed analysis of all the data for the first six months of the year and have rigorously cross-checked comparable data for the same period last year.

2. The Colon of Introduction. The examples given under 1 (d) provide the link to the most characteristic use of the colon: namely, its employment as an introductory device. We said that the colon is used to separate two clauses, the second of which is an explanation, interpretation or amplification of the first. The reverse, as it were, is also true. We can regard the first clause as a preface or introduction to the explanation contained in the second:

> He gave good reasons for his lateness: signal failure had delayed the arrival of his train at Waterloo, and there was a tube and bus strike that day too.

In a celebrated and much-quoted phrase, H.W. Fowler said that the colon in its introductory use had 'acquired a special function, that of delivering the goods that have been invoiced in the preceding words.' In this and all the punctuational uses that remain to be considered, that is exactly what it does.

(a) Between Phrases and Clauses. Either the first or second element of a sentence containing an introductory colon can be an incomplete clause or even a single word.

> Tuesday 11 July: the work was progressing well.

> Only one naturally occurring mineral remains to be discussed: diamond.

> To sum up: research has shown that, of the nine planets in the solar system, only the Earth currently supports life as we know it.

In written communications such as memos or on public notices and official documents containing admonitions, cautions, etc., the colon may generally be followed by a capital letter:

Colon

Warning: Trespassers will be prosecuted.

Attention: No dogs allowed.

To whom it may concern: Any personnel who have not been informed to the contrary by 5.0 p.m. may consider their employment terminated with effect from tomorrow.

(b) Before a List. The colon commonly introduces a list, regardless of whether the items of the list are presented numbered on separate lines or as a continuous string with each item marked off by a comma:

The contents of his briefcase included the following: a copy of *The Times*, a packet of sandwiches, an apple, a paperback novel and several top secret files.

Before 1986 only five moons were known to orbit the planet Uranus. They were the following:

(1) Ariel

(2) Miranda

(3) Oberon

(4) Titania

(5) Umbriel

Note that listed items on separate lines are frequently indented for clarity, as in the previous example.

Words such as *namely, viz, etc.* may or may not be used before the listed items:

Three minerals have yet to be considered: talc, corundum and diamond.

or

Three minerals have yet to be considered: namely, talc, corundum and diamond.

A colon is never used to interrupt the grammatical logic of a sentence. In these two examples, the colon is wrong and should be deleted:

One mineral that we have yet to consider is: diamond.

His briefcase contained: sandwiches, an apple, a copy of *The Times* and some office files.

However, if the list of items is set out with each one on a separate line, a colon may introduce it, because the grammatical logic has already been disrupted by this method of presenting the list:

Until 1986 the five known moons of Uranus were:

(1) Ariel

(2) Miranda

(3) Oberon

(4) Titania

(5) Umbriel

But

> Until 1986 the five known moons of Uranus were Ariel, Miranda, Oberon, Titania and Umbriel.

(For the now old-fashioned use of a dash after a colon at the head of a list, *see* the chapter of Dash.)

(c) Before a Summary. In this particular use a capital letter is sometimes employed after the colon, but it should not be:

> The company's offer therefore amounted to this: it would pay the agreed salary increase but would not back-date it to the start of the fiscal year.

> His whole life could by summed up as follows: he had been the greatest actor in the history of the modern theatre and had used his talent to search for truth.

(d) Before a Direct Quotation. It is easy to overdo this particular instance of the colon by placing it directly after every verb that indicates saying or writing. In these two examples the colon is wrong and should be commuted to a comma or even nothing at all:

> Tom said: 'Don't be so silly.'

> He rushed in and shouted: 'The Russians are coming!'

A more extended introduction to a quotation, however, in which the verb of saying or writing may be implied or even suppressed, needs to be followed by a colon before the quotation:

> Davies began the case for the defence with these words: "Ladies and gentlemen of the jury, imagine if you will the circumstances in which the defendant found himself only two days before the murder of which he is accused."

> He had just two words for his unwelcome visitor: "Get out!"

> In 1959 Kenneth Tynan wrote of Olivier: "The dark imprint of [his] stage presence is something one forgets only with an effort, but the voice is a lifelong possession of those who have heard it at its best."

If the quotation begins a new paragraph, then a colon invariably precedes it. This is especially true when the quotation carries no inverted commas and is indented in smaller type. Here is the colon in front of quotation marks:

> All the while Jones had been listening intently to what his opponent had to say.

Now he got up to make his reply and began:

"Friends, I know that much of what Tom has just said is true. But. 85"

And here is the colon in front of an indented passage:

Kenneth Tynan's admiration of Olivier was considerable, as one of his reviews in the late 1950s made clear:

The dark imprint of Olivier's stage presence is something one forgets only with an effort, but the voice is a lifelong possession of those who have heard it at its best.

(e) Before a Saying or Adage. Allied to the use of the colon before direct quotations is its employment before sayings, as in the examples that follow. (Note that in this instance quotation marks are not used and a capital letter after the colon is permissible.)

My motto is this: Do as you would be done by.

Being a cautious man, my uncle had an old proverb that ruled his every action: Look before you leap.

(f) Before an Example. The practice of placing a colon before a clause or sentence containing or representing an example parallels what was said about the use of 'for example' under the section on the semicolon. In fact, if the connecting words *for example* are used, the colon should be replaced by a semicolon. Note the difference between the following sentences:

Her relatives disliked her intensely: her aunt refused to communicate with her at all.

But

Her relatives disliked her intensely; her aunt, for example, refused to communicate with her at all.

Some dictionaries introduce example sentences or citations with a colon. Here is how one defines the idiom *to break bread*:

to take food or have a meal (with someone): It was his first offer to break bread with me ... (Honey Dec 1974)

And it will not have escaped your notice that the punctuation examples throughout this book have been introduced by colons.

Non-Punctuational Uses

Most of the non-punctuational uses of the colon can be thought of as special instances of the introductory colon. In many cases a larger unit or element precedes (or introduces, if you like) the unit or element that stands next to it in significance. Not all the non-punctuational uses of the colon can be conceived in this way, however, so we shall confine ourselves to the process of merely describing and illustrating each one as we come to it.

1. Business Uses. In the United States, the colon is placed after the salutation at the start of a formal or business letter:

Dear Sir:

Thank you for your inquiry about our product 85

In letters written to friends or relations, the comma is used instead of the colon:

Dear Jim,

It was great to meet up with you at the baseball game last Saturday 85

(Note that in many countries outside the United States, notably Great Britain, a comma is used after the opening salutation in all circumstances. *See* the chapter on Comma. It is also worth mentioning that there is an increasing propensity for dispensing with punctuation marks in this situation altogether, because the new paragraph that invariably begins after the salutation makes punctuation unnecessary.)

Office memoranda are frequently headed by a set list of items detailing the author, recipient(s), date, subject, etc., with a colon introducing each piece of information. For example:

INTEROFFICE COMMUNICATION

To: Jerry Smith

From: Tim Jones

Subject: Preparation of Internal Reports

Date: 7 October 1990

2. Biblical References. In citing passages from the Bible, it is customary to separate chapter and verse numbers with a colon:

Job 24:7   2 Corinthians 6:8 or   II Corinthians 6:8

Some publishers use a full point in this situation, but a colon is clearer. Strings of biblical references should be separated by semicolons, whereas two verses cited from the same chapter should be separated by a comma without repetition of the chapter number. An en rule (short dash) separates the first and last verse numbers in a passage from one chapter and the first and last chapters in a section from the same book. The following examples illustrate all eventualities:

Matthew 21   (Chapter 21 of the Gospel according to St Matthew)

Job 24:7   (Verse 7 of Chapter 24 of the Book of Job)

2 Chronicles 10:6 – 11   (Verses 6 to 11 of Chapter 10 of the second Book of

Chronicles)

Ezra 7:1,6 (Verses 1 and 6 of Chapter 7 of the Book of Ezra)

Genesis 1–4   (Chapters 1 to 4 of the Book of Genesis)

1 Kings 17:1–2 Kings 2:11 (Verse 1 of Chapter 17 of the first Book of Kings to Verse 11 of Chapter 2 of the second Book of Kings)

We may string these references together, using correct Bible order, by means of semicolons:

Genesis 1 – 4; 1 Kings 17:1 – 2 Kings 2:11; 2 Chronicles 10:6-11; Ezra 7:1,6; Job 24:7; Matthew 21.

3. Bibliographical Use. A colon is sometimes used for the following purposes:

(a) Between a title and a subtitle. Note that the subtitle may begin with an initial capital letter:

Cyrus Gordon, *Forgotten Scripts: The Story of their Decipherment*, 1968.

(b) After the place of publication. This is not a common use:

London: Harrap, 1987

Cambridge, Mass.: 1992

(c) Between the volume and page number of a periodical or the volume and page number of a large-scale work (an encyclopaedia, for instance). The volume number may be in Roman or Arabic numerals:

Antiquity XXXII:227 (1958)

Encyclopaedia Britannica (1986) 27:103

A colon is sometimes used between the act and scene numbers in a play, especially a play by Shakespeare:

Macbeth IV:ii:7   Coriolanus II:2:7

4. Use in Dialogue. A characteristic use of the colon is found in the scripts for plays. A colon is placed after the name of a character and immediately before the lines of dialogue assigned to that character. Note that any stage directions relating to the way the character is meant to deliver his or her lines also precede the colon:

Ursula: John, what on earth are we going to do? If Henry finds out –

John: He won't. Darling, trust me. And never forget that I love you.

Sarah [backing away]: You surely don't mean –

William [*smiling mirthlessly*]: Oh yes. I'm the killer they're all looking for.

5. Date and Time. In American usage, the figures representing the date and time in the all-figure format are normally separated by colons:

6:30 p.m.   18:30   2:27:89

Note that in British usage it is customary to use full points to separate the figures of the time and either full points or slashes (solidi) to separate the figures of the date (*see* the chapter on Full point). Note also that in American practice, as exemplified above, the order is month:day:year. British usage favours the slightly more logical ascending order of day:month:year. Hence, using colons, the above date would be rendered as 27:2:89 in the United Kingdom.

6. Ratios. These are expressed in this way:

5:4 is equal to 80:64, not 64:80.

In some countries women outnumber men in the ratio 3:2.

The scale on the old inch-to-the-mile maps was 1:63,360.

For more information on punctuation relating to numbers, *see* the chapter on Numbers.

5

Parentheses

In the section on the comma, we described various types of parenthetical material. A piece of parenthetical material, which we may from now on refer to as a parenthesis, is a word or group of words that stand outside the main grammatical structure of a sentence. A parenthesis can be a single word, a phrase, a clause, or even a whole sentence. The word parenthesis, plural parentheses, is Greek in origin and means literally 'an insertion beside'. The notion of a parenthesis being a kind of insertion is a very helpful one; in fact, a parenthesis is an insertion that disrupts but does not break the logic of a sentence. You could remove a parenthesis and the sentence would remain basically intact.

We have so far seen how a parenthesis can be marked off by using commas. Here and in the next chapter, on the Dash, we shall describe the role of other punctuation marks in carrying out this task.

Symbols of Parenthesis

What we are primarily discussing here is a set of symbols that are usually found in pairs, one sign being the mirror image of the other:

( ) [ ]   < >

The brace too comes as one of a mirror-image pair { } , but its use is rather different from the other signs. We shall return to it later.

Before we get down to details, we need to sort out some confusion in assigning names to the first two of the above symbols. In the United States and among printers and publishers generally, the first pair ( ) are known as parentheses, a term obviously linking them with the parenthesis that we have just been discussing. The second pair [ ] are referred to as brackets. In Britain, parentheses ( ) are known as brackets or, where a distinction seems necessary, round brackets, whereas brackets proper [ ] are usually called square brackets. The other symbols { } and < > are respectively and universally known as curly, or hooked, brackets and angle brackets. For the sake of clarity, and in view of the popular conception in Britain of what brackets are, we shall compromise. We shall talk of parentheses ( ) and square brackets [ ], curly brackets { } and angle brackets < >.

Note for Typists. Old typewriters are generally not able to produce the full range of signs discussed in this section, but virtually all electronic typewriters and word processors include them on their keyboards. If your machine cannot produce at least square brackets in addition to parentheses, you ought to consider upgrading it.

Correctly used and correctly produced square brackets can make a typescript look like a quality production.

Parentheses

The parentheses ( ) were part of the punctuation scene by the start of the sixteenth century. In 1566 Aldus Manutius the Younger, who was one of the earliest people to advocate a syntactical approach to punctuation, wrote of them in his *Orthographiae Ratio* (Spelling Method) as follows:

> Those words ought to be enclosed in a parenthesis,* which are not a part of the sentence, and do not depend upon any word either preceding or following: words whose absence causes no loss to the sentence.

Manutius' sensible point seems incredibly modern, even if his punctuation is not.

Parentheses should be reserved for enclosing anything that is not immediately relevant to the argument of a sentence. Pieces of text in parentheses can either be contained within the sentence or stand outside to form sentences of their own. (*See* later under 'Punctuation in Connection with Parentheses'.)

Parentheses function as a shorthand for such a phrase as 'by the way'. Note the following examples:

> Julie is bringing John (whom she met in Corfu last summer) to our party next week.

> The meeting took place without the presence of Mr West (his wife was due to have her first baby that afternoon) and passed the resolution that you see before you.

Parentheses enclose material that can be classified as one of the following: an afterthought, a comment, an explanation or a reference. We shall give a couple of examples of each.

Afterthought:

> The scent of jasmine pervaded the air (it always does at this time of year), and the crickets chirruped loudly.

> I didn't usually see him on Wednesday (or any other day, for that matter).

Comment:

> Sharon from the typing pool (a very tasty little blonde) sat on the opposite side of the room from Andy.

> He is a top academic (though you wouldn't think it by looking at him) and has gained a number of distinctions and honours.

---

*What we would now refer to as a pair of parentheses

Parentheses

Explanation:

> The Earth is a huge sphere (ball) covered with water, rock and soil, and surrounded by air.
>
> Mr Kurosawa (who is the head of our Japanese client company) is in Britain for a few days and will be visiting our factory here in Swansea.

Reference:

> I have already taken up this point in a previous chapter (see p. 81, n. 3).
>
> In the famous shield passage (Aeneid, VIII, 626–728), Virgil reviews the panoramic history of Rome as though it were a dazzling prophecy.

Life dates, dates of composition and translations of foreign titles of books, plays, paintings, etc., are also placed within parentheses:

> The French writer Stendhal (1783–1842) is famous for his novel *Le rouge et le noir* (The Red and the Black), written in 1830.
>
> Stendhal's most famous novel was *Le rouge et le noir* (1830).

Parentheses have a particular use with abbreviations. They may either enclose the full form following the abbreviation or they may enclose the abbreviation following the full form. This usually happens when the name of an organization, etc., is first mentioned in a piece of text, the abbreviation being used thereafter:

> The strike at the BBC (British Broadcasting Corporation) threatened the coverage of this year's Wimbledon tennis championships. In the event, however, BBC staff did not disrupt the screening of Wimbledon after all.
>
> The British Broadcasting Corporation (BBC) originally offered their staff a 7 per cent pay increase in 1989.

Parentheses serve to indicate an alternative option within a word:

> Police are anxious to track down the person(s) who dug up the twelfth green on Beckenham golf course.
>
> Strong (wo)men required to help set up the staging for Saturday's performance at the Church Hall.

Care should be taken over what constitutes the optional element in the word concerned. This next example is wrong because the optional elements are not properly bracketed off:

> We have a vacancy for a barman(maid).

A slash or solidus should be used here. The advertisement should read:

> We have a vacancy for a barman/barmaid (or a barman/maid).

In the report of a speech, especially a parliamentary one, parentheses enclose interruptions by the audience:

> Mr Speaker, I am happy to tell the House that the siege in Kensington is over and all the hostages are safe. (Loud cheers.)

Parentheses should not be overused, and it is a good rule to use them as little as possible. Their primary purpose is to set off material that really is of purely marginal significance and should be reserved for that use. Thus we prefer to write:

> Mrs Thatcher, Britain's prime minister, visited Paris in July.

because Mrs Thatcher's post as prime minister is of great material significance to her going to Paris. If we were to write:

> Mrs Thatcher (Britain's prime minister) visited Paris in July.

that would imply that Mrs Thatcher's post was of purely academic interest and had very little to do with her being in Paris.

However, there is some merit in using parentheses to avoid a clutter of commas. In the next two examples, (b) is preferable to (a):

(a) Mary, whose shopping basket, a vast portmanteau full of fruit, tinned food, packets of cereal, and all sorts of other groceries, was obviously too heavy for her, struggled unaided out of the supermarket and into the car park.

(b) Mary, whose shopping basket (a vast portmanteau full of fruit, tinned food, packets of cereal, and all sorts of other groceries) was obviously too heavy for her, struggled unaided out of the supermarket and into the car park.

There may be no potential ambiguity in sentence (a), but sentence (b) is preferable largely because it is neater and clearer.

At all costs the text within parentheses must not be too long. In the following example, the reader is kept waiting for ages before the main verb appears without any inkling as to what it is likely to be:

> Closer co-operation between university science departments and local industry (the co-opting of local industrial magnates onto university boards and similar arrangements under which scientific academics representing university departments may become directors of local companies have already proved successful in other countries) will obviously assist in the revitalization of the manufacturing sector in the national economy.

This thoroughly bad sentence is not only a discourtesy to the reader; it is an affront to good English and should be completely recast. Try this:

> Closer co-operation between university science departments and local industry is likely to prove invaluable to the national economy. The co-opting of local industrial magnates onto university boards and similar arrangements under which scientific academics representing university departments may become

Parentheses

directors of local companies have already proved successful in other countries. Such co-operation here will obviously assist in the revitalization of the manufacturing sector.

More words perhaps, but better English and a much clearer message more quickly communicated to the reader.

There is no excuse either for this sentence, quoted in Gowers' *Complete Plain Words*, in which the writer, as well as the reader, gets hopelessly lost:

> ... Owing to a shortage of a spare pair of wires to the underground cable (a pair of wires leading from the point near your house back to the local exchange, and thus a pair of wires essential to the provision of a telephone service for you) is lacking ...

Only this part of the sentence is quoted, but it may be that we can put it right by inserting 'the fact that' after 'Owing to'. It iss still a bad sentence, though – too many references to 'pairs of wires'.

Punctuation and Parentheses

The placing of punctuation marks in relation to parentheses is governed by whether the marks belong to the text enclosed in the parentheses or not. The rule is that the only punctuation allowed inside the parentheses is the punctuation that goes with the text there.

In practice, the only stop likely to cause difficulty is the full point. If the text within parentheses is inside the sentence, there is no full point inside the parentheses, even when the parenthetical text is syntactically a whole sentence itself or actually ends the sentence in which it is contained:

> The main course consisted of roast duck à l'orange (I love roast duck) and two vegetables.

> I have already mentioned this point in an earlier chapter (pp. 81–2).

If the parenthetical text lies right outside the sentence and forms another sentence entirely in parentheses, the full point goes inside the parentheses:

> I have already discussed this matter at length. (*See* Transactions, pp. 81–2.)

When parentheses take the place of commas, never put in the commas as well as the parentheses:

> Curare (which South American Indians have long used to poison their arrows for hunting) is now well established as a medicament.

Not

> Curare, (which South American Indians have long used to poison their arrows for hunting), is now well established as a medicament.

But if text in parentheses comes at the end of a passage already set off by a pair of commas, both those commas remain:

> Jean, who was deep in conversation with Francisco (a handsome Spaniard who was just her type), hardly noticed Tom's departure.

Colons and semicolons generally stand outside parentheses:

> Elijah prophesies drought in these terms (1 Kings 17:1): 'As the Lord God of Israel liveth, before whom I stand, there shall not be dew nor rain these years, but according to my word.'

> To err is human (this we know as a fact); to forgive is divine (this some of us hope and believe).

Question marks and exclamation marks forming part of the text inside parentheses will be included inside the parentheses:

> Jones (the idiot!) then proceeded to kick the ball into his own goalmouth.

> Then the youngest of the Smiths (how many are there, for goodness' sake?) trooped up to collect their prizes as well.

Spaces and Parentheses. Some inexperienced typists put spaces on each side of each of pair of parentheses. These spaces after an open parentheses sign (and before a close parentheses sign) are wrong. In text produced on a word processor, they can generate some very odd effects, the most notable being the lonely sight of a close parentheses sign at the start of a line. If that happens to be the last line of a paragraph, the effect is ludicrous.

> If you type text on a word processor (as many people do), do not put spaces on both sides of your parentheses signs (it can look very silly, as this example will surely show).

So the rule is: include (as part of the first word and) as part of the last, provided that there is no full point. If there is, the) comes straight after it.

Square Brackets

Parentheses (round brackets) deal with material added to a sentence by the author of that sentence. Frequently, some of us (especially editors of books seeking to make things clear for the reader) may add things to sentences written by somebody else. This latter type of addition, a phrase or sentence not included in the original author's text, is enclosed within square brackets [ ]. Square brackets are generally most often encountered with direct quotations and serve to introduce an editorial comment, explanation, correction, or other interpolation:

> John Bunyan's *Pilgrim's Progress* begins: 'As I walked through the wilderness of this world, I lighted on a certain place, where was a den [Bedford jail, where Bunyan was imprisoned for 12 years]; and I laid me down in that place to sleep …'

'… and on the other side, what sighs and groans brast [i.e., burst] from Christian's heart.' Thus Bunyan writes of the fight between Christian and Apollyon.

Similarly they may occur in indented quotations:

On the question of soccer violence, AP of Beckenham writes:

Sir – I feel that the unemployed louts who habitually cause trouble on the terraces [many of the most serious offenders are in fact holding down highly paid jobs in the city] should receive stiff prison sentences, not fines 85

Editors of classical texts or books of inscriptions use square brackets to enclose letters that are thought to be present in the text or inscription but are now illegible. Angle brackets may perform a similar function. This is a very specialized use of square brackets that the ordinary writer is perhaps unlikely to encounter. *See* the chapter on Ellipsis.

A particular use of square brackets that crops up rather more frequently is in enclosing the Latin word *sic*, meaning 'thus', to draw attention to the fact that an old, unusual or incorrect spelling, date, etc., is reproduced exactly as it appears in the original author's work. It amounts to an editorial comment that says 'Yes, the original author really did write that.' The word sic is set as here, in italics. This device should not be overused but should be reserved for cases where sense or clarity might be in momentary jeopardy:

Campbell's London Tradesman (1747) complains bitterly about the type of person setting up in the music selling trade at that time:

The Masters of Musick shops 85 can scarce hum a tune in proper time, but if they new [sic] a little more before they set up the trade, 85 they would have a better chance to thrive.

Note that the spelling 'Musick' is accepted as an ancient one that crops up all the time. It is therefore not deemed incorrect, and so we do not have to insert [sic] after it.

Square brackets are also occasionally put around an editorial or critical question mark. The query may concern the soundness of the original author's text or the content of that text. Many readers do not like this device: some consider it a vulgar intrusion, while others think that it oversteps the bounds of editorial interference. In any event it is ambiguous.

Jones writes: 'Science fiction is more ancient than one might think. As long ago as about AD 180 [?], the Greek satirist Lucian wrote a story about a trip to the moon. …'

In this example, what is the basis of the editor's or reviewer's query? Does he or she disbelieve the date, or is the writer's assertion about the beginnings of science fiction such a surprise? Square brackets around question marks are best avoided.

A special use of square brackets is found in linguistics, in which they are conventionally used to enclose a so-called narrow phonetic transcription. Some dictionaries that provide pronunciations often enclose them in square brackets:

> knight [nait], *n.*, a mounted soldier in the army of a feudal superior 85

Other Types of Brackets

Curly brackets { } and angle brackets < > have a number of specialized uses that ordinary writers and editors rarely encounter. These uses are to do with the preparation of classical texts or books of ancient inscriptions for publication.

Curly brackets enclose letters that are superfluous to the text. Angle brackets enclose letters that should have been in the text but were left out or written down wrongly by the scribe who copied the text. Sometimes the conventions for using square, curly and angle brackets are different from those set out here. They may also call for the use of double square brackets, e.g. for indicating letters that are thought to have been present but were later rubbed out. The way in which these different types of brackets are used is normally explained in the book in which they appear.

Brackets within Brackets

These should be avoided if possible, but if they cannot be, one may use either square brackets or parentheses within parentheses. For example:

> Twenty Thousand Leagues Under the Sea (a novel by Jules Verne [1828–1905]) is one of the best early science fiction novels in the genre.

There are two alternative ways of setting down this sentence:

(a) *Twenty Thousand Leagues under the Sea* (a novel by Jules Verne (1828–1905)). …

(b) *Twenty Thousand Leagues under the Sea* (a novel by Jules Verne, 1828–1905).…

Sentence (b), using commas, is preferable here, but where the parenthesis with a parenthesis is longer, one of the other methods should be used.

Non-Punctuational Uses

There are several non-punctuational uses of parentheses ().

1. In Lists. Parentheses are used purely as a convention to enclose numbers or letters against each item in the list. The items may be written out continuously or on separate lines:

> His writings may be grouped under the following headings:
>
> (a) philosophy; (b) satire; (c) history; (d) pornography.

or

His writings may be grouped under the following headings:

(a) philosophy

(b) satire

(c) history

(d) pornography

Half-parentheses like this) may be employed in lists of this nature:

Subjects under review include the following:

1) Student grants

2) Accommodation

3) Staffing provisions

2. In Mathematics. Elements in mathematical expressions that must be taken together in order for their calculations to be carried out before the solution of the whole expression are placed within parentheses:

$$(x^2 - xy - 6y^2) \text{ B4 } (2x^2 + 4xy + y)$$

For 'brackets within brackets' in mathematical expressions, the parentheses may contain either square brackets or another set of parentheses. (*See* above.)

Half-angle brackets (either < or >) are used in mathematics as signs of inequality. The < implies that the preceding quantity is less than the one following; the > implies that the preceding quantity is greater than the one following.

3. In linguistics. The signs < and > indicate the direction of derivation. As a shorthand used in etymologies given in dictionaries, the sign pointing left < indicates that what follows is the origin of the word or idiom being defined:

iridium, *n.*, a precious metallic chemical element 85 (< New Latin < Latin *iris*, rainbow; named from its iridescence when found in solution)

Braces

The brace is a large version of the curly bracket. Its use is to link related items in a list, especially when they are in a table. It is also used in mathematics and music. But its primary use is to show that one item is comprised of or equivalent to two or more others. These examples show it in action. Mark well the direction in which the kink or hook should face:

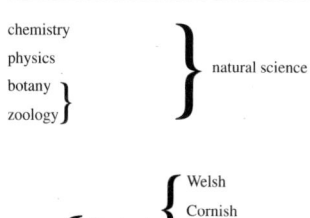

chemistry
physics
botany
zoology
} natural science

Celtic {
  Brythonic { Welsh, Cornish, Breton
  Goidelic { Irish, Scots Gaelic, Manx
}

6
Dash

The dash formally joined the English punctuation scene during the seventeenth century. As a symbol, it is distinguished in being a truly elastic mark of punctuation, both in handwriting and in printing. It does indeed come in different lengths. Printers and editors speak not of the dash as such but of various lengths of rule: the en rule (–), the em rule (—) and the double em rule (——). These ens and ems are printer's measurements (an em is the square of the body of a given size of type; an en is half an em). The length of an em or en rule therefore depends on the type size that the printer is using. To a typist, however, and to you and me as readers or authors with little interest in typographical niceties, all lines that are longer than a hyphen can be regarded as dashes.

In typing, we usually represent the dash as a single hyphen with spaces on each side of it (-). Journalists, working quickly and aware of the realities of editing and typesetting, often represent a dash as a double hyphen with no spaces each side (—). Copy-editors distinguish between an en and an em rule by writing *n* or *N* or *EN* over one type of spaced hyphen and *m* or *M* or *EM* over another. In certain of the usages listed below, a typist can make no practical distinction between a hyphen and a dash, whereas a typesetter would probably make the distinction between a hyphen and an en rule without being told to. In our discussion, we shall try to make such distinctions clear.

Parenthetical Dashes

The most notable function of a dash is to mark off parenthetical material within a sentence. As we have seen, commas and brackets can perform the same function, but the dash does the job with more panache, more flamboyance or sensationalism, and in an altogether more disruptive way:

> The tenor soloist – one wondered at times whether he was actually performing the same piece as the other forces on the platform – sang with such a wayward technique and such a disregard for the conductor's tempi that I felt genuine relief as each of his contributions came to an end.

> When, as an actor, one is selected for a role in a classic play, one simply goes along to the nearest bookshop – Richmond & Page is my local – and buys a copy of it.

Parenthetical dashes come in pairs, as do parentheses and parenthetical commas. As in the case of text enclosed in parentheses, one should be able to take the words between the dashes out of the sentence altogether without damaging the grammatical wholeness of the sentence.

A 'dashed' parenthetical phrase placed at the end of a sentence takes only the first or introductory dash; the second dash coalesces with the full point:

> The title of his book, *The Greening of the Desert*, was powerful – one might almost say dramatic.

A parenthetical sentence between dashes does not end in a full point but can take a question mark or exclamation mark:

> He is – how can I put it? – a raving lunatic.

> Then Nigel – what an idiot he is sometimes! – spilt the whole bottle of wine down my dress.

It is extremely easy to overdo the use of the dash in marking off parentheses. Some journalists employ it at almost every opportunity, mainly because of its impact. Unfortunately, overuse has inevitably led to a weakening of the effect of the dash, so that all too often it is used where a pair of commas would be quite adequate. Note this example:

> Jones – the owner of the car – was surprised at how dirty it was.

The dashes here represent overkill. The information concerning Jones's ownership of the car is not a major digression, as the dashes would naturally imply, but a rather relevant point. This is, admittedly, an extreme example, but it is useful in pointing to a trend that should be discouraged. Dashes should be reserved for barely related digressions, not as a lazy alternative to commas or parentheses. It all comes down to thinking about what one is trying to communicate.

Dashes and Commas. In an extended parenthesis that contains words or phrases linked by commas, it can often be clearer to mark the beginning and end of the parenthesis by dashes. We noted a similar use of round brackets (parentheses) earlier on.

Even here, however, care should be taken to avoid overdoing the dashes. This example shows how effective dashes can be when used in this way:

> A mountain of debris – smashed furniture, papers and books thrown all over the floor, and ornaments shattered to smithereens – was the disheartening sight that greeted him.

It is worth noting, as we did when discussing parentheses, that we do not combine dashes and commas in the same positions in the sentence.

Compound punctuation marks made up of dashes and other stops were used at one time and are described at length by Eric Partridge (*You have a Point There*, pp. 86–8). They are virtually a vanished breed now. But see the reference to the colon and dash before a list in the next part of this chapter.

The Single Dash

1. Before Lists and Summaries. A single dash can take the place of a colon in introducing a list, summary or conclusion:

> All the member nations of NATO were represented – Belgium, Canada, Denmark, France, West Germany, Greece, Iceland, Italy, Luxemburg, the Netherlands, Norway, Portugal, Spain, Turkey, the United Kingdom, and the United States.
>
> Booze, women, gambling – his life was one long round of debauchery.

At one time, it was common practice to introduce a list with a combined colon and dash (: –). Typists used to render it as a colon and hyphen. This practice was particularly used for lists in which the items were set out on separate lines, with each item indented, as in this example:

> The items stolen included the following: –
>
> > A half-hunter watch
> >
> > Jewellery valued at A33,000
> >
> > A set of Meissen figures, value A310,000

This style is now largely obsolete; a colon is sufficient.

2. Introducing the Attribution of a Quotation. This may be used with a direct quotation enclosed in quotation marks:

> 'History is bunk.' – Henry Ford.

or on a separate line, usually ranged right, after an indented quotation not marked off by quotation marks:

> My heart leaps up when I behold
>
> A rainbow in the sky …
>
> – William Wordsworth

3. Introducing an Afterthought or Break in Continuity. The informality and disruptive character of the dash make it an ideal mark for setting off an afterthought – especially an ironic one – at the end of the sentence and for signalling an abrupt change of subject or other break in the flow of a sentence:

> The last time Tom had seen Sam, he looked as if he were at death's door – obviously, death hadn't been at home that day.
>
> John, I've poured you a gin and – oh, I forgot, you only drink orange juice, don't you?

4. Signalling Breaks and Hesitations in Speech. A dash or a number of dashes may be used in writing dialogue to signal hesitancy:

'Mr Henderson, I – ' Lewis broke off as Henderson's secretary entered the office with a tray of coffees.

'I – er – that is – I – don't know who you mean,' stammered Jones.

For the use of an ellipsis in simulating halting speech, *see* the chapter on Ellipsis.

5. Indicating a Change of Speaker. A dash is used to indicate a change of speaker when the text of a conversation is set continuously, like this:

Jones met Smith in the corridor: 'Smith, where have you been?' – 'Don't panic, Jones. I got held up, that's all.'

This is perhaps an old-fashioned use of the dash. In most cases of quoted dialogue, each character's words start on a fresh line. *See* the chapter on Quotation Marks.

6. The Equivalent Use of the Dash. This is a rather informal use, in which the dash does duty for the word 'equals':

+ –   plus

B4 –   multiplied by

7. In Informal Notetaking. This is chiefly a special use of the dash in handwriting, found for example in lecture notes:

1856 – Treaty of Paris ends Crimean War85

This is not a disciplined use of the dash. Like many informalities of handwriting, it may or may not be a trait peculiar to certain people.

En Rule

1. To Distinguish Compounds that are Not Hyphenated Compounds. This is best explained by example:

The blue-green sea (Hyphen)

He suffers from red – green colour blindness (En rule)

2. To Mark off Words where the First Element is not a Modifier of the Second. For example:

The former Liberal – SDP Alliance (En rule)

The Tyson – Bruno fight (En rule)

3. In Date Ranges, Page References, and Linked Places. The en rule is typically used as shown in the following examples:

Dash

The 1914–18 war

The German composer and organist J.S. Bach (1685–1750)

Typographical Note on the Choice of Em and En Rules

The uses of the dash so far discussed can all be represented in typing by a spaced hyphen (-). Typesetters are, however, faced with a choice between two basic alternatives: either they can use an em rule closed up to each of the words on each side—as in this sentence—or they can use an en rule – like this – with a space on each side. The unspaced em rule is the older form, but among modern editors and designers a preference is growing for the spaced en rule. The latter probably has a more up-to-date look, and the choice may also be governed by the size and style of type involved. But in the end it does not much matter which rule is used for the dash, as long as the choice is consistently followed throughout.

In the next section of this discussion, however, the use of en and em rules is more restricted. We shall group our usages in accordance with which rules are to be used, with a note on how they should be represented in a typescript. We shall also mention double em rules as we need to.

(*See* pp. 8–9, 11–13 and 61–2.)

The Gatwick – Malaga flight has been delayed for two hours.

The Chinese – Soviet border

The following sentences wrongly use the en rule:

From 1946–71 she was a lecturer in French at a provincial university. (Write 'From 1946 to 1971 85'.)

We should like to use a second colour in the section of the book between pages 65–80. (Write '85 between pages 65 and 80'.)

En rules meaning 'and' or 'to' do not usually have spaces each side. But there are times when spaces help clarity of reading:

Friday 21 July – Saturday 16 September

c. 1494 – c. 1520

However, be careful not to cause confusion with parenthetic dashes if you are using spaced en rules for these.

4. Denoting Negative Numbers or Quantities. An en rule immediately followed by a number may be used to denote a negative quantity.

– 4.6   – 273^{BA}C

However, it should be noted that most typesetters have a minus sign that is intermediate between an en and an em rule. A typesetter would probably use this automatically for scientific work.

> **Note for Typists**
>
> A typist can represent en rules by hyphens with or without spaces each side. If the typescript is intended to be printed and published, an accompanying typographical specification will say whether parenthetical dashes should be en or em rules. Other dashes will have to be marked up by a copy-editor, especially closed-up hyphens that should be en rules.

Em Rule

1. To Mark Omission. An em rule (or a double em rule, if the em rule is being used for the parenthetic dash) is used to denote a partly or wholly suppressed name or swear word:

> Last summer, she had an affair with Lord —.
>
> I travelled to the small hilltop village of P—, where I stayed the night at a pleasant inn.
>
> Keep your —ing nose out of my affairs.

2. In Indexes and Bibliographies. Em rules or double em rules are used, often as an alternative to indention, to indicate a repeated entry heading in an index or a repeated author's name in a bibliography:

> Dickinson, A.E.F., 'The Legacy of Vaughan Williams: A Retrospect', *Music Review* XIX (1958), pp. 290–304
>
> ——, 'Toward the Unknown Region', *Music Review* IX (1948), pp. 275 ff
>
> ——, *Vaughan Williams*, Faber & Faber (1963)

3. In Tables. Em rules are sometimes used in the columns of a table to indicate a lack of available data or an inapplicable item.

4. To Introduce a Quotation in a Foreign Language. This is encountered in languages such as French:

> — *Comment allez-vous, M Dubois, dit Marie.*

> **Note for Typists**
>
> For the uses of the em rule that we have specified, the double hyphen (—) is preferred, with a suitable explanation to the typesetter if you are preparing a manuscript for the press. Do remember, however, that if you are using an em rule to represent a parenthetical dash, you can type this as a spaced hyphen. copy-editor should mark it up as an em rule if need be.

7

Ellipsis

The Greek word *elleipsis*, a noun taken from the verb *elleipein*, 'to leave behind, leave out, omit', is the origin of our English word ellipsis, the act or an instance of omitting part of a word, sentence or passage, especially in quoted material. A succession of full points, written as … or …. separated by regular spacing, is the signal for an ellipsis. In some languages, such as French, the ellipsis may be set as a single character (…) and is often referred to as 'points of suspension'.

Ellipsis in Quotations

The chief use of an ellipsis is to mark the gap in a quotation resulting from the omission of a word or words from that quotation.

1. Non-Scholarly Use. Three or four dots are normally used for the ordinary ellipsis in non-scholarly usage. Strictly, the typographical form preferred in Britain is three dots, usually with spaces each side, although sometimes American practice is to close up these spaces. A three-dot ellipsis is used to mark an omission of words within a sentence.

Four dots are used when the portion of the quotation just before the omission itself ends with a full point. In such a case, the first dot in a four-dot ellipsis is in fact that full point and is closed up to the end of the preceding word. A four-dot ellipsis is also often used when the final words of a quotation are omitted but what remains makes complete sense.

The following examples illustrate the use of the three- and four-dot ellipsis. They are based on the following source quotation:

> It is of course as a composer that we know Rakhmaninov best today, an artist still speaking to us directly in a musical language that was growing old when he was still young. For Rakhmaninov was the last of the 19th-century Russians, never more at his best than when presenting his listener with a long, flowing melody imbued with what Michael Kennedy has called 'a resigned melancholy'.

The three-dot ellipsis indicates omission within a sentence:

> It is … as a composer that we know Rakhmaninov best today, an artist still speaking … in a musical language that was growing old when he was still young. For Rakhmaninov was the last of the 19th-century Russians, never more at his best than when presenting … a long, flowing melody imbued with what Michael Kennedy has called 'a resigned melancholy'.

The three-dot ellipsis is also used to mark off a quotation broken off without making complete sense:

> It is of course as a composer that we know Rakhmaninov best today, an artist still speaking to us directly in a musical language that was growing old when he was still young. For Rakhmaninov was the last of the 19th-century …

A three-dot ellipsis may also introduce a quotation when it starts in the middle of a sentence, whether the resulting extract makes complete sense or not:

> … an artist still speaking to us directly in a musical language that was growing old when he was still young. For Rakhmaninov was the last of the 19th-century …

The four-dot ellipsis is used when the part of the quotation immediately before the omission is a sentence ending in a full point:

> It is of course as a composer that we know Rakhmaninov best today, an artist still speaking to us directly in a musical language that was growing old when he was still young …. the last of the 19th-century Russians, never more at his best than when presenting his listener with a long, flowing melody imbued with what Michael Kennedy has called 'a resigned melancholy'.

The four-dot ellipsis is also often used to mark a quotation broken off at the end but leaving a remnant that makes complete sense:

> It is of course as a composer that we know Rakhmaninov best today, an artist still speaking to us directly in a musical language that was growing old when he was still young. For Rakhmaninov was the last of the 19th-century Russians ….

It should be noted that this last usage is intended to signal the fact that the quotation has been broken off in mid-sentence. If we had stopped the quotation after 'young', there would have been no need to use an ellipsis at all.

The ellipsis is used whether the quotation is enclosed within quotation marks or set off separately or in smaller type.

When quotation marks are used, the introductory ellipsis may be dispensed with if the quotation is made to form part of the syntax of the sentence; if, however, the quotation follows a colon, the introductory ellipsis is used within the quotation marks. Compare these two examples:

> We learn that Rakhmaninov was 'an artist still speaking to us directly in a musical language that was growing old when he was still young.'

But:

> As a composer, Rakhmaninov owed much to the 19th century. This is how a noted music critic has recently described him: '… an artist still speaking to us directly in a musical language that was growing old when he was still young.'

Ellipsis

2. Scholarly Use. The number of dots (that is, full points) used to signal an ellipsis can vary in scholarly editing. In critical editions of classical texts or historical documents, illegible parts of words are represented by dots, one for each letter that cannot be read or is assumed to be missing. Three dots signal the omission of whole words or passages that are unreadable or missing from the source, while a line of dots stands for a more significant gap. Missing lines of poetry may also be signalled by a row of dots that can run the length of the average line. Dots representing large gaps are normally widely spaced apart. Dots of omission may be used in conjunction with square brackets to clarify the text, as in this example:

> Catherine's diary for August 1889 revealed her feelings. The entry for 7 May ran:
>
> J..n [John] v...t.d me at B..u...on [Broughton]. He promised at 1.st that he wd ... [? marry me] next yr.

Critical editions using dots in this way are of scholarly interest only. More practical editions for the general reader may use square brackets only. Thus the diary entry might be rendered:

> J[oh]n v[isi]t[e]d me at B[ro]u[ght]on. He promised at l[a]st that he w[oul]d [? marry me] next y[ea]r.

Other Uses of Ellipsis

The three-dot ellipsis (any more than three is looked on by most sensible readers and writers as an extravagance or a piece of vulgar sensationalism) is used in fiction to indicate a number of effects.

1. Halting dialogue. For example:

> The wounded soldier spoke with difficulty: 'Doc, you 85 you've got to 85 promise me you'll 85 look after Myra.'

2. Tailing off. An ellipsis marks a trailing away at the end of a sentence. It represents a much less abrupt break than a dash. For example:

> 'The trouble is,' she said, 'I love you and I just can't live without you and ...'
>
> He stood on the outer limits of the town and gazed at the road before him. Beyond the town lay the savannah, and beyond that lay the mountains, and beyond those ... what?

3. To Close an Incomplete List or Endless Series. This is both a general and technical use. The general use may be thought of as rather informal. Here are examples of both:

> A typical geometric progression is this one: 1, 2, 4, 8, 16, 32, 64, 128, ...

Eggs, butter, washing powder, ... Her shopping list had all the usual household items.

4. In mathematical expressions. An ellipsis marks an omission of terms in a series before the *n*th term. For example:

In the sequence of terms, the index *r* takes on the successive values of 0, 1, 2, 3, ..., *n*.

5. The Ellipsis with Exclamation and Question Marks. When required, exclamations or questions may end in an ellipsis. In this case, the exclamation mark or question mark follows the ellipsis. For example:

How I detest his haughtiness, his patronizing attitude, his self- righteousness ...!

Who is going to tell him? John? Alison? Tom ...?

8
Quotation Marks

The translators of the Authorized Version of the Bible, which was published in 1611, knew nothing about quotation marks:

> … and He asked them, saying, Whom say the people that I am? They answering said, John the Baptist; but some say, Elias, and others say, that one of the old prophets is risen again. He said, But whom say ye that I am? Peter answering said, The Christ of God.
>
> – Luke 9:18–20

By the eighteenth century, however, English writers had discovered quotation marks, and punctuation pundits are glad they did, for there is still much to argue about in the use of these marks, not least whether they should be single or double. (*See* the remarks on single and double quotation marks below.)

In typewritten documents, reports or other manuscripts, and also in some pieces of handwritten material, quotation marks are represented either as ' ' or as " ". In printed books and the output from some word processors or desktop publishing equipment, as well as in carefully handwritten manuscripts, the symbols are differentiated, being set down as either ' ' or " ". These latter symbols are what are called inverted commas (or speech marks) in Britain. The term 'inverted commas' has been a generally accepted synonym for 'quotation marks' for a long time, even though only the opening marks are true inverted commas (the closing ones being ordinary commas placed above the level of the letters). In this account, we shall use the more descriptive term 'quotation marks, as we have done elsewhere. We shall also note that they are often called quote marks or quotes for short.

Quotation Marks in a Sentence

The main function of quotation marks is to enclose the actual words said or written by somebody. These words generally have to be introduced, interrupted or otherwise accompanied by a clause or phrase that places them in the context in which they are being quoted – e.g., 'she said' or 'Tom replied'. Such a clause or phrase, not being part of the quotation, goes outside the quotation marks. Some people refer to it as a 'reporting' clause; for convenience, so shall we:

'You, sir,' shouted Colonel Napier, 'are a scoundrel!'

Turning towards him, she said calmly, 'I think that you had better leave.'

Smith tried to keep the emotion out of his voice: 'We have to face it – the spaceship has disappeared.'

'Emma Woodhouse, handsome, clever, and rich, with a comfortable home and happy disposition, seemed to unite some of the best blessings of existence; and had lived nearly twenty-one years in the world with very little to distress or vex her.' So begins Jane Austen's novel *Emma*.

Reporting clauses and Commas. Reporting clauses are regarded as parenthetic phrases and as such are set off from the part of the sentence that forms the quotation by commas like this:

Jean said, 'Jim, I love you.'

'Jim,' said Jean, 'I love you.'

'Jim, I love you,' said Jean.

In these examples, a comma in the original quotation is preserved throughout. But note that in the last example the full point ending the quotation is replaced by a comma. This is because any pause in the quotation coming directly before the reporting clause is conventionally replaced by a comma. This comma is suppressed by a concluding question mark or exclamation mark. (*See* below.)

Note the position of the comma in this sentence:

'You', he thundered, 'will repay every penny you have ever borrowed from my family.'

Because there is no comma in the original quotation ('You will repay every penny …'), a true parenthetical comma placed outside the quotation marks sets off the reporting clause from the rest of the sentence.

Note that in American usage, the comma always goes inside the quotation marks, even in the example above:

'You,' he thundered, 'will repay every penny you have ever borrowed from my family.'

When Commas are Absent. Commas can be omitted after verbs of saying when the quotation is an exclamation functioning as the direct object of the verb concerned or when it is suppressed by an exclamation or question mark in a preceding quote:

He rang the bell and shouted 'Fire!'

'Look out!' he yelled. 'The wall's collapsing!'

'Didn't you hear me?' said the old man. 'I said "Look out!"'

(For the use of double quotation marks in the last example, see the part of this chapter devoted to double and single quotes.)

Note that when the object of the reporting clause's verb is yes or no, quotation marks are in certain circumstances not used:

Quotation Marks

Tom and Jane were asked if they would come but they said no.

Asked if he would like a cup of coffee, John smiled and said, 'Yes, please, I'd love one.'

Quotation Marks in Dialogue. Sections of dialogue in a novel may dispense with reporting clauses, provided that there is no doubt about which person is speaking. Usually, as in the following example, the words assigned to each speaker in a piece of quoted dialogue begin on a new line every time.

… a man and woman were speaking. He listened for a moment to their conversation.

'Come on, Sally, love. Just one.'

'Fred, I told you. I'm not that sort of girl.'

'Well, look – can I take you out tomorrow night?'

'I'm washing my hair tomorrow.'

Quotation Marks and Paragraphs. In long discursive writing, often in translations of Greek or Roman speeches, it is necessary to set out the quoted speech in a series of paragraphs. The convention is to introduce the speech with an 'open-quotation' mark and to repeat this mark at the start of each new paragraph within the speech. The only time that the 'close quotation' mark is used is right at the end of the final paragraph of the speech. The following example illustrates the procedure, although in practice the paragraphs are generally much longer:

There was applause as he rose to speak. Gesturing for silence, he began:

'My friends, I have asked you here today for two main reasons, which I shall be glad to explain to you.

'Firstly, I have been fortunate enough to attain my eightieth birthday and wanted you to help me celebrate it. Some of you I haven't seen for ten years or more.

'And secondly, I'd like to find out which one of you is trying to murder me.'

Double or Single Quotes. H.W. Fowler was the most eminent advocate of the use of single quotations marks for normal use and double ones to enclose quotes within quotes. British publishers have generally followed this practice, but publishers in the United States and elsewhere have stuck to the use of double quotes for ordinary direct speech and singles for quotes within quotes. In a letter or business report, it does not much matter which order is adopted as long as the writer follows a consistent policy. On the whole, it would seem best to use double quotation marks as standard and only use single ones for quotes within quotes, as the Americans do. Authors of books are generally told what to do by their editors. The likely confusion between a single 'close-quote' symbol and an apostrophe is possible, but is perhaps overemphasized. *See* the chapter on Apostrophe.

Quotes within Quotes. Quotations can be nested one inside the other, rather like Russian dolls. We signal the different 'levels' of quotation by alternating between single and double quotation marks (or doubles and singles, if you prefer). Thus a main quotation is marked off by, say, single quotation marks, the quotation within the quotation is marked off by doubles, the quotation within that is marked off by singles, and so on. For example:

> The police inspector referred to his notes: 'When arrested the prisoner said, "All right, I confess." He then asked "Can I please make a phone call?" '

> 'I remember', said Bert, 'my old dad telling me, "Son, your grandfather had a motto. 'Do as you would be done by,' he used to say, and I've never forgotten those words to this day. Nor should you." And, do you know, I never have.'

> Lawson asked, 'Am I right in thinking that Capt. Smith said "I heard the sentry shout 'Halt!' "?'

It is generally impractical to go further than a quote within a quote within a quote. Rather than involve yourself in such complications, you ought to consider using reported speech.

Direct and Reported Speech

Although this book is not a grammar, it is worthwhile mentioning at this point the distinction between direct and reported speech. Direct speech is the verbatim reproduction, enclosed within quotation marks, of what somebody actually said. Any of the earlier examples in this section illustrate it.

Reported speech, by contrast, is a restatement by the writer of the meaning of what someone said. In reported speech, which is also called indirect speech or indirect discourse, the reporting clause introduces or otherwise accompanies a sentence not en-closed in quotation marks. When the reporting clause precedes such a sentence, the two are often linked by the word 'that'. The restated sentence of reported speech, unlike the verbatim quotation of direct speech, agrees in tense with the reporting clause, being removed one step back into the past from the tense of the original words upon which it is based.

It is beyond our province here to go too deeply into the recasting of direct speech into reported speech. These two labelled examples must suffice:

> Tom said, 'I will be glad to come to see you on Friday. Are you still living where you were last year?' (Direct)

> Tom said that he would be glad to go to see her on Friday. He asked if she was still living where she had been the previous year. (Reported)

Thoughts are often expressed as direct quotations without quotation marks. The tense of the part of the sentence expressing the thought may or may not be the same as that of the verb of thinking, and question marks may or may not be retained. Some flexibility is allowed, as these examples illustrate:

(a) Where, he wondered, would he find a hotel in this deserted place? He could see that this job was going to be more difficult than he had realized.

(b) Where, he wondered, am I going to find a hotel in this deserted place? I can see that this job is going to be more difficult than I realized.

(c) He wondered where he was going to find a hotel in this deserted place. He could see … (The sentence continues as for (a))

(d) Where was he going to find a hotel in this deserted place, he wondered. He could see …

(e) Where am I going to find a hotel in this deserted place, He wondered. He could see … (Continue as in (a) – or) I can see … (Continue as in (b))

Other possibilities may be allowed. *See also* the chapters on the Full Point and Question Mark.

The 'That' Trap. Avoid using quotation marks in a that-clause. Quotes are only to be used for the actual words said or written. The following example is wrong:

   Bill said that 'he wasn't going to take that lying down'.

What Bill actually said was: 'I am not going to take that lying down.' To make the sentence correct and still keep the flavour of the quotation, we can move the quotation marks on a bit:

   Bill said that he wasn't going to 'take that lying down'.

But using quotation marks in a that-clause is a style of writing prone to error, and it should be avoided.

Other Uses of Quotation Marks

Quotation marks are used in several ways that do not directly relate to verbatim transcriptions of things said or written. They are conventionally used to enclose the following:

(a) Words or phrases used ironically, sarcastically, technically or in some other way than normal:

   Some people who think of themselves as 'fashionable' are just plain vulgar.

   The decision worried him, but he knew that he had 'burned his boats'.

(Note that well-known idioms such as the one in the second example are not usually enclosed in quotation marks these days.)

(b) Slang words:

>Acapulco is a 'glitzy' resort where the rich and beautiful go to have fun.

(c) Words or phrases to which the author wishes to draw attention – what Eric Partridge called 'words named as words':

>The abstract nouns 'virtue' and 'vice' are complete opposites.

>The word means 'to fall over backwards'.

(d) Titles of paintings, poems, short stories, essays, and chapters within a book:

>'Sunflowers' is one of Van Gogh's finest paintings.

>Have you read Gerard Manley Hopkins? His poem 'Pied Beauty' is one of my favourites.

>'Aristophanes and the War Party' is a brilliant lecture by Gilbert Murray. It was written and delivered in 1928 and included in Murray's Humanist Essays.

(Note that the titles of books, magazines and newspapers are rarely given between quotation marks in printed matter nowadays except when an italic form of a given typeface is unavailable. *See* the chapter on Italics.)

Quotation Marks and Other Punctuation Marks

This is one of the most hotly contested issues in punctuation. In practice, the question boils down to this: should the comma, the full point, and so on, be placed inside or outside the quotation marks? We have already briefly gone over the ground in earlier sections. Here we shall restate some basic principles and provide some further examples.

The underlying rule is that generally stops, exclamation marks and question marks go inside the quotation marks if they belong to the quotation and outside if they do not. Exclamation marks and question marks are relatively uncomplicated in this regard. For example:

>He rang the bell and shouted 'Fire!'

>'Help!' she screamed. 'Let me out!'

>'Where are you, William?' she called. 'Where have you gone?'

>Did he say 'Titan' or 'Triton'?

>Did I hear you shout 'Fire!'?

>To think that you could be so tactless and ask me 'What is love?'!

>How stupid you were to shout 'Fire!'!

>Did Pilate really ask Christ, 'What is truth?'?

In the last two examples, some authorities recommend that one or the other of the two exclamation marks and question marks should be dropped.

Parentheses and square brackets can go inside quotation marks and quotation marks can go inside parentheses and square brackets. Here is an interesting example of the latter, in which punctuation marks seem to pile up:

> I attach copies of the relevant sections (with which, incidentally, Mr Jones said he could 'find no fault'!).

Dashes need to be handled with a little care. If the original quotation contains a phrase between parenthetic dashes, it is wise to break the quote if you must before the first dash and include that dash in the second part of the quote. In this pair of examples, the first is recommended usage:

> 'I bought a pair of jeans,' he said, ' – blue ones they were – in a shop in Croydon.'

> 'I bought a pair of jeans – ' he said, 'blue ones they were – in a shop in Croydon.'

The first sentence avoids confusion as to whether the text has been abruptly broken off rather than being just interrupted. The second example leaves room for doubt.

Commas, semicolons, colons and full stops at the break point in an original quotation are all represented by a comma inside the quotation marks when the quotation is contained within a sentence. If the comma is replacing a full point, semicolon or colon, then the reporting clause (the 'he said' clause) ends with the full point, semicolon or colon as appropriate.

> 'To err is human,' she said; 'to forgive is divine.'

> 'Man proposes,' says the proverb: 'God disposes.'

> 'Come in,' she said. 'Would you like a cup of coffee?'

The Comma, the Full Point and Quotation Marks. The placing of the comma with respect to quotation marks has already been discussed in the parts of this chapter headed 'Reporting Clauses and Commas' and 'When Commas are Absent'. There is no more to add on the positioning of commas, except to repeat that Americans always place the comma inside the quotation marks under all circumstances. The full point is also placed within quotation marks on all occasions by American writers. But in Britain it is not. The full point goes inside quotation marks only if it marks the end of the quotation, and the end of that quotation coincides with the end of the sentence containing it.

> Eric said, 'You have a point there.'

Logic would say that the full point inside the quotation marks ends the quotation only and would demand that another one be placed outside the quotation marks to end the containing sentence. That second full point is, however, suppressed.

The full point goes inside the quotation marks in a sentence that is taken up entirely by a quotation. For example, in dialogue:

She spoke quietly to John: 'How can I make you see the foolishness of all this?'

'You'll never convince me that it is foolishness, Jane.' 'But it is, darling. In fact, it's complete lunacy.'

On the other hand, if the containing sentence ends with only a phrase from the quotation or a portion of it that does not make complete sense, the full point is generally placed outside the quotation marks:

Under no circumstances can this invention be regarded as 'modern and up-to-date'.

He said that he would not 'take this lying down'.

General Use of Quotation Marks

Quotation marks should be used as little as possible in ordinary writing. The ironic, sarcastic or technical uses of them should in particular be controlled to avoid an irritating 'peppering' of quote marks on a page. It is worth noting that once you have given the first mention of a technical or slang word in quotation marks, subsequent mentions need not also be in quotes.

9

Apostrophe

The apostrophe, taken in from the Greek language, joined the English system of punctuation in the seventeenth century. It is symbolized by ' (a superior comma) and therefore appears to be identical with the mark that closes a quotation. This resemblance has led a few authorities to disown the system of using single quotation marks as standard on the grounds of potential, if not actual, confusion. For example:

'Aristophanes' plays were popular with Athens' citizens.'

'The plays of Aristophanes were popular with the citizens of Athens.'

And what happens when the double-quoter needs to use single quotation marks for an internal quotation? For example:

John said, "My professor began his lecture like this:

'Aristophanes' plays were popular with Athens' citizens.'"

Sadly, argument is ultimately fruitless.

For convenience we now divide the uses of the apostrophe into three main groups: the possessive use, the use in marking omissions and the plural use.

The Possessive Use

1. The possessive form is shown by *'s* (apostrophe + *s*) in the case of the following four groups of nouns, whether they are in the singular or in the plural:

(a) Nouns that have the same form in both singular and plural:

sheep   deer   wildebeest   salmon

A wolf in sheep's clothing.

These salmon's spawning areas are in the rivers of Yorkshire.

(b) Nouns in which the vowels and perhaps the way of showing some consonants change:

mouse–mice   man–men   woman–women

goose–geese   tooth–teeth   foot–feet

The mouse's hole – the mice's tails.

The man's house – the men's room.

History of the Apostrophe

The Greek word apostrophos, meaning 'a turning away', is the origin of the English word apostrophe as applied to the ' symbol. As such it provides a very good guide to the basic use of the apostrophe both by the Greeks and by ourselves. In Greek manuscripts of medieval times it was written as part of a word in order to show that letters had been 'turned away' – that is, omitted, or (more technically) elided – from that word. When the English took it over in the seventeenth century, they began by using it for the same purpose – that is, to mark omissions.

Poets welcomed it to show the dropping of unstressed syllables in lines that would not otherwise scan properly. The dropping of v in e'en (for even), e'er (for ever) and o'er (for over) is a literary survival that we readily recognize today, and published editions of Shakespeare often contain such forms as in't (for in it) and th' (for the).

Even when the apostrophe is used to denote possession or an analogous relationship, it is really the extension of the symbol's use as a mark of omission. In the early sixteenth century, early Modern English still retained certain inflexions or word endings from its previous Old and Middle stages similar to those still found in German today. One was the use of -es to mark the genitive, or possessive, case in certain masculine and neuter nouns. In dropping the -e- of the genitive ending, writers of the seventeenth century began to signal its absence with an apostrophe. The resulting 's was then gradually extended to words that had never had the -es ending in the genitive. The general possessive 's became standard practice in the eighteenth century.

One has to accept that the lobby against the use of single quotation marks undoubtedly has a case. Unfortunately, British publishers have taken single quotes to their hearts and would be reluctant to make a change to double quote marks as part of their house styles. There is of course nothing to stop writers of letters, company reports, memos, and the like from using double quotes if they wish, and that is something we have already recommended. British authors, however, usually have to be to be guided by their editors on this point. To be practical and honest, the case of those opposed to single quotes is overstressed. Good writers and editors will recast such a sentence as the above if actual confusion is likely:

(c) Nouns with irregular plurals, some of which are archaic or obsolete:

    child–children   die–dice   penny–pence

    brother–brethren

    The child's chair–the children's playground.

    My brother's car–thy brethren's love.

(d) Nouns forming foreign plurals:

nebula–nebulae   phenomenon–phenomena

stigma–stigmata

The nebula's shape resembles that of a horse's head.

The precise extent of these phenomena's effects is not known.

The *'s* is also used to show the possessive in the case of all singular nouns that form their plurals by adding *-s*.

The boy's bike   The girl's coat   The horse's head   Maurice's boutique

So far we have no problems. Unfortunately, with the remaining groups of nouns we enter a more difficult area.

We continue to use the *'s* (apostrophe + *s*) to signal possession in the following cases:

(i) With most common and proper nouns whose singular forms end in *-s*:

James's reign   Charles's kingdom   William Morris's art

John Williams's guitar   Keats's poetry.

There are now fewer exceptions to this rule than there used to be. Some authorities have recommended that words ending in *-s* having more than one syllable should take only an apostrophe to indicate possession. Thus, we ought to write of John Williams' guitar. This procedure, however, is no longer sustainable in the face of current usage.

(ii) With nouns ending in *-ess* or *-ness*. This is a special case of *-s* above, but is worth picking out because some writers have legislated against the use of *'s*, again flying in the face of modern usage:

The princess's crown   The lioness's cubs

2. *The possessive* is shown by means of the apostrophe alone in the following cases:

(a) The plural form of all nouns whose plurals end in *-s* or in *-es*:

The boys' jackets   The horses' tails   The buses' tyres.

Those girls' bikinis are very revealing.

(b) Most classical and biblical names ending in *-s*:

Euripides' plays   Hercules' strength   Tacitus' Annals

Moses' law   Jesus' miracles.

Thucydides' *History* is an unbiased account of the Peloponnesian War.

Note that this principle extends to people such as St Thomas Aquinas and Paracelsus also:

> Paracelsus' theories paved the way for modern medicine.

(c) Many other foreign names ending in *-s* or *-z*:

> Cervantes' stories   Boaz' wife

(But note that in the latter case 'Boaz's wife' is becoming increasingly common. Note also that the simple apostrophe for signalling the possessive form of French names ending in an unpronounced *-s* or *-x* - e.g. King Louis' reign – is on the way out. Hart's *Rules* did not support it in the 1960s and 1970s, and we have no reason to do so now; thus we prefer 'King Louis's reign'.

(c) Certain nouns ending in *-nce*, especially in set phrases:

> appearance' sake   conscience' sake

(Note also in this context the phrase 'for goodness' sake'.)

The examples under 2(c) are heavily influenced by pronunciation, which is a reasonable guide when it comes to common collocations such as 'for goodness' sake'. But how can one distinguish between 'Charles Dickens' novels', which is the way some people say it, and 'Charles Dickens's novels', which reflects 'other people's habits'. In such a case, apostrophe + *s* is always preferable to apostrophe alone because it follows a general pattern.)

3. Multi-word possessives in which the noun concerned is a tightly bound phrase or involves two or more people acting together, add *'s* or *'* to the last word of the phrase or list

> William and Mary's reign

> Her Majesty the Queen of England's only daughter

Where the people or things on the list are considered as separate, the *'s* or *'* is attached to each person or thing:

> John and Mary's family (The family belong to both John and Mary.)

But:

> John's and Mary's family (The family of John and the family of Mary – two separate families.)

4. The possessive use of the apostrophe + *s* (that is, *'s*) is found in many place names and addresses:

> St John's, Newfoundland   St John's Wood

> St Michael's Mount   Land's End   Lord's Cricket Ground.

But it is also excluded from many such names in modern usage:

Apostrophe

Earls Court	Golders Green	St Albans

Bury St Edmunds

Johns Hopkins University.

5. We use 's informally to designate familiar addresses and locations:

I have an appointment at the hairdresser's.

We can meet at Angela's after the concert.

I shop at Woolworth's.

Note that in the last of these examples the apostrophe is increasingly falling out of use in British English; 'I shop at Woolworths' is almost standard usage.

6. Possessive Before Gerund. A purely grammatical use involves whether or not one should employ a possessive before a gerund (a verbal noun ending in *-ing*). In practice what this means is: Which of these sentences is right?

(i) John singing really annoys me.

John's singing really annoys me.

(ii) I hope you don't mind Tom being here.

I hope you don't mind Tom's being here.

(iii) John came without Sally knowing about it.

John came without Sally's knowing about it.

(iv) He wouldn't hear of me paying back any of the money.

He wouldn't hear of my paying back any of the money.

Which is right? They all are; only the first reads a little awkwardly. The use of the *'s* or *'* form or of the possessive pronoun is more formal and literary. The other* is more likely to be heard in speech. A report might look more polished and less colloquial if the possessive + gerund form is used. But beware of pomposity:

Owing to our department's having been reorganized recently, your original requisition form has been mislaid.

Use in Marking Omissions

1. The apostrophe is regularly used to indicate the omission of a letter or letters in a word or phrase. For example:

'Fraid I haven't seen him. Can't tell you where he is (I am afraid I have not seen him. I cannot tell you where he is.)

---

*Strictly speaking, in non-apostrophe form, the **-ing** word is a present participle.

This use of the apostrophe is more or less confined to the most informal writing. The most typical instances are:

don't, won't	do not, will not
shan't, can't	shall not, cannot
aren't, isn't	are not, is not
hasn't, haven't	has not, have not

The verb 'to be' has the following apostrophe forms for colloquial usage:

I'm, you're, he's	I am, you are, he is
She's, we're, they're	she is, we are, they are

Note also these:

I've, you've, he's	I have, you have, he has
She's, we've, they've	she has, we have, they have
I'll, you'll, he'll	I shall/will, you shall/will he shall/will
she'll, we'll, they'll	she shall/will, we shall/will, they shall/will

And finally these:

I'd, you'd, he'd,	I had, should or would, you
She'd, we'd, they'd	had, should or would, etc.

It's and Its. This continues to be a major problem for some writers, even though the distinction is very easy.

The form *it's* is a shortening of *it is* or *it has*:

It's a nice day.

It's been fun working with you, John.

This is an informal use.

The form *its* is a possessive pronoun parallel with *his* and *her*. For example:

Its leaves have withered.

The museum presents its exhibits to the public in an imaginative way.

This is a standard, non-colloquial use.

The forms *it'll* (= it shall/will) and *it'd* (= it had, or it should/would) are also encountered.

Note that there is no apostrophe in *his, hers, ours, theirs,* and *yours*:

This is an old dress of my mother's

This is an old dress of hers.

But note also that the possessive of the pronoun *one* is *one's*, with an apostrophe:

It is difficult to keep one's hair clean in a grimy city.

Finally, please do not confuse *their, there* and *they're*. Try this sentence as a mnemonic:

They have left their luggage there and they're coming back for it.

2. In names and stock phrases. The prefix *O* in Irish names is conventionally (though wrongly) capitalized and followed by an apostrophe in Anglicized Irish names, presumably on the analogy of *o'* (of) in such phrases as will-o'-the-wisp (*see* below). (In Irish, there is no apostrophe, and the form is lower-case *o* followed by a space (*o* means 'descendant of').) Examples of the accepted Anglicized procedure are:

O'Connorl   O'Casey

In some names of Scottish origin beginning with *Mac* or *Mc*, an apostrophe is occasionally encountered:

M'Dougal   M'Quillian

Other names in which apostrophes represent missing letters include:

D'Cruz   D'Arcy

The apostrophe of omission is found in many stock phrases. For example *o'* replaces *of* in:

John o'Groats (a place name)   cat-o'-nine-tails

will-o'-the-wisp   o'clock (of the clock)

3. Contracted Words. These include many nautical terms and represent spellings that reflect pronunciations.

Fo'c's'le   bo's'n

Note that the forms *forecastle* and *boatswain* are preferred in non-nautical usage.

We no longer write 'flu for flu (influenza), 'cello for cello (violoncello) or 'plane for plane (aeroplane or airplane).

There are a few publishers who would probably like to restore these apostrophe spellings, but they are in a dwindling minority.

4. Contracted Numbers. This usage applies primarily to years and again is an informal use:

I was born in '47 (... in 1947)

The class of '89 (... of 1989)

The book is a brilliant portrayal of life in the '50s (... the 1950s)

The Plural Use

The apostrophe is commonly used before the *-s* that serves to form the plural of letters and words used (often in italics) as letters and words, not as units of meaningful discourse:

Mind your p's and q's.

There are five and's in that sentence.

This practice is justifiable in avoiding confusion between *as*, *is* and *us* on the one hand and *a*'s, *i*'s, and *u*'s on the other. To keep consistency all letters should be treated the same – that is, they should all take apostrophes.

However, the use of the apostrophe is on the wane as a signal of the plural. The sentence 'Mind your *p*s and *q*s' is not hard to understand, especially if the letters are placed in italics and the pluralizing *-s* is left in Roman type. In the second sentence, ands works just as well as and's.

Eric Partridge, however, cites a very good use of the pluralizing apostrophe:

The class includes three Louis's and two Lewises.

Plural Numbers. There is no longer any justification for retaining the apostrophe in 1920s, mid-70s, and similar phrases. It represents needless clutter and looks old-fashioned:

We are getting ready for the new single Europe of the 1990s.

Tomorrow's temperatures will be in the low 30s Celsius.

Somehow these sentences would not look so up to date with apostrophes.

Possessive and Plural Abbreviations

Abbreviations and sets of initials retain their full points – if they have them – when used in the possessive or cited in the plural. A plain *-s* is used to indicate the plural; the apostrophe + *s* is used to indicate possession when the abbreviation is single; and the *s* + apostrophe is used to indicate possession with abbreviations in the plural. Although the apostrophe + *s* has been used to show plurals of abbreviations in the past, there is really no point in perpetuating this waste of charcters.

These examples must suffice to illustrate the usage:

The BBC's revenue comes mainly from licence fees.

Throughout the 1960s Smith & Co.'s profits went up each year by about 2 per cent.

There are four Ph.D.s teaching at this institute.

Yesterday Parliament debated MPs' salaries.

General Point

Several commentators have noted that the apostrophe has been or is being dropped in many areas. Printers often set singular and plural possessives without it. Paradoxically, greengrocers and market-stall owners put it on signs where it either should not be or may be rather unexpected. References to *cox's, tom's* and *pot's* (or *potato's*) are actually not wrong because the apostrophe signals omission of letters; references to *lettuce's* and *cabbage's* are wrong, however, and should be avoided. And anybody who writes the word *baby's* for *babies* cannot spell.

10

Question Mark and Exclamation Mark

The question mark and the exclamation mark are, strictly speaking, not stops, or pause marks, but are in fact marks of expression or tone. An important fact about their function, however, is that they replace the full point at the end of sentences that are interrogative or exclamatory. To this extent at least, they deserve to be classed as punctuation marks. And since they share the nature of being expression marks – rather like crescendo and diminuendo marks in music – they may be conveniently treated together in one chapter of our punctuation survey.

Question Mark in a Sentence

In its most usual employment as a punctuation mark, the question mark (also known as the interrogation mark, the interrogation point, the point or mark of interrogation, or – especially among journalists – the query) replaces the full point in the sentences in which it occurs. However, since it is a tone mark, it may be, and often is, employed in mid-sentence. Its most frequently encountered uses are the following:

1. At the End of a Direct Question. A direct question is a straight, ordinary question. The question may be either real, expecting and getting an answer, or rhetorical, expecting no actual answer but often implying a negative one. For example:

History of Question and Exclamation Marks

The question mark, for which ? is the symbol in English and certain other European languages, was the first of these two tone marks to appear in the punctuation system. Scribes introduced an early form of the question mark, known as the punctus interrogativus, into their Latin manuscripts in the ninth century AD. Some experts now believe that the punctus interrogativus was borrowed from a very early form of musical notation. According to an alternative theory, the ? is a corrupt or stylized form of the first and last letters of the Latin word quaestio, 'a question', or its related verb quaero, 'I question', the q being represented by the top part of the symbol, with the o having been reduced to a dot.

The exclamation mark, for which the symbol ! is used, did not appear until the seventeenth century, by which time nearly all the other punctuation marks were in place. It too is said to have had its origins in a Latin word, in this case the interjection io, an expression of joy equivalent to 'hurray'. The letter i may be seen as being represented by the vertical stroke, with the o again reduced to a dot.

Question/Exclamation Mark

> Do you take sugar?
>
> Is there life on Mars?
>
> Can anyone doubt our leader's sincerity?

All direct questions introduced by the interrogatives *how, what, where, when, which, who* or *why* also end in question marks:

> What's the time?
>
> To whom do you wish to speak, please?
>
> How do you like your eggs done?
>
> Where will it all end?

Interjections introduced by 'How dare ...' may appear to be questions but are regularly treated as exclamations and marked accordingly. *See below.*

2. Questions Framed as Statements. Sentences having the word order of a statement may nonetheless be questions, and this is indicated by means of a question mark. The presence of such a word as 'surely' may also indicate that the sentence is a question. However, 'surely' is also often found in exclamations (*see below*). Examples of statement-questions are:

> You mean you bought that house after all?
>
> You're surely not serious?

Questions framed as statements but containing an interrogative also take a question mark:

> You've done what?
>
> She sings in which choir?

3. Elliptical Questions. Partial sentences functioning as questions end in a question mark. The interrogatives used alone come into this category (*What? Where? When? How? Who?* (or *Whom?*), *Which?* etc.), and so do the following examples:

> Coffee, tea or orange juice?
>
> What for?
>
> Anybody there?
>
> Mr Jones? – Yes?

4. Tag Questions. A question mark is used at the end of sentences in which the writer seeks to confirm the truth of a statement or assertion by tagging a question on the end of it which expects the answer that he needs in order to make that confirmation. In fact, tag questions expect the answer 'yes' or 'no'. For example:

Sounds complicated, doesn't it?

Here are a few other examples:

You come from Wales, don't you?

He wasn't in the car, was he?

She has a great love of music, does she not?

(Note that the last example is rather formal.)

5. Indirect Questions and Polite or Formal Requests

We have already covered these topics under the chapter on the Full Point. We said that an indirect question was a statement with a question embedded in it and that a polite or formal request was a weak command. In neither case is the question mark used. A few further examples here should make the point clear. First, an indirect question:

I want to know who you are and what you want here.

Note that a direct question would have the word order turned in this way:

Who are you and what do you want here?

Note also that in indirect questions the tense of the question agrees with the tense of the main verb of asking:

Where is my wife?

He asked where his wife was.

Under the section on the Full Point, we noted that the following sentence does not generally take a question mark at the end:

What would he be like, she wondered.

However, we did show an alternative, namely:

What would he be like? she wondered.

Some writers dislike placing the question mark in the middle of the sentence in this way. But there are those who feel that, even though the question is 'reported' in the past tense (the same tense as 'wondered'), the question mark makes it more vivid.

Some writers follow the rule that if the verb of thinking or wondering is present, and the thought/question is in the present or future, then a question mark may be placed at the end of the sentence:

What will he be like, I wonder?

Why is she so charming, I ask myself?

If, however, both verbs are in the past tense, then no question mark is used anywhere:

> What would he be like, I wondered.
>
> Why was she so charming, I asked myself.

If the tenses are mixed, though, a question mark is justified in mid-sentence on the grounds that the thought/question is virtually a verbatim quotation:

> What will he be like? I wondered.
>
> Why is she so charming? I asked myself.

The unturned indirect question is a kind of sentence in which the embedded question has not been cast into its usual indirect form. In this kind of sentence, we have to use our judgement. The question mark is a genuine rhetorical device rather than a grammatical one. If in an unturned indirect question the embedded question somehow takes precedence over the sentence as a whole, so that the verb of asking or wondering is virtually parenthetical to it, the question mark should undoubtedly be used. But otherwise it should not be used. Compare these two examples:

> This book attempts to teach us what are the most important points regarding parliamentary procedure. (No question mark.)
>
> If you know, sir, tell me where is my beloved husband? (Question mark.)

A polite or formal request is generally framed like this:

> Could you please send me ten extra copies of your report.
>
> Would all passengers please refrain from putting their feet on the seats?

Such requests are commands, instructions or imperatives cloaked in the garb of questions. But they are not true questions. Compare the use of a question mark with a straight request or inquiry:

> Could I have another piece of cake, please?
>
> May I go to the pictures with Debby tonight please, mum?

Question Marks and Quotation Marks

The question mark is placed inside quotation marks if it belongs to the quotation. Otherwise it is placed outside:

> 'Where are you going?' he asked.
>
> Why did he use the word 'poison'?

If the quotation ends in a question mark and comes at the end of a sentence, the full point ending the sentence is omitted:

> 'John,' she asked petulantly, 'where are you going now?'

Note that these two sentences mean the same:

    The question 'Is there life on Mars?' remains unresolved.

    The question of whether there is life on Mars is unresolved.

The omission of quotation marks from sentences such as the first in this pair of examples is also common:

    The question Is there life on Mars? remains unresolved.

The use of quotes is clearer and less offensive to those who hate question marks in the middle of sentences.

Non-Punctuational Uses

The chief non-punctuational use of the question mark is to signal doubt.

1. In Life-dates. The question mark, usually placed in front of a year of birth or death, signals the author's uncertainty as to whether this is the correct year:

    Hieronymus Bosch (?1450–1516)

Where there is absolutely no clue as to the year concerned, a question mark only may be used:

    The Welsh harpist John Parry (?-1782)

Many publishers, however, prefer this form:

    … John Parry (died 1782)

There is (theoretically, at least) a distinction to be made between the use of a question mark and the use of *circa* or *c*.

The word *circa* means 'about' and denotes an informed guess about the accuracy of the year mentioned. The question mark, by contrast, expresses doubt as to whether the year is actually correct. In practice this distinction seems to be rarely made: most authors and publishers use either one or the other but not both in the same book or article. Note that in

    Hieronymus Bosch (?1450-1516)

doubt is being expressed only about the first date.

2. Surprise or Irony. In this context, the question mark may stand in mid-sentence and is usually enclosed in parentheses or square brackets:

    Tell me about the advantages (?) of living in Docklands.

    He paid just £10,000 (?) for that cottage.

Careful authors fight shy of this use of a punctuation mark sent to do the job that words should do, and authorities on written style loathe it. Some call it vulgar. On the whole, the practice is best avoided.

Above all, do avoid multiplying question marks:

> With you as a friend (??), I don't need any enemies.

3. In Chess Notation. A special use of the question mark as a signal of doubt and surprise is found in the written records of chess games. It is a shorthand way of saying that the move concerned is a mistake. A double question mark signifies a blunder:

> Q × B ?   R × P ??

(For the use of square brackets with a question mark, *see* the chapter on Parentheses.)

Exclamation Mark

This was once called a mark or point of admiration and is now generally known in the United States as an exclamation point. Journalists often call it a bang, largely perhaps because it is regularly used after onomatopoeic words such as Bang! and Crash!

Like the question mark, the exclamation mark replaces the full point at the end of a sentence that is described as exclamatory. The description 'exclamatory' is necessarily a loose one, since it can cover anything from an expression of astonishment to a peremptory command.

While the cases in which we can use a question mark are fairly restricted and easy to define, those covering the exclamation mark are not; we need to be much more discriminating about the way we use this latter mark. Its overuse is frowned on as vulgar, and despite what one sees in print, multiple exclamation marks, such as the pair at the end of this sentence, stand for deplorable sensationalism and ought to be banned!!

It is rare, if not unlikely, that the writer of a business report or an academic paper on anything other than a literary subject will ever need to use an exclamation mark at all. The mark has virtually no place in technical prose, quality journalism or a sober essay. For poets and writers of fiction, however, it may prove a useful adjunct to their list of punctuation symbols. And the tabloid reporter, who regards the exclamation mark as part of his or her stock in trade, would surely be lost without it.

It would be easy enough to recommend complete avoidance of the exclamation mark were it not for the fact that, sensitively placed and properly employed, it can liven up an otherwise dull piece of writing. Although it must be said that no writer should rely upon punctuation to perform a task that choice of language and good prose style ought to perform, we have to acknowledge that the odd exclamation mark will add welcome spice.

1. The Exclamation Mark after Words or Phrases. The most characteristic way in which exclamation marks may be used with reasonable impunity is after interjections or after words that represent a loud, sharp noise.

(a) With Words Representing Sounds. These are also known as onomatopoeic words and include the following:

Splash!   Boom!   Thud!

Crash! went the window

His business has gone phut!

(Note that in the second example the exclamation mark is located in mid-sentence. This is normal when exclamation marks are used with onomatopoeic words.)

We may add to the onomatopoeics a number of 'comic strip' words such as these:

Pow!   Zap!   Splat!

(b) With interjections. Interjections expressing a range of emotions (alarm, anxiety, pain, relief, joy, surprise, amazement, anger, despair, etc.) may be followed by an exclamation mark. We list a few here in the order of the emotions just specified:

Hey! Look out!   Oh! Ow! (or Ouch!)

Ah!   Hurray!

Good heavens!   By Jove!   Bah!   Alas!

(The use of 'Alas!' is of course archaic or self-consciously pompous. 'Ah me!', another expression of despair, is also archaic.)

(d) Sharp Commands or Imperatives. Typical of these are the following:

Halt!   Stop!   Attention!   Quick march!

Present arms!

(e) With Oaths, Obscenities and Expletives. These include not only swearwords but also miscellaneous intensifying expressions. Typical are:

Damn!   Christ!   Well, I'll be blowed!

Gracious me!   So there!   Right you are!

(f) With Insults. These include name-calling and insults that function grammatically as imperatives and subjunctive phrases:

Idiot!   Liar!   You bastard!   Go to hell!

God damn you!

2. Exclamation Marks at the End of Sentences. This is where the greatest caution needs to be exercised. Certain forms of short sentence expressing any of the emotions or feelings mentioned in the previous section regularly take an exclamation mark, but only when an urgent or dramatic effect is present or is being sought.

The following series of examples will suffice to illustrate legitimate use of the exclamation mark in ordinary sentences:

> God, I've lost my key!
>
> Hell, I'll be late!
>
> I can smell gas!
>
> Hello! Is anybody there?
>
> I wish I hadn't eaten those green apples!

Just because a writer feels that a statement or interjection is arresting or full of powerful impact, however, there is no need to assume that it should be followed automatically by an exclamation mark. Take this example:

> Gentlemen, we are at war.

3. Traditional Exclamatory Sentences. The exclamation mark is used, almost by custom or common consent, at the end of certain sentences and phrases following one of a number of set patterns. The patterns, with examples, are as follows:

(a) Non-interrogative Sentences Introduced by 'How' or 'What'. These may be full or elliptical sentences:

> How nice!
>
> How kind you are!
>
> How dare you! (How dare he say that! How dare they!)
>
> What an idiot!
>
> What lovely big eyes you have!

(b) Exclamatory Questions. These are rhetorical questions requiring no real answer and said with a tone of surprise, satisfaction, despair, etc.:

> Isn't she strong!
>
> Wasn't that a marvellous film!
>
> Will I never have any peace!

(c) Phrases introduced by 'That' or 'To think that'. For example:

> To think that I nearly got a job with that firm!
>
> Oh, that I should have lived to see this country go to the dogs with such eagerness!

(d) Expressions of Surprise in the Form of Negative Conditional Clauses Introduced by 'If', 'Well, if', or 'Why, if'. For example:

> Well, if that doesn't take the biscuit!
>
> Why, if it isn't my old friend John Clark!

(e) Wishes Introduced by 'If only'. For example:

> If only I'd known!
>
> If only she could love me as I love her!

(f) Wishes Expressed in a Clause with a Subjunctive Verb. For example:

> Long live the Queen!
>
> God forbid!
>
> God help us!

(g) Blessings or Curses Introduced by 'May'. For example:

> May God have mercy on your soul!
>
> May he be boiled in oil!
>
> May good fortune shine upon you!

(h) Urgent Warnings. For example:

> Take care!
>
> Mind my foot!

(j) Urgent or Brusque Commands. For example:

> Pick up this mess!
>
> Get up to bed at once!

Exclamation Marks and Quotation Marks

The exclamation mark goes inside the quotation marks if it belongs to the quotation. If the end of the quotation coincides with the end of the sentence, the full point is omitted. The following examples illustrate all cases:

> How I love Gainsborough's painting of 'The Blue Boy'!
>
> 'Help!' he shouted. 'I can't swim!'

Non-Punctuational Uses

The exclamation mark in parentheses, expressing surprise, is one of the most frequent non-punctuational uses. For example:

Question/Exclamation Mark

Somebody paid him £500 (!) for his bashed-up old Peugeot. I wouldn't have given him even half that.

The same strictures that were set forth concerning the 'parenthetical' question mark apply here also. Most careful writers avoid the exclamation mark in parentheses as an overdone gimmick.

In chess notation, the exclamation mark indicates that a move is very good. A doubled exclamation mark (!!) indicates an excellent or inspired move:

> White: P × Q !!   Black resigns

It is worth noting that chess reports also make use of different combinations of ? and ! P × Q !? indicates an interesting move that may be dangerous. P × Q ?! indicates a seemingly poor move that may prove to be clever in the long run.

In mathematics, the exclamation mark placed after a whole number represents the factorial of that number, the result obtained by multiplying the number by all the whole numbers below it. Thus:

$$5! = 5 \times 4 \times 3 \times 2 \times 1 = 120$$

11

Capital Letters

We are so used to seeing a mixture of capital letters and 'small' letters, with capitals at the start of each new sentence and at the start of certain words within a sentence, that anything different has major impact because it is so unexpected. The American poet Edward Estlin Cummings provided many instances of this in his work, from which capitals were deliberately excluded. He is better known as e.e. cummings, shunning capital letters even in the preferred orthographical representation of his name (he contended that only God merited a capital).

Printers and editors regularly refer to capital letters as 'upper-case' letters and 'small' letters as 'lower-case' letters. This terminology derives from the days of printing with metal type, which was stored in a divided tray. The two sections of the tray were called cases, the capitals being located in the upper case, with the 'small' letters being in the lower one. Even in the days of word processing and computer typesetting, printers continue to use the old terminology.

Uses of Capital Letters

There is only one genuine punctuational use of capital letters, given as (1) in the list below. The other uses are largely a matter of orthographical convention, and in some cases writers and editors can choose whether to use a capital or not, as long as they follow a consistent policy on the matter.

History of the Capital Letter

Modern English capital letters are of Roman origin. The even, upright letter forms found on such ancient Roman monuments as Trajan's column, erected between ad 106 and 113, were echoed in the so-called majuscule letters of classical and early medieval manuscripts. The majuscules were less angular than the stone-cut letters but still had an even appearance.

With the introduction of minuscule (that is, 'small') letters in the eighth century by the Anglo-Saxon monk Alcuin, Charlemagne's educational adviser, manuscripts lost their even look but gained in legibility. Majuscules, or capitals, now took on a different role. In enlarged and illuminated form they stood at the beginnings of chapters and paragraphs as the first letter of the first word. In the course of time they began to be used within the paragraph, to distinguish the first letter of the first word of each new sentence. Thus, before the age of printing began in the late fifteenth century, the capital letter had already evolved the function for which it is primarily used even today.

Capital Letters

Avoid Unnecessary Capitals. In general, if there is a choice, most authorities recommend the use of lower-case ('small') letters rather than capitals. The reason is that words with an initial capital letter stand out from the majority of words, which take a lower-case initial. There are times when this can be helpful to a reader, showing him or her that words are being used in a unique or specific way. Overuse of capitals vitiates this useful distinction. Therefore avoid capitals if you do not need them.

1. a the Start of Sentences and Paragraphs. For the sake of emphasis the first letter of every paragraph and of every sentence beginning after a full point is a capital letter. This is true whether or not the sentence is in quotation marks. For example:

> The old man said, 'The day war broke out my wife and I got married.' He gazed tearfully at her photograph as he spoke.

New sentences following questions or exclamations also begin with a capital:

> What can this rising new company do for you? A whole array of tasks from manning the phones to emptying the wastepaper baskets.

In certain circumstances a capital letter may follow a colon:

> My father had an old saying: Do as you would be done by.

(*See also* the chapter on Colon for the instances in which capitals are allowed.)

2. At the Start of Each Line in a Poem. Traditionally, the first letter of each line in a piece of verse is a capital:

> If all the good people were clever,
>
> And all clever people were good,
>
> The world would be nicer than ever
>
> We thought that it possibly could
>
> – Elizabeth Wordsworth

3. The Names of People and Places. All proper names (place names and personal names) in English begin with a capital letter:

| Terry Wogan | Birmingham | France | South Africa |

This category includes street names and the names of public houses, cinemas, theatres, national buildings and institutions, and places of public interest:

Oxford Street	The Red Lion	The Odeon
The Comedy Theatre	The British Museum	
Hyde Park	Times Square	

Adjectives and nouns directly derived from proper names also take an initial capital:

  France–French   Jung–Jungian   Marx–Marxism

Names of objects, scientific units, etc., derived from personal or place names are not always written with an initial capital, especially when they have become firmly established in the language:

  balaclava   watt   wellingtons   joule

Adjectives derived from personal or place names are not written with an initial capital when their association with the proper name from which they are derived becomes distant:

  french windows   french horn   brussels sprouts

Most verbs derived from proper names are not written with a capital:

  frenchify bowdlerize   pasteurize

4. Foreign Languages. The names of all languages are treated as proper names in English:

  English   Welsh   French   German

5. Brand Names, Trademarks, etc. All brand names, trademarks, company names, and the objects to which they may refer are written with initial capitals:

  Go out and buy me a packet of Persil.

  I own some shares in British Gas plc.

When a brand name or trademark stands for a particular type of object in regular use, write it with a lower-case initial:

  Would you mind running the hoover over the drawing-room carpet?

  I have to go to the launderette (or laundromat).

6. Modes of Address, Titles, etc. These should in general take an initial cap only when used in front of a personal name:

  Professor Jones   Professor Michael Jones

But:

  Michael Jones is professor of linguistics.

Other examples are:

  Sir Peter Smith   Good morning, Sir Peter.

But:

  Good morning, sir.

Capital Letters

The prizes were presented by His Grace the First Duke of Exton. Following this ceremony, the duke made a fine speech to the whole school.

All the normal modes of address take initial capitals: Mr, Mrs, Ms and Miss.

7. Official Posts. The same rules apply as for (6) above. When the post is given as a title forming part of the name, it takes an initial capital. But otherwise not:

Prime Minister Margaret Thatcher visited Washington for talks with President Bush.

The British prime minister met the US president.

King Charles I reigned from 1625 to 1649.

Charles I was the first king of England to be executed.

Full official titles should be written with initial capitals:

The President of the United States addressed the whole nation from the Oval Office of the White House last night.

8. Unique Things. Initial capitals should be used for such things as the following:

The Statue of Liberty	The British Telecom Tower	
The Crown Jewels	The Oval Office	The White House

This category includes certain specific references, as opposed to general ones. For example, the (British) Government is often given a capital, while the lower-case letter is used when the reference is to any legislative body in general:

The Government has announced …

No government is completely perfect.

Note that official bodies take an initial capital when the names are used in full but not when the names are shortened, as in the following example:

The Department of Health is to be wholly reorganized. Mr C—, the minister responsible for running the department, explained the changes.

9. Initials and Acronyms. These are generally written, typed or set as capital letters, usually without full points:

BBC   CBS   MP   RSC (Royal Shakespeare Company)

UNESCO   USA   USSR

It is good practice to provide the name of the organization, institution, etc., in full at the start of an article, report, etc., with the initials in parentheses, and then to use the initials for all subsequent references. For further information on initials, *see* the chapter on the Full Point. *See also* the chapter on Parentheses.

10. Principal Words in Headings and Titles. The first word and all the main nouns and verbs in the title of a book, play, essay, poem or report, and also in a heading or subheading, are traditionally written with initial capital letters. Pronouns, conjunctions, prepositions, the definite and indefinite articles, and parts of the verb 'to be' are generally written with lower-case initials:

The Corn is Green   *How Green was my Valley*

The Mill on the Floss   *Men and Machines*

A style that is gaining ground, especially in the preparation of bibliographies, is the writing of titles and headings with an initial capital for the first word and thereafter only for words that would take a capital in ordinary usage. Thus we would have, for example:

The corn is green   *Men and machines*

The fall of the house of Usher

This new system has much to recommend it; in particular it parallels many other languages (e.g. French) in which titles and headings are presented in this way. The more traditional use of capitals in titles and headings is still the more prevalent, however.

For further information on titles, *see* the next section on Boldface and Italics and the section on Paragraphs.

11. Miscellaneous Uses. The following are conventional uses of initial capital letters:

(a) The First Person Singular Pronoun, *I*. Example:

I think, therefore I am.

(b) All pronouns referring to God or Jesus Christ. For instance:

God so loved the world that He gave His only begotten son …

With all due respect to e.e. cummings, this is a use that is declining. The Revised Standard Version of the Bible, in the edition known as *The Common Bible* (1973), uses lower-case initials for these pronouns, and perhaps we should too.

(c) Days of the Week, Months of the Year and Geological or Historical Periods. For example:

Clocks go back on the third Saturday in October.

He is an expert on the Pleistocene epoch.

Oliver Cromwell ruled England during the Protectorate.

Capitals and Small Capitals

Writing, typing or printing whole words, phrases or sentences in capitals is fine for titles or chapter headings, to which the reader's attention must be drawn. In ordinary text this practice certainly attracts attention too. Warnings can be especially effective if treated in this way:

> ... you are trying to observe. WARNING: YOU MUST NEVER POINT A TELESCOPE DIRECTLY AT THE SUN. You should always observe the sun by projecting it onto a screen or piece of card ....

However, the use of capitals in the middle of plain text is regarded by many as garish.

Much more discreet but still reasonably emphatic is the use of small capitals. These are characters whose shapes are the same as those of full capitals but whose heights are equivalent to those of lower-case letters.

Small capitals are used for certain abbreviations (AD, BC), for initials and acronyms when full capitals are deemed to be too emphatic (BBC, UHT), and often (with an initial full capital) for the first word or two in the chapter of a book – for example:

> WHEN WE are very young, we regard the ability to ride a bicycle as one of the most highly prized skills ...

In many modern dictionaries, small caps are used to pick out a word, e.g., in an etymology, where further information can be found:

> waistcoat ... [from WAIST + COAT]

Capitals and Alphabetical Order

The traditional method of ordering an alphabetical list when two items are identically spelled but one has an initial capital letter is to put the lower-case form first:

> eye (organ of the body)
>
> Eye (place in Suffolk)

However, many encyclopaedia publishers (*Encyclopedia Britannica*, for example) use the order Person – Place – Thing, which would make capital forms precede lower-case ones. Placing capitals before lower-case forms is also the order that most computers use in generating alphabetic lists. Computers can be programmed to place lower-case forms first, but left to themselves they usually compile the list on the basis of numerical values assigned to letters on the basis of the American Standard Code on Information Interchange (ASCII). It happens that the ASCII codes for capitals come before those for lower-case letters.

Modes of Address within the Family

Finally, capitals are used in sentences such as these:

Capital Letters

Where's my coat, Mum?

Yes, Father, I understand.

Hello, Uncle John.

I'm staying with my Uncle John.

This is my uncle. His name is John Smith.

12

Boldface

Boldface and italic type are typographical terms and used to apply only to typeset or printed material. Nowadays, the dot-matrix or daisywheel printers set up to work with most word processors can produce a passable dark type similar in function to the printer's boldface and a rightward-sloping version of roman that can pass for italic. We shall come to italic in the next chapter.

Boldface, or bold type, is a heavier version of the roman type belonging to a particular fount or typeface normally used for text. It is possible to have a bold italic in some modern typefaces, but generally the most widely available style of bold is a roman one. Small capitals are generally not available in boldface.

Authors who write for publication should indicate boldface not by printing it as such on their word processors or typewriters but by typing ordinary text and underscoring it with a wavy line.

Newton's Early Life. Newton was born at Woolsthorpe, Lincolnshire ...

Uses of Boldface

Boldface is used exclusively for emphasis or contrast. Its main use is in headings and subheadings. Usually such headings are the same point size as the text face or a point or two larger. But boldface may also be used in a much bigger point size for display headings, book or chapter titles, etc. The chapter titles and main headings in this book are in bold.

Boldface may be used in the middle of ordinary (roman) text to pick out specific words.

I must have **all** your forms in by the end of this week.

This usage is often found in reference-books, dictionaries, encyclopaedias, etc. A dictionary definition may, for example, use different strengths of bold type:

harmless adj. not causing or likely to cause harm or hurt —**harmlessly** adv.— **harmlessness** n.

(Usually this means that the stronger or primary bold type is a point larger than the secondary, which in its turn is the same size as the text face.)

Use in Indexes and Bibliographies. Page references in an index may be set in bold when they point to the most substantial or significant treatment of the indexed item in the book concerned. For example:

Tiglath-Pileser III, 274, **276–80**, 285, 315, 316

(In the above citation, the bold type indicates that the major reference to Tiglath-Pileser III is to be found on pp. 276–80.)

In bibliographies in scientific books, where dates of publication, volume numbers, page numbers and column numbers may cause confusion, the page numbers are frequently in boldface:

Heller, H. & Lederis, K. 1958. Paper chromatography of small amounts of vasopressin and oxytocin. *Nature*, London, **182**, 1231–2

(The above example is quoted in Judith Butcher, *Copy-editing: The Cambridge Handbook*.)

In Mathematical Books. Vector and tensor quantities are set in boldface italics:

($\mathbf{s} + \mathbf{t}$)a = sa + ta

(Needless to say, this is a very specialized use.)

Punctuation and Boldface

Any punctuation directly following a bold title, heading or word in text is usually included in the boldface. Note the appropriate examples above and this one:

balalaika: A triangular stringed musical instrument popular in Russia . ...

13

Italics

Italic type (italic, or italics, for short) is an elegant, light, almost cursive, rightward-sloping style of type used for various forms of emphasis. It is the typographical equivalent of underlining a word or words in a piece of handwritten text, and indeed authors and editors preparing typescripts for the press signal italicized words and passages to the printer by putting a straight line underneath them.

Most typefaces that one encounters in books, newspapers and magazines have an italic form, and the dot-matrix printer forming part of virtually every office's word-processing equipment these days can produce a sloping version of its standard roman fount that provides sufficient contrast to function as a passable italic type.

Francesco Griffo cut the very first italic typeface in 1500 for the great Venetian printer Aldus Manutius the Elder. It was based on an informal kind of handwriting used in the papal chanceries during that period. This compact, humanistic style of type was at first used as a main text face – Griffo used it for the Aldine edition of the poems of Virgil in 1501. It can still be attractive as a text face even today, but it is more commonly encountered in the emphatic uses described here.

Uses of Italics

We use italics in the following ways:

1. Emphasis. For example:

> You *must* ensure that all the necessary arrangements are completed by Friday.
>
> We shall *under no circumstances* be responsible for property lost or damaged in transit.

Careful writers avoid excessive italicization for emphasis.

2. Chapter Headings and Subheadings. In this respect italic type is used in a similar way to boldface. Two illustrations will suffice:

> *The Solar System*
>
> Nine planets orbit the Sun along with meteoroids, asteroids and comets, to make up …
>
> *Newton's Discoveries.* Newton's scientific work spanned the fields of optics, mechanics, …

3. Drawing Attention to a Letter, Word or Phrase for its own Sake. Another instance of 'naming a word as a word'. We met a similar use under the section on quotation marks:

> I cannot stand people who use the constructions *different to* or *different than*. The correct phrase is *different from*.
>
> *Catherine* has nine letters.
>
> There are two *l*s in artillery.

In the last example, note that the letter *l* is in italics but the pluralizing *-s* is in roman.

4. Foreign Phrases. Italics are used for words or phrases that do not yet seem to have become fully naturalized in the English language:

> In 1820 Schubert wrote a one-act opera that achieved a modest *succès d'estime*.
>
> The Soviet orchestra's tour had been made possible by the new climate of *glasnost*.

But italics are not used for words and phrases that are naturalized:

> She offered him a canapé as they continued to talk.
>
> The general's coup d'état took place at dawn on Thursday.

5. Names of Ships, Aircraft and Other Vehicles. For example:

> We went to America on the *QE2*.
>
> The first victim of the German ship *Bismarck* was HMS *Hood*.
>
> The *Bluebird*'s design was revolutionary.

Note in the last example the fact that *Bluebird* is in italics but the possessive *'s* is in roman.

6. Titles of Books, Plays and Long Poems. The titles appear in italics for self-contained publications (full-length novels, plays, long poems, non-fiction works, etc.). Chapters, articles, essays or short poems that form part of larger collections are left in roman between quotation marks:

> Have you read *War and Peace*, by Leo Tolstoy?
>
> Last night we saw Tom Stoppard's play *Professional Foul*.
>
> D.B. Fry, 'Speech Reception and Perception', *New Horizons in Linguistics*, edited by John Lyons. Penguin, 1970.
>
> T.S. Eliot wrote *The Wasteland* and a short poem called 'Gerontion'.

To these may be added musical plays and films:

Oklahoma and *South Pacific* are still among the best musicals that Rodgers and Hammerstein ever wrote.

Dustin Hoffman is outstanding in *Rain Man*.

7. Musical Compositions (Symphonies, Operas, Ballets, etc.). Named musical compositions (especially those on a large scale) are generally placed in italics:

Handel's oratorio *Israel in Egypt*.

Beethoven's *Pastoral Symphony*.

Compositions that are identified merely by a genre and a number are left in roman.

Beethoven's Symphony No. 6.

Prokofiev's Piano Sonata No. 7.

8. Magazines, Newspapers and Periodicals. The word *The* is only included in the italic title if it appears on the publication's mast-head:

I read it in *The Daily Telegraph*.

I saw the story in the *Daily Mail*.

However, whether it stands as part of the italicized title or not, the definite article can be missed out when necessary:

Have you seen this morning's *Daily Telegraph*?

9. Latin Genus and Species Names of Plants or Animals. Note that (a) genus names begin with an initial capital letter and species names never do, even when they are derived from proper names, (b) if a genus name needs to be repeated only the italic form of its initial capital letter is given, followed by a full point, and (c) all divisions above that of genus are written in roman:

The dog (*Canis familiaris*) and the wolf (*C. lupus*) both belong to the family Canidae.

The garden contained two fine buddleias, one a specimen of *Buddleia davidii*, the other of *B. globosa*.

10. Mathematics. Most variables in mathematics are set in italics by printers.

$x^2 + 2x + y^2$

11. Italics as Punctuation. In a piece of text the mere change from roman (or normal) type to italics may under certain circumstances obviate the need for any other punctuation. For example:

... From Late Latin *incarnare* to make flesh, from Latin IN[2] + *caro* flesh

In the above example, taken from an etymology in a dictionary, we might have expected commas after *incarnare* and *caro*. The use of italics allows the commas to be omitted.

12. Italics within Italics? Emphasis by means of italics when the typeface is already italic is clearly impossible. In such cases it is legitimate to use quotation marks. Compare these:

He wrote a brilliant assessment of *Pilgrim's Progress*.

His book was called *An Assessment of 'Pilgrim's Progress'*.

Another conventional device is to set in roman those words that would normally be italicized when the main text is in italic (such as a caption):

This illustration shows a fine example of Buddleia davidii *and its usual congregation of butterflies.*

14

Numbers in Text

Numbers are of two main types: arabic numerals (popularly called 'figures', especially by printers) and Roman numerals (often called just 'numerals' by printers). In typed or printed matter arabic numerals may either be 'lining' (that is, aligned with each other) or 'non-lining' (that is, with the six and eight extending above the average height of the other figures and three, four, five, seven and nine extending below it. Non-lining figures are a little old-fashioned these days, and most modern typefaces have lining figures. There is no problem about this, except that if you are referring to lines in a poem it may be best to write 'lines 11–13' rather than '11. 11–13'.

Arabic Numerals

1. Figures or Words? In ordinary text it is safest to use words for small numbers (that is, below 10 or below 11) and figures for the rest. The only real exception occurs in text that is typeset in narrow measure: that is, a book where the length of the lines of type is relatively short. Many publishers have a rule about numbers below 10 or 11 enshrined in their house style. If a range or series of numbers is involved, do not mix words and figures. The following examples illustrate the customary practice.

He held a teaching post for seven or eight years.

The encyclopaedia caters for readers between the ages of 7 and 30.

(*See also* the discussion on ranges of numbers below.)

Round numbers may also be expressed in words (twenty, thirty, forty, ... a hundred, two hundred, ... a thousand, two thousand, etc.). With round numbers above a million, the most prevalent style is to use a figure or figures followed by the words 'million' or 'billion': e.g. population, 3 million; A3320 billion; $7 billion (or 7 billion dollars).

It is a rule that numerals should not be used at the start of a sentence. In these examples, therefore, (a) is preferred to (b):

(a) Forty-four people were killed in yesterday's air disaster . ...

Not:

(b) 44 people were killed . ...

Billion or Thousand Million? The British billion (that is, a million million, or 1,000,000,000,000) is virtually a thing of the past. All the British press, everyone working in the City of London, and even British school children have so completely accepted the American billion (that is, a thousand million, or 1,000,000,000) that there seems little point in drawing attention to the distinction any longer. Those who wish to stand by the British billion, however, are welcome to do so.

2. Four and More Figures and the Decimal Point. Writers have a choice in the ways in which they represent numbers consisting of four or more digits.

(a) To comma off from the right (starting at the immediate left of the implied or actual decimal point) all numbers greater than 999.99 ... :

   2,759   21,796.75   234,853.625   13,089,654.875

(b) To write four-figure numbers without commas and to comma off from the right all numbers above 9999.99 ... :

   2759   21,796.75   (*See* the remaining numbers in (a).)

(c) To write four-figure numbers without commas and to use standard or thin spaces instead of commas in numbers above 9999.99 ... (this is now common usage in scientific journals such as *Nature* and *New Scientist*, and is also found in many science textbooks):

   2759   21796.75 234853.625 13089654.875

(d) To write all numbers out continuously with no spaces or commas and no breaks other than the decimal point, as in most books on mathematics:

   2759   21796.75 234   853.625   13089654.875

In the last two cases (using spaces or using no breaks at all), a decimal point may be represented by a comma in accordance with practice on the continent of Europe:

   21796,75   234   853,625   13 089   654,875

In normal British usage, the decimal point is either a full point (.) or a centred dot (·).

Figures following the decimal point are generally written out as a continuous string:

   The value of pi (to nine decimal places) is 3.141592654

3. Percentages. In ordinary writing percentages are usually given in figures followed by the word 'per cent' (or 'percent' in normal American usage). There is no full point after 'per cent'.

   5 per cent   8.8 per cent   23.9 per cent

You can also use the sign % in ordinary text:

   Wheat accounted for 18% of the country's gross national product.

Numbers in Text

And you should always use the % sign in tables, often in the heading to one of the columns (e.g. a column might be entitled 'Proportion of Population under 18', and underneath would be written '(%)').

4. Number Ranges. If you use the 'x to y' or 'between x and y' constructions when quoting number ranges, page references, date ranges, etc., you must include the whole of the numbers involved:

> From 1956 to 1987 he taught in a Roman Catholic seminary in West Africa.
>
> You will find a table of English monarchs and their reign dates between pp. 254 and 257.

The other way of expressing ranges of numbers is by separating the numbers with an en rule (*see* the chapter on the Dash). When using this style remember that the second number (the one to the right of the en rule) is often not given in full. Part of it is omitted, or elided. Authors may find that publishers' preferences vary as to whether the last one or the last two digits are retained in the elided number. Retaining the last two is on the whole clearer, even if it does entail one more keystroke. The following examples illustrate the recommended procedure:

> *See* pp. 5–7, 9–11, 11–18, 20–23, 31–34, 45–51, 96–102, 113–16, 118–23, 134–36, 211–16, 244–47, 256–61, 291–307, 1014–16, 1025–26, 1078–81, 1098–1105.
>
> Fred Smith (1896–1961) had a son called John Smith (1918–87). Fred fought in the 1914–18 war. John was a prisoner of war in World War II during the period 1941–45.

The rule is to elide as much as possible without destroying clarity. Some publishers require the last digit to be retained except in the 'teens' of any hundred, where two are kept. For example, 112–14, but 141–6. This is obviously a workable system, but the one illustrated above is less ambiguous and easier to remember.

Date Ranges BC. Note that in dates between the tenth and first centuries BC, all the figures should be repeated for clarity.

> Pericles (495–429 BC)   Socrates (470–399 BC)
>
> Julius Caesar (100–44 BC)

To be crystal clear, we should properly repeat the 'BC' after both dates:

> Julius Caesar (100 BC – 44 BC)

Some writers also extend this 'all the figures' rule to dates between AD 1 and AD 1000, although there is no need to repeat AD before each date:

> Offa was king of Mercia during the period AD 757–796.

5. Dates. Exact dates should be shown in the following form:

Wednesday 6 September 1989

There is no need for any commas in this formula, except when the date is followed by another number:

On Wednesday 6 September 1989 I completed my book on punctuation.

On Friday 2 September 1939, 21 people died in a German air raid on Warsaw, Poland.

This method of showing the date is logical and reflects general British practice, following an ascending order from day to year. An older method, showing month-day-year, is also widely used, especially in the United States. It requires commas:

On Wednesday, September 6, 1989, I finished my latest book.

or:

On Wednesday, September 6th, 1989, I finished my latest book.

The first method (day-month-year) gives a more up-to-date and less cluttered appearance.

All-figure Formats for Dates. The figures representing the date in this abbreviated form of representation are separated by full points, colons or slashes (solidi). Remember that the British and American formats differ. In this example we note the main British and American ways of showing the date 6 September 1989:

British	6/9/89	6.9.89	6:9:89
American	9/6/89	9:6:89	9.6.89

The forms 06:09:89 (UK) and 09:06:89 (USA) are also encountered.

Years. All years consisting of four figures are written without commas. Five-figure years take commas.

AD 1066   1500 BC   13,000 BC

Note that, as in the examples given here and earlier, AD precedes the year, while BC follows it. Even though we may popularly refer to 1066 AD, careful writers always render that year as AD 1066.

6. *Time*. Ways of showing the time of day have been discussed in the chapters on the Full Point and the Colon. The best way of showing times in races, astronomical events, etc., is exemplified in this illustration:

Smith's time of 2h 12m 14.2s shattered the previous record of 2:13:06.3, set last year by Bert Jones.

7. *Measurements*. In quoting most measurements, especially ones containing decimal quantities, it is clearer with a space between the number and the unit of

Numbers in Text

measurement:

    208.6 cm   300 kg

Some publishers, however, insist on:

    208.6cm   300kg

A thin space should be used by printers in setting temperatures, but typists and those who write by hand can ignore such refinements.

Do not elide measurement ranges, e.g. temperature ranges, to avoid confusion between ascending and descending scales:

    Tomorrow's temperatures will be in the range 21–23°C

8. Catalogue Numbers, Telephone Numbers, etc. There are many variations in usage in this area, but some items in this category – for example, the international standard book number at the front of this volume – have a standardized format within an internationally accepted system. The same applies to American Library of Congress catalog numbers. In quoting an ISBN, do use spaces between the groups of digits, not hyphens.

British Telecom recommends that telephone numbers should be shown in one of the forms below:

    British Telecom recommends that telephone numbers should be shown in one of the forms below:

    London numbers01-234 5678

    Other cities, e.g. Birmingham021-234 5678

    Other UK codes, e.g. Aylesbury, Bucks(0296) 81234

    Other telephone networks, e.g. Mercury, may have recommended methods of showing their telephone numbers that differ from the above.

    When British Telecom changes the numbering system, the above formulas may alter. For example, from May 1990, London will be divided into 071 and 081 areas. A number in central London might therefore read 071-287 0214.

    International numbers vary, but American numbers usually follow this pattern:

    (010 312) 245-1234 (for a number in Chicago)

    Postcodes follow an established system in Britain, consisting of two groups of letters and numbers separated by a space. They are not written as a continuous string. US ZIP (Zoning Improvement Plan) codes consist of continuous strings of figures.

    BR3 3LJ (a UK postcode) 60653 (A US ZIP code)

9. Numbers in Lists. Numbers introducing items in a list may be plain, may be followed by a full point or a single closing bracket, or may be enclosed in brackets (parentheses). *See also* the chapters on the Full point and on Parentheses.

Roman Numerals

Roman numerals may be shown as upper- or lower-case letters or small capital letters.

Full capitals are used for titles such as Queen Elizabeth II or Pope John XXIII.

In biblical usage, LXX (in full capitals) signifies the Septuagint.

Small capitals (if they are present in the particular fount being used) are employed for all other purposes, chiefly for volume numbers in bibliographies:

Antiquity XXXII:226 (1958)

(Note that small capitals do not look attractive with lining figures; they look better with non-aligning figures.)

Lower-case numerals are used to number the preliminary pages of a book, and are sometimes employed in act-and- scene references to Shakespeare's plays:

Macbeth, Act 2, scene ii, lines 13-14

Using lower-case roman numerals for the month in all- figure dates is a practice that is still occasionally encountered:

27.ii.47

But this is rather old-fashioned nowadays.

15

Accents, Diacritics and Textual Symbols

This section is a mixed bag of signs and symbols, some of which apply to foreign languages. The contents are necessarily selective, partly because space is limited and partly because our purpose is to concentrate on conventional symbols in English, not to provide a typographer's textbook on foreign language setting.

Diacritics, or diacritical marks, are signs written above or below characters or letters to show that they have a different sound quality from that which is normal or is expected, or that they are pronounced with a special stress or intonation. Accents are a specific type of diacritic written above a vowel (*a, e, i, o, u*) or a letter functioning as a vowel, such as *w* or *y* in Welsh. Most European languages have a considerable array of diacritics, but English is exceptional in having virtually none. Consequently, most mechanical typewriters have never been designed to print such symbols and cannot reproduce them, although some electronic typewriters, word processors and typesetting machines can.

Because of such deficiencies, the use of appropriate accents on foreign words in English has become relatively uncommon during this century. Even as links with Europe continue to be strengthened during the 1990s, it seems likely that the avoidance of accents will continue. Long-established foreign phrases generally lack their accents anyway. However, there are some words that tenaciously retain their accents, and foreign names, especially in a literary context, should be spelled with the appropriate diacritics.

Textual symbols – for the purposes of this discussion – include such items as footnote symbols (asterisks, daggers, superior figures, etc.), the ampersand, currency symbols, and foreign language punctuation marks, where these are likely to be encountered.

We shall deal with the items in this section in alphabetical order, saying what each one is and providing short remarks and examples where necessary.

Acute Accent (´)

This accent mark distinguishes a certain vowel quality in French and is used for stress on other languages such as Spanish and Italian. In English it marks the strong syllables in poetry:

I wándered lónely ás a clóud

The acute accent is retained on foreign imports largely to aid correct pronunciation:

attaché; blasé; cliché; communiqué; éclat; élan; emegré; fiancé (and fiancée);

passé; protégé; touché.

Ampersand (&)

Originally 'and per se and', meaning the sign for 'and' itself, the ampersand is a textual symbol used as a shorthand for the word 'and'. The sign probably arose as a scribal contraction of the Latin word *et* ('and'). It was much used in early printed books, as was the symbolic abbreviation *&c* (for 'etc.'). These uses are now gone. Its usual modern use is in quoting the names of commercial companies and firms: Marks & Spencer, Sears & Roebuck.

Asterisk (*)

This textual symbol, which is not called an *asterix* – that is the name of a French comic-strip hero – has a variety of uses.

It serves as a symbol indicating a footnote. It follows a word in text on which a footnote gives further information. If an asterisk covers a whole sentence, it follows the full point closing the sentence.

   Text: Anthony Brown* has suggested a possible solution to this difficult problem. ...

   Note: *Philosophical Transactions, xii (1945), pp. 2325.

The asterisk is the first of a series of footnote symbols that are used in turn on each page. The sequence is * † ‡ § ? ¶.

In mathematics and computer work, the asterisk is used as a multiplication symbol. In linguistics it designates a hypothetical linguistic form, sentence, etc., or one not attested in the written record:

   *John elapses books.

   Dot [from ME *dot, from OE dott, head of a boil]

When placed before a date, an asterisk indicates that it is a birthdate:

   Bach, Johann Sebastian *1685 861750.

Breathings

The rough and smooth breathings (*spiritus asper* ʽ and *spiritus lenis* ʼ) are accents placed over initial vowels and the letter *rho* in writing and setting classical Greek texts. They resemble, but are not the same as, the 'open-quotation' (rough) and 'close-quotation' (smooth) marks. Similar-looking accents are used over Arabic or Hebrew vowels.

Breve (˘)

This curved accent written over vowels (*a, e, i, o*) indicates that they are metrically or phonetically 'short'. It is used primarily as a linguistics and classical scansion symbol.

Cedilla (¸)

This is a diacritic written beneath the letter *c* (appearing as ç) before *a, o,* or *u* in French and Spanish to indicate that it is to be pronounced as an *s*. In English it may be omitted from *facade* (originally *façade*), but is retained in *soupçon*. It also appears in such phrases as *comme ci, comme ça*, occasionally used in fictional dialogue.

Circumflex (^)

This accent is retained on such French words as these (some of which may also be italicized):

> bête noire; coup de grâce; crêpe-suzette; papier mâché; pâté (pâté de foie gras); raison-d'être; tête-à-tête.

It is also required in certain Welsh terms as Meibion Glyn Dwr, a Welsh nationalist organization.

Currency Symbols

In most cases, the amount follows the sign for the currency involved, e.g. £300 or $300. The most common currency symbols are:

Cent	¢
Dollar	$
Euro	€
Pound	£
Yen	¥

The international currency symbol # is also occasionally encountered.

Dagger (†)

This is a textual symbol used as a footnote indicator just as the asterisk is. It comes second in the footnote system outlined under the earlier paragraph on the Asterisk.

The dagger is also used in linguistics to signal an obsolete form:

> The word *broad* comes from an earlier †*brad*.

The dagger also signals a deathdate:–

> Bach, Johann Sebastian, *1685 †1750.

The double dagger (‡) is used only as a text indicator and corresponding footnote symbol.

Diaeresis (¨)

This accent, called a dieresis in the United States, is used in ancient Greek, and by extension in French and other languages, to mark the fact that two vowels which would normally have coalesced to form a diphthong are to be pronounced separately. The same sign does duty for the German umlaut, which 'modifies' ä, ë, and ö. It is generally not preserved for Greek and French borrowings, except in the mythological-astronomical name Boötes and the French word noël used as a name (i.e., Noël), when it is placed over the second vowel of the pair. It is usually omitted in naive (originally naïve or naïve). The German umlaut is preserved in many names, but in some, such as *Schönberg*, it is can be correctly rendered by leaving out the umlaut and adding an *e* to the vowel, giving *Schoenberg*. The diaeresis, once used in such words as *coöperate, coördinate*, etc., proved only a temporary trend and is no longer normally encountered in these words.

Foreign Language Symbols

In French, German and Spanish, special symbols exist for showing quotation marks.

In French, special signs called guillemets (« ») are used to signal ordinary or isolated quotations:

> *Qu'est-ce que vous dites,* «franglais?»

Dialogue is shown by means of a double em rule preceding each character's speech:

> ——*Bonjour, M Dubois, dit Marie.*
>
> ——Bonjour, Marie. dit M Dubois.

In German, two main methods exist for displaying verbatim speech in quotation.

(1) To enclose the speech within double commas, the second pair being inverted or turned:

> „Wie geht es Dir, Hans?" fragte Rudolf.

(2) To enclose the speech between inward-pointing guillemets:

> »Wie geht es Dir, Hans?« fragte Rudolf.

It is also worth noting that in German *all* nouns (not merely proper nouns) are capitalized.

In Greek, the question mark is identical with the English semicolon (;), while the colon is represented by a superior full point (·). Note also that Greek uses the acute, circumflex and grave accents, even in its modern form. The breathings, however, are used only in classical Greek.

In Spanish, the same method of showing quotations is used as that for French. But note that all questions are prefaced by a turned question mark (¿) and followed by a normal question mark (?), and all exclamations are prefaced by a turned exclamation

Accents/Textual Symbols

mark (A1) and followed by a normal one (!).

Grave Accent (`)

This accent is retained for reasons of pronunciation in the following French words:

à la (in such phrases as à la carte, à la king); crème de la crème; *père* (as in Alexandre Dumas *père*); pied-à-terre.

Hacek (ˇ)

The hacek, an angular symbol, not curved like the breve, is used in modifying certain consonants and vowels in Czech names. In ordinary use it is often omitted from Dvorák, which is a well-established name in English, but is still used for such people as Leos Janácˇek (which also takes an acute accent).

Inferior Numerals

These are figures set in smaller type below the level of the line of printed text ($_1$, $_2$, $_3$, etc.). They have a variety of scientific uses, the best-known of which is perhaps to be found in chemical formulae such as H_2O. *See* the later paragraphs on Superior Numerals.

Macron (¯)

This accent, placed over vowels (a, e, i, o, u), indicates that the vowel concerned is phonetically or metrically long. It is the counterpart of the breve, for example *kolon*.

Mathematics and Science

Variables (*a, b, c, x, y, z*) are generally in italic. Chemical formulae are set in roman. The mathematical operators + (plus), − (minus), × (multiplied by) and ÷ or / (divided by), together with parentheses, brackets and braces, are only part of the great panoply of signs and symbols that the typing or setting of mathematics requires. Greek letters and symbols, including a large sigma (Σ) used in integration, as well as a long strokeless ∫, also used in integration, all form part of the mathematician's fearsome armoury. Set theory is also replete with unusual signs, such as ∪ (indicating the union between two sets).

This is a highly specialized area. Editors as well as authors who work in these fields regularly are usually qualified mathematicians and scientists. There is, however, a publication to which the experts and novices can refer: Chapter 13 of Judith Butcher's *Copy-editing: The Cambridge Handbook*, CUP (1981, 2nd edition) gives an invaluable rundown of everything science and maths authors and editors need to be aware of.

Paragraph Marker (¶)

The paragraph marker (also known as a pilcrow) is used to introduce a paragraph that in some way needs to be isolated from the main text, usually because it contains additional information of marginal rather than primary signfance or indeed because it needs to be emphasized. For example, a dictionary editor might use a ¶ to set off a note on usage from the rest of the definition or etymology.

In addition to this basic use, the paragraph marker is also employed in the footnote system along with the asterisk and dagger (*see* earlier).

Per Cent Sign (%)

This is typed or printed close up to the figure concerned. The same also applies to the less common per thousand ‰ symbol:

    23.6%   18.5‰

Section Marker (§)

This is a textual symbol that is used primarily to divide up a chapter into main sections. It precedes a figure or figures and is usually accompanied by a section heading.

    §3: Medieval Punctuation

The section marker is also used in the asterisk-dagger footnote system. *See* the earlier paragraph on the Asterisk.

Superior Numerals

These are figures in small type written above the line of the text (^{1}, ^{2}, etc.). They are used as text and footnote indicators as an alternative to the asterisk, dagger, etc. In mathematics superior figures are used to show that a number or variable has been raised to a power specified by the figure (it is an exponent).

Superior numerals are used in chemistry and atomic physics to denote isotopes (where the numeral is the mass number):

    ^{90}Sr ^{238}U ^{238}Pu

although Sr-90, U-238 and Pu-239 are accepted and easier to typeset.

Note also that superior letters can be used in a similar way to figures. For further information on the functions of superior and inferior figures and letters, see Judith Butcher, op. cit.

Superior Ring

This accent occurs on top of å in Danish and is also found in Czech in names such as Martinů. In the Danish name Ångstrøm, we can also see the use of the 'stroked o'. The modifications produced by these changed letters give the name a pronunciation something like [ONG *strurm*].

Accents/Textual Symbols

Tilde (~)

This accent marks the fact that an ñ in Spanish is to be pronounced *ny*. It also indicates that certain sounds in Portuguese are pronounced with a nasal quality. The tilde is retained in such words as these:

mañana; piña (as in piña cloth); señor; sertão (the countryside of northern Brazil).

The tilde is used in phonetics to indicate the nasalization of a vowel. An enlarged, centrally placed tilde, also known as a swung dash (~), has a number of applications, e.g. in lexicographical work.

16

Paragraphs, Indention and Headings

Everything we write concerns a subject or theme. It does not matter whether the piece of writing is a letter about one's holiday, a business report, an article for a women's magazine or the chapters of a book on fly-fishing. There may be only one subject or theme in it or there may be several different ones. Even if there is only one, it will almost inevitably be divided into different topics or aspects, each looking at the whole subject from a different angle or explaining or introducing different parts of it. We show the division of a subject or theme into topics or aspects by arranging the sentences dealing with these topics or aspects into paragraphs.

The importance of the paragraph is easy to overlook. It is in fact part and parcel of good communication. In 1905 T.F. and M.F.A. Husband, writing in *Punctuation: Its Principles and Practice*, said:

> ... the paragraph, while itself only part of a larger whole, is the expression of continuous and unified thought; ... there is running through it a central nerve of thought which dominates the secondary systems; and ... these secondary systems or groups of ideas are set forth sentence by sentence, according to the character of each and its relation to the whole, some of them taking short sentences as their fittest form, others long.

The writer's duty is to make sure that the 'central nerve of thought' is crystal clear to his or her reader.

Paragraphs may be long or short, consist of one sentence or many, or contain a single topic or a set of closely related ones. The writer must choose the arrangement that best suits the material or information that he or she is trying to put across and the medium – newspaper, book, magazine – through which he or she is communicating with the reader. For instance, short one-sentence paragraphs in a newspaper or advertisement are not just there for the ignorant masses with short attention spans, despite what G.V. Carey and other pundits might say. Even busy readers of *The Times* and *The Guardian* strap-hanging their way into work appreciate the one-sentence paragraphs in the front-page stories that allow them to assimilate the data quickly. In a serious novel or a work of non-fiction, however, short paragraphs might have a breathless effect that may be out of place. In general, a mixture of different lengths of paragraph is usually best.

Although the need for paragraphs as so far described is a rhetorical one (that is, we need paragraphs, for example, to make clear the steps in an argument or the important points in a piece of narrative), careful writers also take account of the visual appearance of the printed page. There is nothing more intimidating than a page with no paragraphs on it.

A comprehensive book on the use of English – Eric Partridge's *Usage and Abusage*, for instance – will tell readers more about paragraphs than we are able to do in this book. Our main concern here is to explain a little about how to treat them in writing or on the printed page.

Layout of Paragraphs

The Greeks signalled a change of topic in a piece of writing by drawing a line next to the text at the point where the new topic began. This was called a *paragraphos* ('a line drawn beside'). The Romans accomplished the same task by starting the line of text in which the new topic began with a large capital letter that jutted out into the left-hand margin. In medieval times this capital became further enlarged and beautifully illuminated. Since the illumination was done last, the scribe copying the manuscript would leave room for it by commencing the rest of the first line of the paragraph some way in from the left-hand margin.

The business of taking a bite out of paragraphs in this way is called indention (a word derived from the Latin word *dens*, 'a tooth'), and we say that the first line of each paragraph is indented. Paragraph indention was carried over into printing and applied even to paragraphs that were not to be illuminated. From the seventeenth century it became standard and continues to be the prevailing practice today, although typists and typesetters also practise the art of not indenting paragraphs but setting them flush with the left-hand margin and with a line or half-line of space between them:

> This is an example of the non-indention of paragraphs. Note that a half-line space between these paragraphs can look attractive.
>
> The effect works very well for letters, press releases, pamphlets and technical manuals, where a fast intake of information is needed. It can also have a racy feel to it, which suits some types of fiction.
>
> In serious novels or non-fiction books, where the reader is considered to have time to digest what he or she reads, this form of paragraph layout is less appropriate. Some would say that it gives the book a cheap and cheerful effect.

How big a bite should a writer, typist or printer take when indenting the first line of a paragraph? There are some fairly sensible guidelines on this point, but to explain them we need to remind you about ems and ens. In the chapter on the Dash we met em and en rules, long and short horizontal lines. Here we meet ems and ens of space, usually represented for the benefit of the printer as rectangular boxes. In fact em spaces only are shown like this, and in practice we need only concern ourselves with em spaces.

With short lines of type, known to a typesetter or printer as narrow measure, such as that encountered in a newspaper column or a certain type of dictionary, it is sufficient to set the normal paragraph indention to one em space. Often this amount of indention is also sufficient for books. But if the lines of type are long, the first lines of paragraphs should generally be indented two ems space.

Other Forms of Indention

We normally set off long quotations in a book, article or report by indenting them. In this way we make a clear distinction between the quotations and the rest of the text. Typists usually use a different line spacing for such indented text. The main text may be double-spaced, while the indented text may be one-and-a-half-spaced or even single-spaced. Printers also use different line spacing and also use a smaller size of type, usually one point smaller than the main text. We shall explain more about points in the section on the space.

All the examples in this book are indented, so that you can readily see that they are examples. This one shows indention within indention:

> Regarding the question of indention, Horace Hart makes the following pronouncement:
>
> Indention of first lines of paragraphs to be generally one em for full measures. Sub-indention [that is, indention within indention] should be proportionate: the rule for all indention is not to drive too far in.

This rule about not driving too far in is often broken by trendy printers who think nothing of indenting 8 picas in lines that are only 19 picas long. The waste of space is colossal and the effect, when the last line of the previous paragraph is short, is ludicrous.

> You can see just how ludicrous this can be by looking at this example of a line indented by 7 picas, just under half the length of a line in this book!

Indention within indention finds its most beneficial use in indexes, where complexity can be lessened by this device.

> *Hanging Indention.* A typographical device often employed in reading lists, tables, and so on, is hanging indention, in which the first line of an entry is set full out (that is, flush left), while the turnover lines (the remaining lines resulting from the fact that not all the information can be accommodated on a single line) are indented. The amount of indention is again one or two ems of space, depending upon the measure involved:

> *Places of Interest in Lincolnshire*
>
> Boston is famous for The Stump, a church tower over 80 metres high from which visitors have excellent views of the surrounding area.
>
> Grantham, the birthplace of Margaret Thatcher, Britain's first woman prime minister, has a good museum and a fine church housing a chained library. …

Quotation Marks and Paragraphs

In a quoted conversation, the speech assigned to each character taking part is given a fresh paragraph each time:

> 'The trouble with today's youth, Mr Jones,' said Mrs Lampton, 'is that most of them have got too much money and time on their hands and haven't the least idea how to make use of that time and money.'
>
> 'Surely the problem is that their energies are not being properly channelled,' said Jones. 'Kids need guidance – '
>
> 'Kids need discipline,' Mrs Lampton interrupted. 'They loaf around without a thought for anybody else. They vandalize property and get away with it – '

In a quotation that extends over several paragraphs an 'open-quotation' mark introduces each separate paragraph, but the corresponding 'close-quotation' mark appears only once, at the end of the last paragraph of the quote. (For an example of this, see the chapter on Quotation Marks.)

Headings and Subheadings

In book chapters, articles or reports, headings can prove a useful aid in guiding the reader through the various topics of the author's argument. These should, however, be used in moderation.

Headings can be of three main types: centred headings, or cross heads, printed at the top of a chapter, article or major section; side headings, or shoulder headings, printed above a paragraph; and run-on side headings, which actually form the start of a paragraph and may be indented if style requires it.

Centred headings and shoulder headings can be printed in bold or italic type, in capitals or small capitals. Run-on side headings usually appear in bold or italic, but are rarely printed wholly in capitals. Run-on side headings can be followed by a full point to help set them off more clearly from the text that follows, but they may also form part of the first sentence of the paragraph.

Neither centred headings nor shoulder headings, which lie outside the paragraph, should be followed by full points. For the use of capitals in headings, which should be the same as that in titles, see the chapter on Capital Letters.

We shall conclude this section with a few examples of headings:

Centred Heading:

Newton's Discoveries

> Newton was compelled by an outbreak of plague to leave Cambridge in …

Shoulder Heading:

Nature's Medicine Cupboard

Alkaloids, extracted from many plants throughout the world, are among the most powerful poisons we know; yet in small enough doses their effects can be made to work minor medical miracles. ...

Run-on Headings

Triton. The largest of Neptune's eight satellites, Triton was revealed by the *Voyager 2* probe to be a beautiful blue and red world full of the activity of what can only be described as ice volcanoes. ...

17

Space

People who write by hand and never have anything to do with a typewriter, word processor or typesetting machine may wonder why there is a chapter on Space in this survey. The fact is that, while a handwriter starts wherever he or she likes on the page, and picks up the pen between words leaving a little gap each time, a typist has to remember to position the paper properly and press the space bar or the carriage return to achieve the same effects. Word spaces for the typist or keyboard operator are as much characters as are the letters, numerals and punctuation marks.

For the traditional printer, space was anything but a matter to be taken for granted. In letterpress printing, only the raised letters carried on pieces of type were inked and made marks on the paper. But they had to be secured in a special frame called a chase by pieces of flat metal that surrounded the type and were lower than the printing surface. The spaces between the words were not empty gaps either, otherwise individual letters would have moved or fallen out.

Rectangular flat pieces of metal of various sizes, which were also below the level of the printing surface, marked the word spaces and held the type tight. All these bits of metal were known as quads, or quadrats. Large quads (called quotations) filled up the last lines of paragraphs and the indention of the first lines. Long thin pieces of metal called leading could be inserted between the lines of type to provide space between the lines of text on the page. The leading, quads and quotations, including the metal surrounding the type area (giving the finished page its margins), were all referred to as 'furniture'.

We still put spaces between the lines of text we print or type as an aid to readability, and in typesetting we still refer to such spacing as leading. Mechanical typewriters have special mechanisms that allow the carriage return lever to rotate the platen by differing preset amounts corresponding to half-line, single-line, one-and-a-half, double- and even triple-line spacing. Electronic typewriters, word processors and modern typesetting machines have an electronic equivalent of this mechanism written into their software.

If you are an author, you may have heard your editor say (for example) that a book is to be set in 9 on 10-point, or in 9-point, 1-point leaded (or even 9-point, with 1-point leading). All this is printer's jargon and refers to the size of the type to be used for the main text (in this example 9 point) and the amount of space to be left between each line (1 point). This section includes an account of points and picas, the printer's measuring units. But the reader must bear in mind that this book is not intended to be exhaustive on matters of pure typography, and further information should be sought from a more specialized book.

Ems, Ens and Thins

Both the pica and point are absolute units of measurement, corresponding to an agreed standard. Our old friends the em and en are not. Originally pieces of metal below type height, they were used for spaces in letterpress work. The em is equal to the square of the point size of the type concerned and is thus different in each type size. An en is half an em. They are still type-size sensitive, even in their more modern role of determining the lengths of rules and spaces.

Ems and ens function therefore as relative measuring units.

> ### Points and Picas
>
> European and American printers differ on the actual size of units involved, but the terms point and pica remain universal, even in spite of the sweeping changes to metric measures that are going on. Both points and picas are units of length. Often in typesetting, points are used for vertical measurement, and picas are units of horizontal measurement.
>
> The point in both the United States and Britain equals 0.351 millimetres, and there are about 72 points in one inch. The size of a piece of type (the vertical dimension of the type body) is given in points. In the case of a piece of 9-point type, for example, this is 3.16 mm (about an eighth of an inch).
>
> The pica, equal to 12 points, is used to work out the horizontal extent of lines of type across the page. Printers call this figure the measure to which the type has been set.

A smaller horizontal unit called a thin, also originaly used for spacing, equals a fifth of an em. (Other old terms for spaces include a nut, equal to half an em; a thick, equal to a third; and a mid, equal to a quarter.)

Old-fashioned printers varied the use of ems, ens, thicks, thins, nuts and quotations to achieve proportional spacing, line centring, paragraph indention, and justification (an even appearance on both right and left of the lines of text). The work must have been laborious. Computerized setting has removed the drudgery, but some of the old names remain.

White Space

The amount of empty space at the top and bottom and around the sides of a page help to focus our attention upon the text area. But the text area itself often benefits from having some empty space (white space) within it – below chapter titles, above subheadings, between lines in display headings, etc. It is not our province to go into the aesthetics of the printed page, but the author or report writer would be wise to acquire some knowledge on the subject as an aid to learning good presentation.

Space

All the vertical spacing mentioned in the previous paragraph is measured in points, as when an editor or designer writes 'Insert 3 pts space' above a heading.

Spaces between Words

Word separation by spaces was invented in the eighth century by Anglo-Saxon, German and Irish monks. It evolved gradually among a clerical population for whom Latin was a foreign language. Short words, such as prepositions, remained tacked on to other longer words even after spacing was introduced, but by about the end of the fourteenth century the full use of the space was standard.

There is no need to exemplify word-spacing, because you can see it in every page of this book. We should say something, however, about spacing between sentences. Normal typing practice is to tap the space bar twice after the full point ending a sentence, and this should be followed. It should be noted, though, that some publishers ask their authors to type each line to a specified character count, and they may also tell the authors to key only one space between sentences. This is especially likely when the measure is narrow – i.e., when the lines are short. And do not forget that word spaces should be included in such a character count.

Letter-spacing. In certain circumstances very thin spaces are inserted between the letters of a word. This is now rare in English, but is occasionally encountered in German, especially in books set in the older style of German type. It is used for emphasis, much as italic type is used in English. Here is an example:

> *Du wirst es n i e m a l s verstehen.*

Spaces in Indention. We have already explained that these are measured in ems. For further information on this subject, *see* the section on *Paragraphs, Indention* and *Headings.*

Ligatures. Certain letter combinations used by printers in the English language were once cast on one piece of type. They include ff, fi, ffl, and fl. Other ligatures represented certain sounds in Old English, such as æ and œ. These latter ligatures and some others are occasionally encountered in linguistics or phonetics. They should not be used to render the diphthongs *ae* and *oe* in Latin words such as *Caesar* or *coeli.*

One Word or Two

Pairings such as *blood stream/bloodstream, cabinet maker/cabinetmaker,* and *post horn/posthorn* illustrate the problem of whether certain compounds should be spelled as one word or two. With normal British usage continuing to abandon the hyphen, these are often the only choices. Busy writers may take the line of least resistance on such compounds and spell them solid (that is, as one word). However, words such as *posthorn, tophat* and *swamphen,* give rise to letter combinations that at first sight are misleading. Consequently, these should be spelled as two words to avoid ambiguity.

There are no guidelines to give here, except these: make a choice and stick to it, try to be aware of possible ambiguities and avoid them, and if you have any doubts, let a good modern dictionary be your guide.

18

Slash, Solidus, Oblique or Virgule

This mark, shown by the / symbol, is known by all the above names and a few more besides, such as the diagonal, slant, slash mark or shilling stroke. The names slash (mark), slant and oblique are predominantly British; the names virgule and diagonal are American. When reading out loud, people often register its presence by calling it simply a stroke, especially in legal or official usage. Thus 'Form PN/13' will be referred to in speech as 'Form PN stroke 13'.

> ### History of the Slash
>
> The slash preceded the invention of printing by a century or two and was originally used as a light pause mark. In writing, it degenerated into a short curved stroke written next to the bottom of the preceding letter and eventually became our modern comma. However, other uses of the slash arose in the course of time – e.g., as a currency symbol. The Italian monetary system of libri, solidi and denarii gave Roman pre-decimal sterling the signs for its units, one of which was the / symbol – hence the name solidus.

The slash today has a variety of conventional uses that we can broadly divide into the ordinary and the technical.

Ordinary Uses

1. Signalling Alternatives. The slash between one word and another means that what is being said in the sentence applies equally to either word. Thus the slash signifies a straight-forward option or alternative:

> Each student attending the lecture is asked to bring his/her own writing materials.

And/or. In the special case of and/or, a three-way choice is signified:

> There is space under the dashboard for fitting a stereo radio and/or cassette recorder.

In the last example, the space can accommodate a radio only, a stereo cassette recorder only or both a radio and a recorder.

To signal a choice between words that have letters in common, the slash can be used in the middle of a word:

Bookshop manager/ess required. Apply within.

Everyone must do what s/he considers appropriate.

This use of the slash has become widespread as a method of avoiding sexist language and of complying with legislation on equal opportunities.

2. Expressions of Date. When an event or process takes place over successive years, seasons, months, or days, the appropriate time units are separated by a slash.

Our interview with stuntman Fred Smith will appear in the August/September issue of *Heroes of Sport*.

The 1988/9 soccer season was marred by the tragedy of Hillsborough.

Gower and Botham missed the 1989/90 tour to the West Indies.

On the night of 15/16 October, a great storm ravaged England.

(A purely historical use results from the fact that before 1752 Britain and America used the Old Style Julian calendar and started the year on 25 March. A few historians still acknowledge this fact by using a formula such as 4 February 1621/2. People's life dates may also appear as 1629/30–1687, for example. The use of the slash in this way is, however, a technicality and many writers avoid it.)

The date is informally shown in an abbreviated all-figure format with slashes separating the figures. Note that British usage requires the day-month-year sequence, whereas American writers employ the order month-day-year.

3/9/90 means 3 September 1990 in Britain and 9 March 1990 in the United States.

See the chapters on Full Point and Numbers.

3. Fractions and Ratios. The slash is often used as the visual representation of a division sign in mathematics and is consequently used to represent fractions, especially when these are not available on a typewriter. Certain typefaces also make use of the slash, separating a superscript figure for the numerator from a subscript figure for the denominator:

A half may be represented by 1/2 or ½

Awkward fractions may be treated in this way:

(Note that the % symbol makes use of the solidus, as does the less common 'per thousand' sign ‰).

4. Sections and Subsections. In legal or official usage, a slash may often be used between the main section of a document and a subsection or paragraph.

'*See* Section B/13*a*' is an instruction to see Paragraph 13*a* of Section B.

Slashes

5. Abbreviational Use. The slash appears in abbreviations such as c/o ((in the) care of) and a/c (bank or financial account of):

To: Fred Smith, c/o Mrs R. Peterson, 'Sunnyview', …

a/c R.T. Parkinson

6. In Lines of Verse. When lines of poetry are written out in a continuous format to save space, the line breaks are signified by slashes:

Mid pleasures and palaces though we may roam, / Be it ever so humble, there's no place like home.

– John Howard Payne

Technical Uses

The following are generally restricted to technical contexts.

1. Replacement of 'per'. A special use of the slash used as a division sign is found in scientific writing, as in the following examples:

The Earth's escape velocity is in excess of 40,000 km/h.

The acceleration due to gravity is 9.80665 m/s^2, and the atmospheric pressure at sea level is about 1.03 kg/cm^2.

(The previous sentence means that the Earth's escape velocity exceeds 40,000 kilometres per hour, its free-fall acceleration is 9.80665 metres per second per second, and its sea level atmospheric pressure is 1.03 kilograms per square centimetre.)

2. Linguistic Use. The technical linguistic use, found in journals and academic papers on the subject and also in a few general dictionaries, is to enclose a broad phonetic transcription within a pair of slashes:

thyme / taim /, *n.* a plant belonging to the mint family and constituting the genus *Thymus* …

19

Hyphen

The hyphen (-) fulfils a triple role in writing and printing. Its purely punctuational use is of minor importance and causes few problems. Its other functions are apparently paradoxical and are fraught with difficulty in terms of their applications. These uses may be classified under the headings of 'Joining and Compounding' and 'End-of-Line Division'.

Life (for a writer) would be much easier if there were no such thing as the hyphen. The unwillingness of writers of English – British ones especially – to adopt a consistent approach to this troublesome little symbol has led to an inability on the part of any authority to come up with a rational system of guidelines for its use. Broad principles have been worked out, mainly by lexicographers, who have to make consistent decisions about the forms of words, but exceptions to these principles abound.

Any discussion of the hyphen has to start from the acceptance that, although we can make any number of 'rules', usage does not have to abide by them. This seems especially true of the hyphen, and many writers find it such a nuisance that they avoid it. American writers use the hyphen far less often than their British counterparts in similar contexts, and a continuing process of abandoning the hyphen has been going on even in Britain since the 1950s.

Punctuational Uses

We shall clear the decks for more serious discussion by quickly disposing of four uses of the hyphen in the sentence.

The History of the Hyphen

The word *hyphen* is Greek; its derivation – from the words *hypo*, 'under' and *hen*, 'one', hence meaning something like 'under one (word or meaning)' – reveals its primary function in joining or combining parts of words. Aristophanes of Byzantium, the early second-century BC librarian at Alexandria who was the first to devise a punctuation system for Greek, used a curving mark to do the job of a hyphen, but it did not catch on.

Towards the end of the tenth century AD, scribes began using a special sign to mark the point where a word had to be divided at the end of a line because there was not enough space to fit it all in. The rest of the word began the next line. This sign was the – and from the fourteenth to the eighteenth centuries it was frequently doubled, =. Proofreaders, especially in the United States, still use the = to signify

> the instruction to insert a hyphen. In due course the end-of-line hyphen was joined by the compounding hyphen to perform the task originally intended by Aristophanes' curve.
>
> (It is interesting to note that some publishers, e.g. J.M. Dent & Sons, Ltd., were using the tilde, or 'swung dash' (~) as an end-of-line hyphen in certain of their books well into the twentieth century.)

1. With Stems, Endings and Affixes of Words. This is a technical usage mostly encountered in linguistics textbooks:

> Nouns whose plurals end in *-s* or *-es* are very numerous in English.
>
> The prefixes *ante-*, *pre-* and *post-* are of Latin origin.

2. To Represent Speech Impediments or Nervousness in Quotations. The hyphen conventionally signals stammering in quoted speech:

> 'I d-d-don't know w-what you m-m-mean,' stammered Trevor. 'I've n-not s-s-seen her s-s-since F-F-Friday.'

(Compare the use of dashes to represent hesitation.)

3. In Linking. Typists especially use the hyphen to link years, places, and other things:

> The 1939-45 War
>
> The London-New York flight
>
> The Spurs-Aston Villa match

Printers use the en rule in this context, and if what you are writing is to be printed and published, you should see to it that all such uses of the typed hyphen as this one are marked up as en rules. *See* the chapter on the Dash.

4. The suspended hyphen. A hyphen followed by a space is used in lists of words that have certain letters (stems, prefixes, etc.) in common. The hyphen isolates the parts that are different:

> The car is available as three-, four- and five-door models.
>
> The medical unit is equipped to deal with all ante-, peri-and postnatal problems. (Some writers prefer 'antenatal, perinatal, and postnatal'.)

Joining Uses

The use of the hyphen as a joining symbol consists in helping to form compound words, usually adjectives, nouns or verbs. These can be temporary compounds, formed for one use and probably never to be used again – rather like Dylan Thomas's 'fishingboat-bobbing sea', or they can be permanent, such as the words T-shirt or cure-all.

It used to be said that newly coined compound nouns consisting of two words ought to be spelled as two separate words at their birth. As they grew to be more accepted they would pass first through the stage of being hyphenated (that is, written with a hyphen) and then, after full acceptance, they would become solid (that is, written as one word). For example, *blood stream* would have first become *blood-stream* and finally *bloodstream*.

The reality today is that authors, editors and publishers, who cannot be bothered with the hyphen, either spell a compound noun as one word or two, depending on their own predilections or on which dictionary they use for their house style. Not for them the pedantic justification of *walking-stick* by the Fowlers, who said that the hyphen was essential to prevent the reader from interpreting 'walking stick' as 'a stick that walks'. Today's publishers might at a pinch accept *walkingstick* one day (many Americans already do), but for the majority 'walking-stick' is out, and 'walking stick' is in.

Having said all that, however, we must acknowledge that hyphens are not a completely useless adjunct to our compound-formation process. The following list of cases illustrates usual modern practice, although (as we have already said) exceptions are rife.

1. Hyphen of Readability. Certain prefixes, such as *anti-, co-, micro-, pre-, pro-, semi-*, etc., are usually hyphenated when they are followed by words or word elements that begin with the same vowel as that with which the prefix ends:

anti-imperialism	pre-eminent
co-opt	pre-oestrus
micro-organism	semi-industrial

Otherwise words introduced by these prefixes are solid. Note also that *co-ordinate/coordinate* and *co-operate/cooperate*, and their derivatives, nowadays tend to drop the hyphen.

These remarks are also true of the prolific prefix *re-*. Note such words as *re-entry, re-estimate*, but *rearrange, reinforce, reorder*, and *reunite*.

When a tripled consonant appears in the middle of a word, a hyphen should be included at the affix boundary purely on grounds of readability:

The ordinary garden slug is almost shell-less.

His home is in what used to be called the county of Inverness-shire.

The daffodil has a bell-like flower.

Hyphen

Words such as *de-icer* and *de-mister* also take a hyphen of readability to preserve correct pronunciation.

2. Hyphen for Removing Doubt. Use a hyphen to remove all ambiguity, however fleeting, from the reader's mind:

There are only three pound tickets left. (= three tickets at a pound each.)

There are only three-pound tickets left. (= an unspecified number of tickets, each costing three pounds.)

The hyphen distinguishes between certain compounds introduced by the prefix *re-*. Thus we write *recover* (to regain one's health, composure, etc.), but *re-cover* (to furnish with a new cover) and recreation (relaxation), but *re-creation* (creation anew or for a second time). Other pairs distinguished by hyphens include:

reform (change)   re-form (form again)

react (register an effect)   re-act (act again)

3. Hyphen Before Capitals. All prefixes or combining forms occurring before a capital letter take a hyphen:

pre-Christian   anti-Nazi   Pan-Hellenic   pro-Iranian   un-American

4. Non- Words. Up to the end of the 1970s, it could fairly be said that, whereas American writers spelled such words as *nonindustrial, nonliterary, noneconomic*, etc., without a hyphen, British writers spelled them with one: *non-industrial, non-literary, non-economic*, etc. The only exception, as far as British authors and editors were concerned, was *nonconformist* (often *Nonconformist* in its specialized religious meaning), which did not take a hyphen. At the end of the 1980s we can discern the erosion of the hyphen in words beginning with *non-*. Few people are now shocked to see words such as *nonindustrial* in print, even in a British textbook. This is yet another nail in the coffin of the hyphen. Having said that, however, we would advise British writers to use the form *non-profit-making*, for the American term *nonprofit*.

5. The Hyphen in Word-plus-Word Compounds. In this part of the discussion, we shall deal not with prefixes but with free words in combination.

(a) Compound Nouns. Hyphens should be generally avoided in favour of one word or two and a modern dictionary should be consulted in case of doubt, except in the following categories:

(i) Spelled-out numbers between 21 and 99, excluding multiples of ten:

She is thirty-two years old

The number is eight hundred and twenty-three

Spelled out fractions:

| two-thirds | three-fifths |
| forty-one | sixty-fourths |

Three-quarters of those voting were women. (British use. Americans prefer 'Three fourths' …)

The reaction lasted twenty-one six-hundredths of a second.

(ii) Noun + noun compounds. These are often spelled with an en rule in print, but typists may use a hyphen:

Sir Henry Irving was a great actor-manager.

Athens and Sparta were rival city-states in Greece.

(iii) Onomatopoeic (sound-effect) words. These 'reduplicated' formations take a hyphen not only as nouns but also as verbs, adjectives and adverbs:

He heard the clip-clop of the horse's hooves fading into the distance.

The horse and its rider clip-clopped along the road.

The horse's hooves made a lively clip-clop sound.

The horse went clip-clop along the road.

(iv) Compounds containing a possessive. Among these are words such as *bull's-eye* and several plant names:

The garden is full of mare's-tails.

Venus's-hair is a delicate tropical fern.

(v) Fixed phrases. These also include many popular plant names:

You and I must have a heart-to-heart, my dear.

We're having a get-together at my house on Thursday.

The forget-me-nots look lovely in the spring.

Love-lies-bleeding is a most attractive sight in the British countryside.

Also included in this category are such phrasal nouns as *go-as-you-please, give-and-take* and the slightly old-fashioned *n'ere-do-well.*

(vi) Military ranks and other terms. These are still generally hyphenated and include combinations ending in *-general* and *-major*, especially when used as titles. The term *court-martial*, either as a noun or verb, is also hyphenated. Its plural is courts-martial:

Brigadier-General Sheringham-Smythe is visiting the barracks today.

He was a regimental sergeant-major during the last war.

(vii) Family relationships. These include all the *great-* and *-in-law* connections, but those beginning with *grand* are solid:

Mother-in-law	father-in-law	son-in-law
daughter-in-law	brother-in-law	sister-in-law
Great-grandmother	great-grandfather	great-granddaughter
great-grandson	great-aunt	great-uncle.

(viii) Noun + gerund of a transitive verb. These have generally been hyphenated in the past, and quite a few still are, but under American influence some of these are moving to solid or two-word compounds:

... famous for steel-making, wood-engraving, and lager-brewing.

But:

woodworking   metalworking   bricklaying

The agent-nouns associated with these formations – wood-engraver, woodworker, etc. – are treated in the same way.

(ix) Other verb-based noun compounds. Hyphens are customary in the following:

do-gooder; cure-all; has-been; make-believe; runner-up; passer-by; go-between; hanger-on; flare-up

But there are plenty that are spelled solid, such as *rundown, shutdown, breakthrough, breakup, Passover, flypast, flyby,* ...

(x) Letter + noun. Some writers prefer to drop the hyphen in these, but British and US usage continues to support it:

T-shirt   V-neck   X-rays

(Note that the verb 'to X-ray' must be hyphenated.)

(xi) Scientific and analogous units. These include the following:

kilowatt-hour   foot-pound   man-week

(b) Compound Adjectives. Almost any adjective composed of two or more words can be hyphenated when it precedes the noun:

He walked up the stairs to his third-floor office.

But

His office was on the third floor.

He was an entertaining after-dinner speaker.

But

He gave an entertaining speech after dinner.

The adjectives in the above example are hyphenated when preceding the noun (in attributive position) but not elsewhere. As can these:

> The house lay above a thickly-wooded hillside.
>
> The hillside was thickly wooded.
>
> They reached a dried-up river valley.
>
> The riverbed was dried up.
>
> He had an up-to-date car but out-of-date ideas.
>
> His car was up to date but his opinions were out of date.
>
> He carried a worn-out coat over his arm.
>
> The coat he carried was worn out.

The following are hyphenated in all positions:

Adjective + adjective: A red-hot news story; this is red-hot.

Adjective + participle: A foul-smelling plant; this plant is foul-smelling; deep-fried fish; I love my fish deep-fried.

(i) Adjective + noun: A first-class choir; our choir is first-class.

(ii) Adjective + noun + *-ed*. She was a big-boned woman; she was big-boned.

(iii) Noun + adjective: A country-wide reputation; news of his escape was now country-wide. (Note that some of the compounds in this class are often written solid: *foolproof, worldwide, waterproof*.)

(iv) Compound adjectives involving numbers and units. These are hyphenated:

> A six-foot-tall man.   A five-metre wall.
>
> A 30-kilometre journey (or a 30-km journey).

Note that the following are also hyphenated in all positions:

air-cooled	devil-may-care	far-flung	far-reaching
lantern-jawed	life-giving	long-awaited	never-ending
poverty-stricken	quick-acting	quick-fire	sure-fire

Some hyphenated compound adjectives rarely if ever occur anywhere in the sentence other than in attributive position:

> real-time – A computer's real-time clock.
>
> sabre-toothed – A sabre-toothed tiger (or sabretoothed tiger).

In some cases a hyphenated form means something different from an unhyphenated form:

Hyphen

Her cat was black and white.

Her television was black-and-white.

Note the absence of hyphens in these examples:

A Foreign Office spokesman.

The United States Ambassador.

A House of Lords debate.

An Old Testament prophecy.

A Friends of the Earth representative.

(v) *Better-, best- ill-, little-, well-, worse-* and *worst-*compounds. These are usually hyphenated in attributive positions but not elsewhere:

A well-known journalist	A little-known journalist
His plan was ill advised	His plan was well thought out.
An ill-advised decision	A well-thought-out scheme.
The worst-paid workers	Few workers were worse paid.

An attributive adjective preceded by an adverb ending in *-ly* is not hyphenated to the adverb.

A richly deserved reward.   Her reward was richly deserved.

(c) Compound Verbs. Common hyphenated forms include:

dry-clean	French-polish	cold-shoulder
cold-hammer	bad-mouth	goose-step
sweet-talk	power-lift	stir-fry

(d) Compound Adverbs. These include the following:

big-headedly	hard-heartedly	half-heartedly

They crashed head-on.

He learned his lines parrot-fashion.

(e) Miscellaneous Compounds. Hyphens are customary in the following situations:

(i) Words ending in *-elect: President-elect*, but prefer *Vice President elect* (as in American usage).

(ii) *by-blow, by-law, by-election, by-form.* But *byname, byword*.

(iii) Words beginning with *ex-: ex-wife, ex-president*. But *ex prime minister*.

(iv) Words beginning with *off: off-licence, off-chance, off-drive, off-putting*. But *offset, offshoot, offspring*.

(v) Among words beginning with *on*, prefer *on-drive*, but write all other words solid:

oncoming, ongoing, onset.

(vi) Most adjectives, but not verbs or nouns, beginning with over: *over-proud, over-dignified.* But *overbearing.*

(vii) Words beginning with *self-*. All these are hyphenated apart from *selfsame, selfconscious.*

(viii) Words beginning with *un-*. Do not hyphenate directly after un-. But do write *unco-operative, unco-ordinated.*

(ix) Words ending with *-like*. All these are written solid, except when the first element is a proper name or ends in double *l*: catlike, fatherlike. But *bell-like, A California-like climate.*

(x) Virtually all Latin- and Greek-based prefixes are unhyphenated with only a few exceptions, especially where the last consonant or vowel of the prefix is the same as the first consonant or vowel of the rest of the word, although even here the cases are few. Note also the following:

counterculture	counter-revolution
infra-red	infrastructure
quasi-judicial	quasi scholar (USA)
ultra-ancient	ultraviolet (despite infra-red)
ultra-right-wing party	(but on the ultra-right wing of the party)
vice-president	Vice President of the United States
vice-chairman	viceroy (and viceregent)

End-of-Line Hyphenation

The principles of end-of-line hyphenation are in process of change in Britain, from a traditional system based on etymology to a more rational system practised in the United States, which is based on pronunciation and the shape of the word.

End-of-line hyphens should be avoided if possible, because they are obviously not an aid to readability. Most printers do not break words when the setting is unjustified (has a ragged appearance on the right-hand side), especially in narrow measure. End-of-line division should not be completely avoided in unjustified setting, though. A total absence of it reduces the number of words that can be set and can cause some extremely ugly 'gappy' effects on the right-hand side.

The principles of end-of-line hyphenation that we have followed in preparing the word list in the rest of this book are as follows:

1. Words are broken at natural syllable boundaries according to pronunciation: *man-age-ment, mana-gerial.*

Hyphen

2. One-syllable words are not to be divided: *asked, bathed*.

3. Words are broken between two or more consonants, usually after the first one: *illus-trate, prob-lem*.

4. But consonants that form one sound are not divided: *warm-est, bro-ther*. Compare *Beet-hoven*.

5. Break words after a prefix or before a suffix: *pre-amble, un-loved, train-er*.

6. Words ending in *-ing* may be broken before the suffix: *shin-ing, bor-ing*.

7. A doubled consonant before *-ing* or (if the word is polysyllabic) before *-ed* may be divided: *run-ning, rot-ted*; but not *drop-ped*.

8. Misleading word-division must be avoided: *re-adjust*, not *read-just*; *thera-pist*, not *the-rapist*; *extrac-tor*, not *ex-tractor*.

Words such as *women, often*, etc., should generally not be broken.

9. Words must not be broken at points where the result would leave one letter at the end of a line or one letter at the beginning of a line. Therefore, do not divide *about, above, baby, rainy*.

10. Word breaks leaving two letters at the end or beginning of a line are also to be avoided, except in the case of a two-letter prefix, such as *un-, de-, re-: un-known, de-moralized, re-vive*.

11. Where a word is already spelled with a hyphen, the word must be broken at that hyphen and not anywhere else: *one-horse* (a *one-horse* town), *has-been*. (*Court-mar-tial* should be avoided.)

12. Ambiguous word breaks must be avoided: Thus we may break *re-creation* and *re-form* at the hyphen, but we should not break recreation, reform (without hyphens). *See also* Principle No. 8, above.

13. American authorities prefer not to break personal names at the ends of lines, but forms such as *Steven-son, Priest-ley*, are more-or-less acceptable in British English. We have, however, excluded names from our list for reasons of space. Nouns and adjectives derived from personal names are subject to end-of-line division: *Marx-ism, Keynes-ian*.

14. A line must not end in the middle of a set of initials: *J. S. Bach* is wrong; you should instead use the form *J.S. Bach*.

15. Figures and units should likewise never be separated. *33 km* is unacceptable. The same applies to dates given with BC or AD and also to the time of day.

Hyphenation Dictionary

aard/vark
ab/ac/ti/nal
aba/cus
aba/lone
aban/don
ab/at/toir
ab/bess
ab/bey
ab/bot
ab/brevi/ate
ab/brevi/ation
ab/di/cate
ab/di/ca/tion
ab/do/men
ab/domi/nal
ab/du/cent
ab/duct
ab/er/rant
ab/er/ra/tion
abey/ance
ab/hor
ab/id/ing
abil/ity
ab/ir/ri/tate
ab/ject
ab/la/tion
ab/lu/tions
ab/ne/gate
ab/nor/mal
ab/nor/mally
ab/nor/mal/ity
ab/norm/ity
ab/ol/ish
ab/ol/ition
ab/om/in/able
ab/or/igi/nal

abor/tion
abort/ive
ab/ra/ca/dab/ra
ab/ra/sion
ab/ras/ive
ab/re/ac/tion
ab/ridge/ment
ab/ro/gate
ab/rupt
ab/ruptly
ab/rupt/ness
ab/scess
ab/scond
ab/sence
ab/sent
ab/sen/tee
ab/sen/tee/ism
ab/sinth
ab/so/lute
ab/so/lutely
ab/so/lu/tion
ab/so/lut/ism
ab/solve
ab/sorb
ab/sorb/ent
ab/sor/ber
ab/sorp/tion
ab/stain
ab/ste/mi/ous
ab/stemi/ous/ness
ab/sten/tion
ab/ster/gent
ab/stin/ence
ab/stract
ab/strac/ted
ab/strac/tion

ab/struse
ab/surd
abun/dance
abun/dant
ab/use
ab/us/ive
abut/ted
abys/mal
abys/sal
aca/cia
aca/demic
acad/emy
acan/thus
ac/cede
ac/cel/er/ate
ac/cel/er/ation
ac/cel/er/ator
ac/cent
ac/cen/tor
ac/cen/tu/ate
ac/cept
ac/cess
ac/cess/ible
ac/ces/sion
ac/cess/ory
ac/ci/dent
ac/ci/den/tal
ac/ci/den/tally
ac/cipi/ter
ac/claim
ac/cla/mation
ac/cli/mat/iz/ation
ac/cli/mat/ize
ac/col/ade
ac/com/mo/date
ac/com/mo/dat/ing

ac/com/mo/dation
ac/com/pani/ment
ac/com/pany
ac/com/plice
ac/com/plish
ac/com/plish/ment
ac/cord
ac/cord/ance
ac/cord/ingly
ac/cord/ion
ac/cord/ion/ist
ac/cost
ac/count
ac/count/able
ac/count/ancy
ac/count/ant
ac/coutred
ac/cou/tre/ment
ac/credit
ac/cre/tion
ac/crue
ac/cu/mu/late
ac/cu/mu/lator
ac/cur/acy
ac/cur/ate
ac/cursed
ac/cu/sing
ac/cus/tom
acerb/ity
acet/ate
acet/one
acet/yl/ene
achieve/ment

Hyphen

Achil/les' heel	ac/tu/ate	ad/junct	adul/ter/ate
ach/ing	acu/ity	ad/just	adul/terer
ach/ro/matic	acu/men	ad/just/able	adul/ter/ess
acid/u/lous	acu/punc/ture	ad/just/ment	adul/tery
ac/knowl/edge	acute/ness	ad/ju/tant	ad/vance
ac/knowl/edge/ment	ada/mant	ad/meas/ure	ad/vance/ment
aco/lyte	ad/apt	ad/min/is/ter	ad/van/tage
ac/on/ite	adap/ta/bility	ad/min/is/tra/tion	ad/van/ta/geous
acous/tic	ad/ap/ta/tion	ad/min/is/trat/ive	ad/vent
ac/quaint	ad/dax	ad/min/is/trator	ad/ven/ti/tious
ac/quaint/ance	ad/ded	admir/able	ad/ven/ture
ac/qui/esce	ad/den/dum	ad/miral	ad/ven/tur/ous
ac/quire	ad/der	ad/mire	ad/verb
ac/qui/sition	ad/dict	ad/mir/able	ad/ver/bial
ac/quisi/tive	ad/dic/ted	ad/mir/ably	ad/ver/sary
ac/quit	add/ing	ad/mir/ation	ad/verse
ac/quit/tal	ad/di/tion	ad/mi/rer	ad/versely
acre/age	ad/di/tive	ad/mi/ringly	ad/ver/sity
ac/rid	ad/dress	ad/miss/ible	ad/vert
ac/ri/mo/ni/ous	ad/dres/see	ad/mis/sion	ad/vert/ence
acri/mony	ad/duce	ad/mit	ad/ver/tise
ac/ro/bat	ad/emp/tion	ad/mit/tance	ad/ver/tise/ment
ac/ro/batic	ad/en/oids	ad/mit/tedly	ad/ver/tiser
ac/ro/po/lis	ad/equate	ad/mix	ad/ver/tis/ing
ac/rylic	ad/here	ad/mix/ture	ad/vice
act/ing	ad/her/ence	ad/mon/ish	ad/vis/able
ac/tion	ad/her/ent	ad/mon/ition	ad/vise
ac/tion/able	ad/he/sion	ado/les/cence	ad/vis/edly
ac/ti/vate	ad/he/sive	ado/les/cent	ad/viser
ac/tive	ad/hibit	adop/tion	ad/vis/ory
ac/ti/vist	ad/ia/batic	ad/ore	ad/vo/cacy
ac/tiv/ity	adi/pose	ad/or/able	ad/vo/cate
act/ress	ad/ja/cent	ad/or/ation	ae/gis
ac/tual	ad/jec/ti/val	ad/orn	aepy/ornis
ac/tu/al/ity	ad/jec/tive	ad/orn/ment	aer/ial
ac/tu/ally	ad/join	ad/ren/alin	aero/batic
ac/tu/ar/ial	ad/journ	adroit/ness	aer/obic
ac/tu/ary	ad/ju/di/cate	ad/sorb/ent	aero/drome
	ad/ju/di/ca/tion	adu/la/tion	aero/dy/nam/ics

aero/foil	after/care	aim/lessly	al/go/rithm
aero/naut/ical	af/ter/math	air/borne	alien/ate
aero/naut/ics	after/noon	air/brake	ali/men/tary
aero/plane	after/shave	air-con/di/tion	ali/mony
aero/sol	after/thought	air/cooled	al/kali
aero/space	after/wards	air/craft	al/ka/line
aes/thete	aga/pan/thus	air/craft/man	al/lay
aes/thet/ic	ag/ate	air/craft/woman	al/le/ga/tion
aes/thet/ically	agen/das	air/crew	al/lege
affa/bility	ag/glom/era/tion	air/field	al/legedly
af/fable	ag/grand/ize	air host/ess	al/le/gi/ance
af/fably	ag/gra/vate	air/ily	al/leg/or/ical
af/fa/bil/ity	ag/gra/vat/ing	air/lift	al/leg/ory
af/fair	ag/gra/vation	air/plane (US)	al/ler/gic
af/fect	ag/gre/gate	air/port	al/lergy
af/fecta/tion	ag/gres/sion	air/ship	al/levi/ate
af/fect/ing	ag/gress/ive	air/sick	al/levi/ation
af/fec/tion	ag/gressor	air/sick/ness	al/ley
af/fec/tion/ate	ag/grieved	air/strip	al/li/ance
af/fer/ent	ag/gro	air/tight	al/lied
af/fi/da/vit	agil/ity	air/worthi/ness	al/li/ga/tor
af/fili/ate	agit/ate	ala/bas/ter	al/lit/er/a/tion
af/fili/ation	agi/ta/tion	alac/rity	al/loc/ate
af/fin/ity	agit/ator	al/ba/core	al/lo/ca/tion
af/firm	ag/nostic	al/ba/tross	al/lo/morph
af/firm/ative	ag/on/ized	al/bin/ism	al/lot
af/firm/atively	ag/on/iz/ing	al/bino	al/lot/ment
af/fix	ag/ony	al/bum	al/low
af/flict	ago/ra/phobia	al/bu/men	allow/able
af/flic/tion	ag/rar/ian	al/chem/ist	al/low/ance
af/flu/ence	agree/able	al/chemy	al/loy
af/flu/ent	agree/ment	al/co/hol	al/lude
af/ford	agri/cul/tural	al/co/holic	al/lure
af/for/est/ation	ag/ri/cul/ture	al/cove	al/lur/ing
af/fray	ag/ro/nomic	al/der	al/lu/sion
af/fright	ail/eron	Al/ex/an/drian	al/lu/vial
af/front	ail/ing	al/fresco	al/lu/vium
afore/men/tioned	ail/ment	al/gae	al/manac
Af/rica	aim/less	al/ge/bra	al/mighty

Hyphen

al/mond	am/bi/ence	am/pli/fier	an/gel
al/most	am/bi/guity	amp/lify	an/ger
alms/house	am/bigu/ous	am/poule	ang/ler
along/side	am/bi/tion	am/pu/tate	an/gli/cism
alo/pe/cia	am/bi/tious	amuse/ment	an/gora
al/pha/bet	am/biva/lent	amus/ing	an/grily
al/pha/beti/cal	am/bler	ana/chron/ism	an/guish
alp/ine	am/bro/sia	ana/chron/istic	an/gu/lar
al/ready	am/bu/lance	an/ae/mia an/e/mia	ani/mal
al/sa/tian	am/bush	(US)	ani/mate
al/tar	ameli/or/ate	an/ae/mic	ani/ma/tion
al/ter	ameli/or/ation	an/aes/thesia	ani/mos/ity
al/ter/ca/tion	amen/able	an/aes/thetic	ani/seed
al/ter/nate	amend/ment	an/aes/thet/ist	ank/let
al/ter/nately	amen/ity	an/aes/thet/ize	an/nal
al/ter/na/ting	Am/er/ica	ana/gram	an/neal
al/ter/na/tive	ameth/yst	an/al/gesic	an/nex
al/ter/nator	ami/able	an/al/o/gous	an/nexe
al/though	ami/ably	an/al/ogy	an/ni/hil/ate
al/ti/meter	am/ic/able	ana/lyse	an/ni/hil/ation
al/ti/tude	amic/ably	anal/y/sis	an/ni/ver/sary
al/to/gether	am/meter	ana/lyst	an/no/tate
alu/min/ium	ammo/nia	ana/lyt/ical	an/nounce
alu/min/um (US)	am/mon/ite	an/ar/chist	an/nounce/ment
alum/nus (US)	am/mu/ni/tion	an/ar/chy	an/noun/cer
al/ways	am/ne/sia	an/ath/ema	an/noy
alys/sum	am/nesty	an/at/omy	an/noyed
am/al/gam	amoe/bas amoe/bae	an/cestor	an/nual
am/al/gam/ate	am/or/ous	an/ces/tral	an/nually
am/al/gam/ation	amorph/ous	an/ces/try	an/nuity
ama/teur	amor/tize	an/chor	an/nul
ama/teur/ish	am/pE8re	an/chor/age	an/nul/ment
am/aze/ment	am/per/sand	an/chovy	an/ode
amaz/ing	am/phet/amine	an/cient	an/od/ize
am/bas/sador	am/phib/ian	an/cil/lary	an/om/aly
am/bas/sa/dress	am/phib/i/ous	an/droid	anom/al/ous
am/ber	am/phi/theatre	an/ec/dote	an/ony/mous
am/ber/gris	am/phora	an/er/oid	an/ony/mously
am/bi/dex/trous	amp/li/fi/cation	an/eur/ism	an/orak

Hyphen

an/or/exia ner/vosa	an/ti/quary	apo/logy	ap/praisal
an/other	an/ti/quated	apo/plectic	ap/preci/able
an/swer	an/tique	apo/plexy	ap/preci/ably
an/swer/able	an/tiquity	apos/tate	ap/preci/ate
an/swer/ing	an/tir/rhin/um	apos/trophe	ap/preci/ation
an/tag/on/ism	an/ti/sep/tic	ap/pal	ap/preci/at/ive
an/tag/on/ist	an/ti/social	ap/pal/ling	ap/pre/hend
an/tag/on/ize	an/ti/thesis	ap/pal/lingly	ap/pre/hen/sion
Ant/arc/tic	ant/ler	ap/par/atus	ap/pre/hen/sive
ant/eater	an/vil	ap/parel	ap/pren/tice
ante/ce/dent	an/xi/ety	ap/par/ent	ap/pren/tice/ship
ante/date	any/body	ap/par/ently	ap/proach
ante/dil/u/vian	any/how	ap/par/it/ion	ap/proach/able
ante/lope	any/one	ap/peal	ap/proach/ing
ante/natal	any/place	ap/peal/ing	ap/prob/ation
an/ten/na	any/thing	ap/pear	ap/pro/pri/ate
an/terior	any/way	ap/pear/ance	ap/pro/pri/ation
ante/room	any/where	ap/pease	ap/prove
an/them	aor/tic	ap/pease/ment	ap/prov/ing
ant/hill	apart/heid	ap/pend	ap/proxi/mate
an/thol/ogy	apart/ment	ap/pen/di/citis	ap/proxi/mation
an/thra/cite	apa/thetic	ap/pen/dix	ap/ri/cot
an/thro/po/logi/cal	apa/thy	ap/per/tain	Ap/ril
an/thro/pol/ogist	aperi/ent	ap/pet/ite	ap/ron
an/thro/pol/ogy	aperi/tif	ap/pet/izer	ap/ti/tude
an/ti/biotic	ap/er/ture	ap/pet/iz/ing	apt/ness
an/ti/body	aph/or/ism	ap/plaud	aqua/lung
an/tici/pate	aph/ro/dis/iac	ap/plause	aqua/marine
an/tici/pa/tior	api/ary	ap/pliance	aquar/ium
an/ti/climax	api/cul/ture	ap/plic/able	Aquar/ius
an/ti/clock/wise	ap/ing	ap/pli/cant	aqua/tint
an/tics	apla/sia	ap/pli/ca/tion	aque/duct
an/ti/cy/clone	apoc/a/lyptic	ap/ply	aqui/line
an/ti/dote	apoc/ryphal	ap/point	ar/ab/esque
an/ti/freeze	apo/gee	ap/pointed	Ara/bia
an/ti/his/ta/mine	apol/it/ical	ap/point/ment	ar/able
an/tip/athy	apo/lo/getic	ap/por/tion	arach/nid
an/tip/odes	apo/lo/get/ically	ap/posite	arach/noid
an/ti/quar/ian	apo/lo/gize	ap/praise	Ara/maic

Hyphen

ar/bit/rar/ily	ar/ith/metic	ar/tiste	as/sas/sina/tion
ar/bit/rary	ar/ith/meti/cal	ar/tis/tic	as/sault
ar/bit/rate	ar/mada	ar/tis/ti/cally	as/semble
ar/bor	ar/ma/ment	art/less	as/sem/bly
ar/cade	ar/ma/ture	as/bes/tos	as/sent
archae/olo/gical	arm/band	as/bes/tosis	as/sert
archae/olo/gist	arm/chair	as/cend	as/ser/tion
archae/ology	arm/ful	as/cend/ancy	as/ser/tive
ar/chaic	arm/is/tice	as/cend/ant	as/sess
arch/angel	ar/mour	as/cer/tain	as/ses/sor
arch/bishop	ar/mor (US)	as/cetic	as/set
arch/ery	ar/mour-plated	as/cor/bic	as/sidu/ous
arche/typal	arm/oury	as/cot	as/si/du/ity
arche/type	arm/pit	as/crip/tion	as/sign
archi/pel/ago	aro/matic	as/dic	as/sig/nation
archi/tect	ar/range	asex/ual	as/sign/ment
archi/tec/ture	ar/range/ment	ash/can (US)	as/simi/late
archi/trave	ar/ray	ash/en	as/sist
arch/ives	ar/rears	ash/lar	as/sist/ance
arch/iv/ist	ar/rest	ash/pan	as/sist/ant
arch/way	ar/rive	ash/tray	as/sizes
arc/tic	ar/ro/gance	Asi/atic	as/so/ci/ate
ar/dent	ar/rog/ant	as/in/ine	as/sorted
ar/dently	ar/row	as/par/agus	as/sort/ment
ar/dour ar/dor (US)	ar/senal	as/pect	as/suage
ar/du/ous	ar/sen/ic	as/pen	as/sume
ar/du/ously	ar/son	as/per/ity	as/sump/tion
Ar/gen/tina	ar/terio/scler/osis	as/per/sions	as/sur/ance
ar/gon	ar/tery	as/phalt	as/sure
ar/gu/able	ar/tesian	as/phyxia	as/sur/edly
ar/gue	art/ful	as/phyxi/ate	as/ter
ar/gu/ment	arth/ritis	as/phyxi/ation	as/ter/isk
ar/gu/men/ta/tive	ar/ti/choke	as/pir/ate	as/ter/oid
arid/ity	art/icle	as/pire	asth/matic
Ar/ies	ar/ticu/late	as/pir/ation	as/tig/matic
ar/is/toc/ra/cies	arti/ficial	as/pirin	as/tig/mat/ism
ar/is/to/crat	artil/lery	as/sail/ant	as/ton/ish
ar/is/to/cratic	ar/tisan	as/sas/sin	as/ton/ish/ing
	ar/tist	as/sas/sin/ate	as/ton/ish/ment

Hyphen

as/tound	at/tenu/ate	au/then/ti/cate	avoid/ance
astrin/gent	at/tic	au/then/tic/ity	avoir/du/pois
as/tro/loger	at/tire	au/thor	avow/able
as/tro/logy	at/ti/tude	auth/ori/tarian	avun/cu/lar
as/tro/naut	at/tor/ney	auth/ori/ta/tive	awaken/ing
as/tro/nomer	at/tract	au/thor/ity	aware/ness
as/tro/nomi/cal	at/tract/ive	au/thor/iza/tion	aw/ful
as/tro/nomy	at/tract/ively	au/thor/ize	awk/ward
as/tute	at/tribu/table	au/tis/tic	awk/wardly
asy/lum	at/tri/bute	auto/bio/graph/ical	awk/ward/ness
asym/met/rical	at/tri/tion	auto/bio/graphy	awn/ing
asyn/chron/ous	au/ber/gine	autoc/racy	ax/iom
at/av/is/tic	au/burn	auto/crat	ax/io/matic
athe/ism	auc/tion	auto/crat/ic/ally	aya/tol/lah
ath/lete	auc/tion/eer	auto/cue	aza/lea
ath/let/ics	au/da/cious	auto/graph	bab/bler
At/lan/tic	au/da/city	auto/matic	ba/bel
at/las	aud/ible	auto/mati/cally	ba/boon
at/mo/sphere	au/di/ence	auto/ma/tion	ba/by/ish
at/mo/spheric	au/dio-vis/ual	auto/maton	baby-sit/ter
atom/izer	au/dit/ing	auto/mo/bile	bac/ca/rat
aton/al/ity	au/dit/ion	auton/omous	bac/cha/nal
atone/ment	aud/itor	auton/omy	bach/elor
at/ro/cious	aud/it/or/ium	aut/opsy	ba/cil/lus
at/ro/city	aug/ment	au/tumn	back/ache
at/tach	aug/ment/ation	au/tum/nal	back/bit/ing
at/tachE9	au/gur	aux/ili/ary	back/bone
at/tach/ment	Au/gust	avail/abil/ity	back/break/ing
at/tack	aur/icle	avail/able	bab/bler
at/tain	au/rora	ava/lanche	ba/bel
at/tain/able	aus/pi/ces	av/ari/ce	ba/boon
at/tain/ment	aus/pi/cious	av/ari/cious	ba/by/ish
at/tempt	aus/tere	av/enue	baby-sit/ter
at/tend	aus/ter/ity	av/er/age	bac/ca/rat
at/tend/ance	Aus/tral/asia	aver/sion	bac/cha/nal
at/tend/ant	Aus/tra/lia	avi/ary	bach/elor
at/ten/tion	Aus/tra/lian	avi/ation	ba/cil/lus
at/ten/tive	Aus/tria	avo/cado	back/ache
at/tent/ively	au/then/tic	avoid/able	back/bit/ing

Hyphen

back/bone	bal/boa	ban/ner	bar/rel
back/break/ing	bal/cony	ban/quet	bar/ren
back/cloth	bal/der/dash	ban/shee	bar/ren/ness
back/date	bal/een	ban/tam	bar/ri/cade
back/fire	bale/ful	ban/ter	bar/rier
back/gam/mon	bal/lad	bap/tis/try	bar/ring
back/ground	bal/last	bap/tis/tery	bar/ris/ter
back/hand	ball/cock	bap/tize	bar/room (US)
back/ing	bal/ler/ina	bara/thea	bar/row
back/lash	bal/let	bar/bar/ian	bar/ter
back/less	bal/lis/tics	bar/baric	bas/alt
back/log	bal/loon	bar/bar/ous	bas/cule
back/pedal	bal/loon/ing	bar/be/cue	base/ball
back/side	bal/lot	bar/bell	base/board
back/stage	ball/point	bar/ber	base/less
back/stairs	ball/room	bar/bit/ur/ate	base/ment
back/stroke	bal/ly/hoo	bar/bule	bash/ful
back/ward	ba/lo/ney	bare/back	bash/fully
back/ward/ness	bal/sam	bare/faced	ba/sic
back/water	bal/us/ter	bare/foot	ba/sic/ally
back/woods (US)	bal/us/trade	bare/headed	ba/si/lica
back/yard	bam/boo	bare/ness	ba/sin
ba/con	bam/boozle	bar/gain	ba/sis
bac/terio/logi/cal	ba/nana	bar/gain/ing	bas/ket
bac/teri/olo/gist	band/age	ba/ri/tone	bas/ket/ball
bac/teri/ology	ban/died	bar/ium	bas/ket/work
bac/terium	ban/dit	bark/ing	bas/set
bad/min/ton	band/master	bar/ley	bas/si/net
baf/fling	ban/do/lier	bar/maid	bas/soon
ba/ga/telle	bands/man	bar/man	bas/tard
bag/gage	band/stand	bar/nacle	bas/tion
bag/pipes	band/wagon	barn/yard	bath/mat
Ba/ha/mas	ban/ish	ba/ro/meter	bath/robe
bail/iff	ban/ish/ment	ba/ro/met/ric	bath/room
baili/wick	ban/is/ters	bar/on/ess	bath/salts
bake/house	ban/jo	bar/onet	bath/towel
ba/la/clava	bank/note	ba/roque	bath/tub
ba/la/laika	bank/rupt	bar/rack	bathy/sphere
bal/ance	bank/ruptcy	bar/rage	bats/man

bat/tal/ion	be/deck	be/holden	be/ne/vol/ent
bat/ted	be/devil	be/lated	be/nign
bat/ten	bed/jacket	be/lay	bent/wood
bat/ter	bed/lam	be/lea/guered	be/queath
bat/tery	bed/pan	bel/fry	be/quest
bat/tle/field	bat/tle/drag/gled	Bel/gian	be/rate
bat/tle/front	bed/ridden	Bel/gium	be/reaved
bat/tle/ments	bed/rock	be/lie	be/reave/ment
bat/tle/ship	bed/room	be/lieve	be/reft
bat/tling	bed/side	be/little	beri/beri
baux/ite	bed/spread	bell/la/donna	ber/ry
bay/onet	bed/time	bell-bot/toms	ber/serk
bay/wood	beef/burger	bell/boy bell/hop (US)	be/ryl/lium
ba/zaar	beef/eater	bel/li/cose	be/seech
ba/zooka	bee/hive	bel/li/ger/ent	be/set
beach/comber	bee/keeper	bel/li/ger/ency	be/set/ting
beach/head	bee/keep/ing	bel/low	be/side
beach/wear	bees/wax	bel/lows	be/sides
bead/ing	beef/bur/ger	bell/push	be/siege
beag/ling	beet/root	belly/ache	be/som
bean/bag	be/fore	belly/flop	be/sot/ted
bear/able	be/fore/hand	belly/ful	be/sought
beard/less	be/friend	be/long	be/spoke
bear/garden	beg/gar	be/long/ings	bes/tial
bear/ing	beg/garly	be/loved	be/stow
bear/skin	beg/ging	be/low	best/sel/ler
beast/li/ness	be/gin	belt/ing	be/tray
be/atif/ic	be/gin/ner	be/moan	be/trayal
beau/ti/cian	be/gin/ning	be/muse	bet/ter
beau/ti/ful	be/go/nia	be/neath	bet/ting
bea/ver	be/grudge	be/ne/dic/tion	be/tween
be/calmed	be/half	be/ne/fac/tor	be/velled
be/came	be/have	be/ne/fac/tress	bev/el/ling
be/cause	be/ha/vi/our	be/ne/fi/cent	bev/er/age
be/come	be/ha/vi/or (US)	be/ne/fi/cial	be/ware
be/dazzle	be/head	be/ne/fi/ci/ary	be/wilder
bed/clothes	be/hest	be/ne/fit	be/wil/der/ment
bed/cover	be/hind	be/ne/vol/ence	be/witch
bed/ding	be/hold		be/witch/ing

Hyphen

be/yond	bi/ling/ual	birth/right	blan/dish/ments
bi/an/nual	bil/ious	bis/cuit	blan/ket
bi/an/nually	bil/la/bong	bi/sect	blas/pheme
bi/ased	bill/board (US)	bi/sex/ual	blas/phe/mer
bi/ath/lon	bil/let	bish/op/ric	blas/phem/ous
bib/li/cal	bill/fold (US)	bis/muth	blas/phemy
bib/lio/graph/ical	bil/liards	bi/son	bla/tant
bib/lio/ma/nia	bil/ling	bis/tro	blaz/ing
bib/lio/graphy	bil/lion	bitch/ily	blaz/onry
bib/lio/phile	bil/low	bit/ing	blem/ish
bibu/lous	bill/poster	bit/ten	bless/ing
bi/car/bon/ate	bi/met/al/lic	bit/ter	blind/fold
bi/cen/ten/ary	bi/mil/len/ary	bit/terly	blind/ness
bi/cen/ten/nial	bi/mil/len/nium	bit/ter/ness	bliss/ful
bi/ceph/al/ous	bi/nary	bit/tern	blis/ter
bi/ceps	bind/ery	bitu/men	blith/er/ing
bi/colour	bind/ing	bi/valve	blitz/krieg
bi/corn	bind/weed	bi/vouac	bliz/zard
bi/cycle	bin/nacle	bi/zarre	block/ade
bid/dable	bin/ocu/lar	blab/ber/mouth	block/age
bid/der	bio/chem/ist	black/beetle	blood/bath
bi/det	bio/chem/istry	black/berry	blood/curd/ling
bi/en/nial	bio/de/grad/able	black/bird	blood/hound
bi/en/ni/ally	bio/graph/ical	black/board	blood/less
bi/fari/ous	bio/graphy	black/currant	blood/shed
bi/focal	bio/lo/gical	black/fly	blood/shot
bi/fo/li/ate	bio/lo/gist	black/guard	blood/stain
bi/fur/cate	bio/logy	black/head	blood/stream
bi/fur/ca/tion	bi/onic	black/ish	blood/thirsty
big/am/ist	bio/physics	black/leg	blos/som
big/am/ous	bio/plasm	black/list	blotch/ier
big/amy	bi/par/ous	black/mail	blot/ter
big/head	bi/par/ti/san	black/ness	blow/fly
big/oted	bi/ped	black/out	blow/lamp
big/otry	bi/plane	black/smith	blow/out
bi/kini	bird/seed	blad/der	blub/ber
bi/lat/eral	birth/day	blad/der/wrack	blud/geon
bil/berry	birth/mark	blame/less	blue/bell
bil/harzia	birth/place	blanc/mange	blue/berry (US)

Hyphen

blue/bottle	bon/bon	bo/sun	braini/ness
blue/print	bond/age	bo/tan/ical	brain/less
blu/ish	bone/less	bot/an/ist	brain/power
blun/der	bone/shaker	bot/any	brain/wash
blun/der/buss	bon/fire	bother/ation	brain/wave
blun/der/ing	bon/net	bot/tle	bra/less
blus/ter	bo/nus	bot/tle/neck	bran/dish
board/ing	booby/trap	bot/tling	bras/si/ere
board/room	book/able	bot/tom	bra/vado
boast/ful	book/binder	bot/tom/less	brav/ery
boat/hook	book/bind/ing	botu/lism	braz/enly
boat/house	book/case	bou/doir	bra/zier
boat/swain	book/ing	boul/der	Bra/zil
bob/bies	book/ish	boul/evard	bread/crumbs
bob/bin	book-keep/ing	boun/cing	bread/line
bobo/link	book/let	boun/dary	bread/win/ner
bob/sleigh	book/maker	boun/ti/ful	break/able
boc/age	book/mar/ker	bou/quet	break/ables
bod/ice	book/sel/ler	bour/bon (US)	break/ages
bod/ies	book/shelf	bour/geois	break/away
bod/kin	book/shop	bour/geoisie	break/down
body/guard	book/stall	bou/tique	break/fast
body/work	book/worm	bo/vine	break/ing
bo/gey	boom/er/ang	bow/ler	break/neck
bog/gle	boom/ing	bow/line	break/through
bo/gie	boor/ish	bowl/ing	break/up
bo/gus	boon/doggle	bow/sprit	break/water
bois/ter/ous	bor/acic	box/ing	breath/alyser
bois/ter/ous/ness	bora/cite	box/room	breath/ing
bold/ness	bor/dello	boy/cott	breath/less
bol/lard	bor/der	boy/friend	breath/tak/ing
boll/worm	bor/der/ing	boy/hood	breed/ing
bol/shie	bor/der/line	brace/let	brevi/ary
bol/ster	bor/eal	bra/chio/pod	brev/ity
bom/bard	bore/dom	brack/ish	brick/layer
bom/bard/ment	bore/hole	brad/awl	brick/work
bom/bas/tic	bor/ing	brag/ging	bride/groom
bomb/shell	bor/row	brah/min	brides/maid
bon/anza	bor/stal	brain/child	bridge/head

Hyphen

bridle/path	bucket/ful	bur/dock	cad/die
bridle/way	buck/teeth	bur/eau/cracy	cad/dis fly
brief/case	buck/wheat	bur/geon	cad/dy
brief/ing	Bud/dhism	burg/lar	ca/dence
brig/ade	Bud/dhist	bur/lesque	ca/det
briga/dier	bud/ding	bur/row	cad/mium
brig/and	bud/dleia	bur/sar	ca/du/ceus
bright/ish	bud/geri/gar	bur/sary	ca/du/city
bright/ness	buf/falo	bury/ing	cae/sar/ean
bril/liance	buf/fer	bush/man	caf/et/eria
bril/liant	buf/fet	busi/ness	caf/fein
brim/ful	buf/foon	busi/ness/like	ca/gey/ness
brim/ming	buf/foon/ery	busi/ness/man	ca/hoots
Brit/ain	bug/bear	bus/man	cais/son
brit/tle	bu/gler	bus/sing	ca/jole
brit/tle/ness	build/ing	bu/tane	cake/walk
broad/cast	bul/bous	but/cher	cal/a/boose (US)
broad/cast/ing	bulk/head	but/ler	cal/amine
broad/loom	bull/dog	but/ted	ca/lam/it/ous
broad/min/ded	bull/doze	but/ter	ca/lam/ity
bro/cade	bul/let	but/tock(s)	cal/car/eous
broc/coli	bul/letin	but/ton	cal/ci/fer/ous
bro/chure	bull/fighter	but/tress	cal/cium
bron/chial	bull/finch	buz/zard	cal/cu/lable
bron/chitis	bull/frog	by/gone	cal/cu/late
broom/stick	bul/lion	by/pass	cal/cu/lation
brother/hood	bul/lock	by/stander	cal/cu/lator
brow/beat	bull/ring	by/word	cal/cu/lus
brown/ish	bul/rush	cab/a/ret	ca/le/fac/tory
brow/ser	bumble/bee	cab/bage	cal/en/dar
bru/nette	bum/per	cab/in	ca/len/dula
brush/wood	bump/tious	cab/inet	cali/brate
bru/tal	bun/ga/low	cab/man	cal/ibre
bru/tal/ity	bun/gling	ca/boose	cali/ber (US)
brut/ally	bun/ion	cack/ling	cal/ico
bub/ble	bunt/ing	ca/co/graphy	cal/iph
bub/bling	buoy/ancy	ca/co/phony	call/boy
bub/bly	buoy/ant	cac/tus	cal/li/grapher
buc/can/eer	bur/den	ca/da/ver/ous	cal/lig/raphy

Hyphen

call/ing	can/cer/ous	can/yon	cara/way
cal/li/pers	can/de/la/bra	cap/ab/il/ity	car/bine
cal/lis/then/ics	can/des/cent	cap/able	car/bo/hy/drate
cal/lous	can/did	cap/ably	car/bolic
cal/lus	can/di/date	ca/pa/ci/tance	car/bon
calm/ness	can/di/dature	ca/pa/citor	car/bon/ate
cal/orie	can/died	ca/pa/cious	car/bonic
cal/or/ific	can/dour can/dor	ca/pa/city	car/bon/ifer/ous
calo/type	(US)	ca/per	car/boy
cal/um/ni/ate	candy/floss	ca/per/cail/lie	car/buncle
cal/umny	candy/tuft	ca/pil/lary	car/bur/ation
ca/lypso	can/ine	capi/tal	car/bur/et/tor
ca/lyx	can/is/ter	capi/tal/ism	car/case car/cass
ca/ma/ra/derie	can/ker	capi/tal/ist	car/ci/no/gen
cam/ber	can/na/bis	capi/tal/iz/ation	car/da/mom
cam/bium	can/ni/bal	capi/ta/tion	card/board
ca/mel/lia	can/ni/bal/ism	ca/pitu/late	car/diac
ca/meo	can/ni/bal/ize	ca/pitu/lation	car/di/gan
cam/era	can/nier	ca/pon	car/dinal
cami/sole	can/ning	cap/puc/cino	car/dio/gram
camo/mile	can/non	ca/price	car/dio/graph
cam/ou/flage	can/non/ball	ca/pric/ious	car/di/ologist
cam/paign	can/not	Cap/ri/corn	car/di/ology
cam/pan/ile	ca/noe	cap/size	car/dio/vas/cu/lar
cam/pa/nol/ogy	canoe/ing	cap/stan	ca/reer
cam/pan/ula	canoe/ist	cap/sule	care/free
cam/phor	ca/noni/cate	cap/tain	care/less
camp/ing	can/on/ize	cap/taincy	care/less/ness
camp/site	can/opy	cap/tion	ca/ress
cam/pus	can/tan/ker/ous	cap/tiv/ate	care/taker
cam/shaft	can/tata	cap/tive	Ca/rib/bean
Can/ada	can/teen	cap/tiv/ity	ca/ri/bou
ca/nal	can/ter	cap/ture	ca/ri/ca/ture
ca/nary	cant/icle	capy/bara	ca/ril/lon
can/asta	can/ti/lever	ca/rafe	car/mine
can/can	can/ton	cara/mel	carn/age
can/cel	can/vas	cara/pace	car/nal
can/cel/la/tion	can/vass	cara/van	car/na/tion
can/cer	can/vas/sing	cara/van/ning	car/ni/val

Hyphen

car/ni/vore	cas/sock	cat/kin	cel/list
car/ni/vor/ous	cas/ta/nets	cat/sup (US)	cel/lo/phane
ca/ro/tid	cast/away	cat/tery	cel/lu/lar
ca/rou/sel	cast/ing	cat/tle	cel/lu/lose
car/pal	cas/tel/lated	cau/cus	Cel/sius
car/pel	cas/tig/ate	caul/dron cal/dron (US)	ce/ment
car/pen/ter	cas/trate	cau/li/flower	cem/et/ery
car/pet	cas/ual	cause/way	ceno/taph
car/pet/ing	casu/alty	caus/tic	cen/ser
car/port	cata/clysm	caus/ti/cally	cen/sor
car/pus	cata/combs	cau/ter/iz/ation	cen/sor/ious
car/sick	cata/falque	caut/er/ize	cen/sor/ship
car/riage	cata/lepsy	cau/tion	cen/sure
car/riage/way	cata/logue cata/log (US)	cau/tious	cen/sus
car/rier	cata/lyst	cav/al/cade	cen/ten/arian
car/rion	cata/ma/ran	ca/va/lier	cen/ten/ary
car/rot	cata/pult	cav/alry	cen/ten/nial
cart/horse	cat/ar/act	cave/fish	cen/ti/grade
car/ti/lage	ca/tarrh	cave/man	cen/ti/litre
cart/load	ca/tas/trophe	cav/ern	cen/ti/liter (US)
car/to/grapher	cata/strophic	cavi/ar(e)	cen/ti/metre
car/to/graphy	cat/call	cav/ity	cen/ti/meter (US)
car/ton	catch/ment	ca/vort	cen/ti/pede
car/toon	catch/word	cay/enne	cent/ral/ize
cart/ridge	cat/echism	cay/man	centre/piece
cart/wheel	cat/ech/ize	cease/fire	cen/tri/fugal
car/very	cat/eg/ori/cal	cease/less	cen/tri/petal
car/ving	cat/egory	ce/dar	cen/tur/ion
cary/atid	cat/er/pil/lar	ce/dilla	cen/tury
cas/cade	ca/ter/waul	ceil/ing	cepha/lo/pod
case/ment	cat/fish	cel/eb/rate	ce/ramic
cash/ier	cat/gut	cel/eb/ration	ce/re/bel/lum
cash/mere	ca/thed/ral	cel/eb/rity	ce/reb/ral
cas/ing	cath/er/ine wheel	cel/ery	ce/re/mon/ial
cas/ino	cath/eter	ce/les/tial	ce/re/mon/ious
cas/ket	cath/ode	cel/ib/acy	ce/re/mony
cas/sava	cath/olic	cel/ib/ate	cer/tain
cas/ser/ole	cath/oli/cism	cel/lar	cer/ti/fic/ate
cas/sette			cer/tify

Hyphen

cer/ti/tude	char/ac/ter/ize	chem/ical	chlor/ine
ce/ru/men	cha/rade	che/mise	chloro/form
cer/vi/cal	char/coal	chem/is/try	chloro/phyll
cer/vix	charge/able	cher/ish	choc/olate
ces/sa/tion	char/ger	che/root	choir/boy
ces/sion	cha/risma	cher/ubic	choir/master
cess/pit	cha/ris/matic	cher/ubs	cho/king
chaf/finch	char/it/able	cher/vil	chol/era
cha/grin	char/ity	chess/board	cho/les/terol
chair/lift	char/lady	chess/men	chop/per
chair/man	char/la/tan	chest/nut	chop/sticks
cha/let	charm/ing	chev/ron	cho/reo/graphy
chal/ice	char/ter	chi/cane	cho/reo/grapher
chal/lenge	char/woman	chick/weed	chor/ister
chal/leng/ing	chas/sis	chic/ory	chow/der
cham/ber	chas/tise	chief/tain	chris/ten
cham/ber/maid	chas/tise/ment	chif/fon	Chris/tian
cham/ber/pot	chast/ity	chil/blain	Chris/ti/an/ity
cha/me/leon	chat/eau	child/ren	Christ/mas
cham/fer	chat/tel	child/ish/ness	chro/matic
cham/ois	chat/ter/box	child/like	chro/mium
cham/pagne	chauf/feur	chil/li/ness	chro/mo/some
cham/pion	chau/vin/ism	chim/ney	chron/icle
cham/pion/ship	chau/vin/is/tic	chim/pan/zee	chron/icler
chan/cel	cheap/ness	chin/chilla	chro/no/logical
chan/cel/lery	cheat/ing	Chi/nese	chro/no/logi/cally
chan/cel/lor	check/list	chi/nois/erie	chro/no/meter
chan/de/lier	check/mate	chip/board	chrys/alis
chand/ler	check/out	chip/munk	chrys/an/the/mum
change/able	check/up	chi/po/lata	church/goer
change/over	cheek/bone	chip/pings	church/war/den
chan/nel	chee/ki/ness	chi/ro/pod/ist	church/yard
chan/nelled	cheer/ful	chir/rup	chur/lish
chan/ter/elle	cheer/leader	chis/elled	chur/lish/ness
chap/eron	cheer/less	chis/el/ler	chut/ney
chap/lain	cheese/cake	chi/sel/ling	ci/cada
chap/ter	cheese/cloth	chit/chat	ci/gar
char/ac/ter	cheese/paring	chiv/al/rous	ci/gar/ette
char/ac/ter/istic	chee/tah	chlor/in/ate	cili/ate

Hyphen

cin/ders	clam/mier	cliff/han/ger	coch/in/eal
cin/ema	clam/our	cli/mate	cock/ade
cine/mato/gra/phic	clam/our/ous	cli/ma/to/logy	cock/atoo
cin/namon	clam/or/ous (US)	cli/max	cock/chafer
cinque/foil	clamp/down	cli/nic	cock/erel
ci/pher	clan/des/tine	clit/oris	cock/ney
cir/clip	clan/nish	clob/ber	cock/pit
cir/cuit	clap/per	clock/wise	cock/roach
cir/cuit/ous	clap/per/board	clock/work	cock/sure
cir/cu/late	clap/trap	clois/ter	cock/tail
cir/cum/cise	cla/rify	close/ness	co/co/nut
cir/cum/fer/ence	cla/ri/net	clo/thing	co/coon
cir/cum/navi/gate	cla/rin/et/tist	cloud/burst	cod/dle
cir/cum/scribe	clar/ity	cloudi/ness	co/deine
cir/cum/scrip/tion	clasp/knife	cloud/less	co/di/cil
cir/cum/spect	clas/sic	club/foot	co/di/fy
cir/cum/stance	clas/si/cal	club/house	co-di/rec/tor
cir/cum/stan/tial	clas/si/cism	clue/less	co-edu/ca/tional
cir/cum/vent	classi/fi/ca/tion	clum/sily	co/efficient
cir/cus	clat/ter	clum/si/ness	coel/ac/anth
cir/rho/sis	claus/tro/phobia	clus/ter	co/erce
cir/rus	clavi/chord	clut/ter	co/er/cion
cis/tern	clav/icle	co/agu/late	co/exist
cit/adel	clean/ing	co/alesce	co/exist/ence
ci/ta/tion	clean/li/ness	co/al/es/cence	cof/fee
citi/zen	clean/sha/ven	coal/field	cof/fers
citi/zen/ship	clear/ance	coal/hole	cof/fin
cit/reous	clear/way	co/ali/tion	co/gent
cit/ric	clea/vage	coal/mine	cog/it/ate
cit/rus	cle/ma/tis	coarse/ness	cog/nate
civ/ico	clem/ency	coast/guard	cog/niz/ance
civ/il/ian	clem/ent	coast/line	co/habit
civ/ility	clem/en/tine	co/balt	co/here
civi/liz/ation	clere/story	cob/bler	co/her/ence
civ/il/ize	clergy/man	cob/ble(stone)	co/her/ent
clad/ding	cler/ical	co/bra	co/hes/ive
claim/ant	clever/ness	cob/web	co/hort
clair/voyant	cli/ent	co/caine	coif/fure
clam/ber	cli/en/tele	coc/cyx	coin/age

Hyphen

co/in/cide	Col/or/ado beetle	com/menda/tion	com/pact
co/in/cid/ence	col/or/ific	com/mend/at/ory	com/pan/ion
co/in/cid/ental	col/os/sal	com/men/sur/ate	com/pany
co/lan/der	col/os/sus	com/ment	com/par/able
cold/ness	col/os/trum	com/men/tary	com/para/tive
cole/slaw	col/our col/or (US)	com/men/tator	com/pare
col/itis	col/our/ful	com/merce	com/pari/son
col/lab/or/ate	col/or/ful (US)	com/mer/cial	com/part/ment
col/lab/or/ation	col/um/bine	com/mer/cial/ize	com/pass
col/lage	col/umn	com/mis/erate	com/pas/sion
col/la/gen	coma/tose	com/mis/sar	com/pas/sion/ate
col/lapse	com/bat	com/mis/sion	com/pati/bility
col/lap/sible	com/bat/ant	com/mis/sion/aire	com/pat/ible
col/lar	com/bat/ive	com/mis/sioner	com/pat/riot
col/late	com/bin/ation	com/mit	com/pel
col/la/tor	com/bine	com/mit/ment	com/pel/ling
col/lat/eral	com/bust/ible	com/mit/tal	com/pen/sate
col/league	com/bus/tion	com/mit/tee	com/pen/sa/tion
col/lect	come/back	com/modi/ous	com/pE9re
col/lect/ive	come/down	com/mod/ity	com/pete
col/lect/or	co/me/dian	com/mo/dore	com/pet/ence
col/lege	com/edy	com/mon	com/pe/tent
col/legi/ate	come/up/pance	com/moner	com/peti/tion
col/lide	com/fort	com/mon/place	com/peti/tive
col/lie	com/fort/able	com/mon/wealth	com/peti/tor
col/lier	com/forter	com/mo/tion	com/pile
col/liery	com/fort/less	com/mu/nal	com/pla/cent
col/lis/ion	com/mand	com/mune	com/plain
col/lo/quial	com/man/dant	com/mun/ic/able	com/plaint
col/lo/quial/ism	com/man/deer	com/muni/cate	com/plais/ance
col/lu/sion	com/man/der	com/muni/cation	com/ple/ment
co/logne	com/mand/ment	com/muni/ca/tive	com/plete
col/onel	com/mando	com/muniquE9	com/pletely
co/lo/nial	com/mem/or/ate	com/mun/ism	com/plete/ness
co/lo/nial/ist	com/mem/or/ation	com/mun/ity	com/pletion
col/on/ist	com/mence	com/mut/able	com/plex
col/on/ize	com/mence/ment	com/mu/ta/tion	com/plex/ion
col/on/nade	com/mend	com/mute	com/plex/ity
col/ony	com/mend/able	com/mu/ter	com/pli/ant

Hyphen

com/pli/cate	con/cen/tric	con/do/min/ium	con/found
com/pli/ca/tion	con/cept	con/done	con/front
com/pli/city	con/cep/tion	con/dor	con/fron/ta/tion
com/pli/ment	con/cern	con/du/cive	con/fuse
com/pli/men/tary	con/cern/ing	con/duct	con/fus/edly
com/ply	con/cert	con/duc/tion	con/fus/ing
com/pli/ance	con/cer/ted	con/duc/tor	con/fu/sion
com/pli/ant	con/cer/tina	con/duc/tress	con/geal
com/pon/ent	con/certo	con/duit	con/gen/ial
com/pose	con/ces/sion	con/fab	con/geni/tal
com/posi/tor	con/chol/ogy	con/fect	con/ges/ted
com/post	con/cili/ate	con/fec/tion	con/ges/tion
com/pos/ure	con/cili/atory	con/fec/tion/ery	con/glom/er/ate
com/pound	con/cise	con/fed/er/acy	con/glom/era/tion
com/pre/hend	con/cise/ness	con/fed/er/ate	con/gratu/late
com/pre/hen/sible	con/clave	con/fed/er/ation	con/gratu/la/tions
com/pre/hen/sion	con/clude	con/fer	con/gratu/la/tory
com/pre/hen/sive	con/clu/sion	con/fer/ence	con/gre/gate
com/press	con/clu/sive	con/fess	con/gre/ga/tion
com/pres/sor	con/coct	con/fes/sion	con/gress
com/prise	con/coc/tion	con/fes/sional	con/gres/sional
com/prom/ise	con/comi/tant	con/fes/sor	con/ical
com/pul/sion	con/cord	con/fetti	con/ifer
com/pul/sory	con/cord/ance	con/fide	con/if/er/ous
com/punc/tion	con/cor/dat	con/fid/ant	con/jec/ture
com/pu/ta/tion	con/course	con/fid/ante	con/jec/tural
com/pute	con/crete	con/fide	con/jugal
com/puter	con/cre/tion	con/fi/dence	con/ju/gate
com/rade	con/cu/bine	con/fi/den/tial	con/ju/gation
com/rade/ship	con/cur	con/fine	con/junc/tion
con/cave	con/cur/rent	con/firm	con/junc/ti/vitis
con/ceal	con/cus/sion	con/fir/ma/tion	con/jun/cture
con/ceal/ment	con/demn	con/fis/cate	con/jure
con/cede	con/dense	con/fis/ca/tion	con/jurer
con/ceit	con/des/cend	con/flag/ra/tion	con/jur/ing
con/ceive	con/de/scen/sion	con/flict	con/ker
con/ceiv/able	con/di/ment	con/form	con/nect
con/cen/trate	con/dition	con/form/ist	con/nec/tion
con/cen/tra/tion	con/dole	con/form/ity	con/ning tower

Hyphen

con/nive	con/soli/date	con/sum/mate	con/tour
con/niv/ance	con/soli/da/tion	con/sum/ma/tion	con/tra/band
con/nois/seur	con/sommé	con/sump/tion	con/tra/cep/tion
con/note	con/son/ant	con/sump/tive	con/tra/cep/tive
con/quer	con/sort	con/tact	con/tract
con/quer/ing	con/sor/tium	con/ta/gious	con/trac/tion
con/queror	con/spicu/ous	con/tain	con/trac/tor
con/quest	con/spir/ator	con/tainer	con/trac/tual
con/science	con/spir/at/or/ial	con/tam/in/ate	con/tra/dict
con/scien/tious	con/spire	con/tam/ina/tion	con/tra/dic/tion
con/scious	con/stable	con/tem/plate	con/tra/dic/tory
con/scious/ness	con/stab/ul/ary	con/tem/pla/tion	con/tralto
con/script	con/stancy	con/tem/pla/tive	con/trap/tion
con/scrip/tion	con/stant	con/tem/por/ary	con/trari/ness
con/sec/rate	con/stel/la/tion	cont/emp/or/an/eous	con/trary
con/se/cra/tion	con/ster/na/tion	con/tempt	con/trast
con/secu/tive	con/sti/pated	con/tempt/ible	con/tra/vene
con/sen/sus	con/sti/pa/tion	con/temp/tu/ous	con/tra/ven/tion
con/sent	con/stitu/ent	con/tend	con/tre/temps
con/se/quence	con/sti/tute	con/ten/der	con/trib/ute
con/se/quen/tial	con/sti/tu/tional	con/tent	con/tri/bu/tion
con/se/quently	con/strain	con/tent/edly	con/trite
con/serve	con/straint	con/ten/tion	con/tri/tion
con/ser/va/tion	con/strict	con/ten/tious	con/trive
con/ser/va/tive	con/stric/tion	con/test	con/tri/vance
con/ser/va/tory	con/struct	con/tes/tant	con/trol
con/sider	con/struc/tive	con/text	con/trol/ler
con/sid/er/able	con/struc/tor	con/ti/nent	con/tro/ver/sial
con/sid/er/ate	con/strue	con/ti/nen/tal	con/tro/versy
con/sid/er/ation	con/sul	con/tin/gency	con/tu/sion
con/sid/er/ing	con/su/lar	con/tin/gent	con/un/drum
con/sign	con/su/late	con/tinu/ally	con/ur/ba/tion
con/sign/ment	con/sult	con/tinu/ation	con/val/esce
con/sist	con/sul/tant	con/tinue	con/val/es/cence
con/sist/ency	con/sul/ta/tion	con/ti/nu/ity	con/val/es/cent
con/sist/ent	con/sul/ta/tive	con/tinu/ous	con/vec/tion
con/sist/ently	con/sul/ting	con/tort	con/vene
con/so/la/tion	con/sume	con/tor/tion	con/venor
con/sole	con/sumer		con/veni/ence

Hyphen

con/veni/ent	copy/right	cor/res/pon/ding	coun/ter/point
con/vent	copy/wri/ter	cor/ri/dor	coun/ter/poise
con/ven/tion	cor/dial	cor/rob/or/ate	coun/ter/sign
con/ven/tional	cordi/al/ity	cor/rob/or/ation	coun/ter/sink
con/verge	cordi/ally	cor/rode	coun/try
con/ver/gence	cor/dite	cor/ro/sive	coun/try/side
con/ver/gent	cor/don	cor/ru/gated	coup/ling
con/ver/sant	cor/du/roy	cor/rupt	cou/pon
con/verse	cork/age	cor/rupt/ible	cour/age
con/ver/sa/tion	cork/screw	cor/rup/tion	cour/ageous
con/ver/sion	cor/mor/ant	cor/set	cour/gette
con/vert	cor/nea	cor/ti/sone	cour/ier
con/ver/ter	cor/ner	cos/me/tic	cour/teous
con/vert/ible	cor/net	cos/mic	cour/tesy
con/vex	corn/flakes	cos/mo/naut	court/room
con/vey	corn/flour	cos/mo/pol/itan	court/ship
con/vey/ance	cor/nice	cos/set	court/yard
con/veyor	corn/starch	cost/li/ness	cov/en/ant
con/vict	co/rol/lary	cos/tume	Cov/en/try
con/vic/tion	co/rona	cot/tage	cov/er/age
con/vince	cor/on/ary	cot/ton	cover/let
con/vin/cing	cor/on/ation	coty/ledon	cov/ert
con/viv/ial	cor/oner	couch/ette	cov/et/ous
con/vo/ca/tion	cor/onet	coun/cil	cow/ard
con/voke	cor/poral	coun/cil/lor	cow/ar/dice
con/vol/vu/<?>us	cor/por/ate	coun/sel	cow/boy
con/voy	cor/por/ation	coun/sel/lor	cow/hand
con/vulse	cor/por/eal	count/down	cow/herd
con/vul/sion	cor/pu/lence	coun/ten/ance	cow/pat
con/vul/sive	cor/pu/lent	coun/ter	cow/shed
cool/ant	cor/puscle	coun/ter/bal/ance	cow/slip
co/oper/ate	cor/rect	coun/ter/blast	cox/swain
co/op/er/at/ive	cor/rec/tion	coun/ter/charge	coy/ness
co-ord/in/ate	cor/rec/tive	coun/ter/feit	coy/ote
co/pilot	cor/rel/ate	coun/ter/foil	crack/ling
cop/ing	cor/re/la/tion	coun/ter/mand	craft/ily
cop/ious	cor/res/pond	coun/ter/meas/ure	crafti/ness
cop/per	cor/res/pon/dence	coun/ter/pane	crafts/man
cop/pice	cor/res/pon/dent	coun/ter/part	cram/pon

Hyphen

cran/berry	criti/cal	cu/cum/ber	cus/tard
cra/nium	criti/cism	cud/dle	cus/to/dian
cra/ter	criti/cize	cud/gel	cus/tody
cra/vat	cro/chet	cul/in/ary	cus/tom
cray/fish	crock/ery	cul/min/ate	cus/tom/arily
craz/ily	cro/co/dile	cul/mi/na/tion	cus/tom/ary
crazi/ness	cro/cus	cul/pable	cus/tomer
cream/ery	crook/edly	cul/pa/bil/ity	cus/toms
cre/ate	crop/per	cul/prit	cut/icle
cre/ation	cro/quet	cul/ti/vate	cut/lery
cre/ative	cro/quette	cul/ti/va/tion	cut/let
cre/ativ/ity	cross/bar	cul/ti/va/tor	cy/an/ide
cre/ator	cross/check	cul/ture	cy/ber/net/ics
crea/ture	cross/eyed	cul/tural	cyc/la/men
cre/den/tials	cross/fire	cum/ber/some	cyc/lic
cred/ible	cross/legged	cumu/la/tive	cyc/li/cal
credi/bil/ity	cross/roads	cum/ulus	cyc/ling
cred/ibly	cross/wind	cu/nei/form	cyc/list
credi/table	crossword	cun/ning	cyc/lone
credi/tably	crot/chet	cup/board	cyg/net
credi/tor	crou/pier	cup/ful	cyl/in/der
credu/lity	crow/bar	cu/pid/ity	cym/bals
credu/lous	cru/cial	cur/able	cyni/cal
cre/ma/tion	cru/cible	cur/ate	cyni/cism
cre/ma/tor/ium	cru/ci/fix	cur/ator	cy/press
cre/mate	cru/ci/fix/ion	cur/few	Cy/prus
creo/sote	cru/cify	curi/os/ity	cys/ti/tis
cres/cent	crude/ness	cur/iously	Czecho/slo/vakia
crest/fal/len	crum/pet	cur/lew	dab/chick
cre/vasse	cru/sade	cur/rant	dachs/hund
crev/ice	cru/sader	cur/rency	daf/fo/dil
crew/cut	crus/ta/cean	cur/rent	dag/ger
crim/inal	cryp/tic	cur/ricu/lum	da/guer/reo/type
crim/in/ology	crys/tal	cur/ry/comb	dah/lia
crim/son	crys/tal/lize	cur/sory	dain/tily
crip/ple	crys/tal/lo/graphy	cur/tail	dairy/maid
cri/sis	cu/bicle	cur/tain	dairy/man
crisp/ness	cu/bism	cur/va/ture	dal/ma/tian
cri/ter/ion	cu/bist	cush/ion	dam/age

Hyphen

dam/ask	de/base	dec/lar/ation	de/fen/dant
dam/na/tion	de/bate	de/cline	de/fen/sive
damn/ing	de/bauch/ery	de/clutch	de/fer
damp/ness	de/ben/ture	de/coc/tion	de/fer/ence
dam/sel	de/bili/tate	de/code	de/fer/en/tial
dam/son	de/bil/ity	de/com/mis/sion	de/fi/ance
dan/de/lion	de/bon/air	de/com/pose	de/fiant
dan/druff	de/brief	de/con/tam/in/ate	de/fi/ciency
dan/ger	deb/ris	de/cor	de/fi/cient
dan/ger/ous	de/bunk	dec/or/ate	de/fi/cit
dan/gle	dE9/but	dec/or/ations	de/file
Dan/ish	de/cade	dec/or/ator	de/fine
dap/per	dec/ad/ence	dec/or/um	defi/nitely
dark/ness	de/caf/fein/ated	dec/or/ous	defi/ni/tion
dark/room	de/can/ter	de/coy	de/flate
dar/ling	de/cap/it/ate	de/crease	de/flect
dart/board	de/cath/lon	de/cree	de/fo/li/ate
dash/board	de/cay	de/crepit	de/formed
dash/ing	de/cease	ded/i/cate	de/form/ity
date/less	de/ceased	ded/i/ca/tion	de/fraud
daugh/ter	de/ceit	de/duce	de/fray
daunt/less	de/ceive	de/duct	de/freeze
dav/en/port	De/cem/ber	de/duc/tion	de/frost
day/break	de/cent	de/face	de/funct
day/dream	de/cen/tral/ize	defa/ma/tion	de/fuse
day/light	de/cep/tion	de/fama/tory	de/gen/er/ate
day/time	de/cep/tive	de/fault	de/grad/ation
daz/zle	dec/ibel	de/fault/er	de/grad/ing
dea/con	de/cide	de/feat	de/gree
de/ac/ti/vate	de/cid/edly	de/feat/ism	de/hy/drate
dead/line	de/cidu/ous	de/feat/ist	de/ity
dead/lock	deci/mal	de/fe/cate	de/jec/ted
dead/pan	deci/mate	de/fect	de/ject/edly
deaf/ness	de/cipher	de/fec/tion	de/jec/tion
deal/ings	de/cis/ion	de/fec/tive	de/lay
death/bed	de/cis/ive	de/fec/tor	de/lec/table
death/trap	deck/chair	de/fence	del/eg/ate
dE9/bE2cle	de/claim	de/fense (US)	dele/ga/tion
de/bar	de/clare	de/fend	de/lete

Hyphen

de/le/tion	dem/on/strate	de/port/ment	des/cen/dant
de/let/eri/ous	dem/on/stra/tion	de/pose	des/cent
de/lib/er/ate	dem/on/stra/tor	de/pos/it	de/scribe
de/lib/er/ation	de/moral/iz/ation	de/pos/ition	de/scrip/tion
deli/cacy	de/mor/al/ize	de/posi/tor	de/scrip/tive
deli/cate	de/mur	de/posi/tory	de/sec/rate
de/li/ca/tes/sen	de/mure	de/pot	de/sert (abandon)
de/li/cious	den/drite	de/praved	des/ert (dry region)
de/light	de/nial	de/pre/cate	de/ser/ted
de/light/ful	deni/grate	de/pre/ci/ate	de/ser/ter
de/lin/eate	den/izen	de/pre/ci/ation	de/serve
de/lin/quency	Den/mark	dep/re/dation	de/ser/vedly
de/lin/quent	de/nom/in/ation	de/press	de/ser/ving
de/li/ri/ous	de/nom/in/ator	de/pres/sant	de/sic/cate
de/li/rium	de/note	de/pres/sing	de/sign
de/liver	de/nounce	de/pres/sion	des/ig/nate
del/phin/ium	den/sity	dep/ri/va/tion	de/sir/able
de/lude	den/tist	de/prive	de/sire
de/luge	den/tures	de/pu/ta/tion	de/sist
dema/gogue	de/nun/ci/ation	de/pute	desk/top
de/mand	de/odor/ant	de/puty	des/ol/ate
de/mand/ing	de/odor/ize	de/rail	des/ola/tion
de/mar/ca/tion	de/part	de/rail/ment	des/pair
de/mean/our	de/part/ment	de/ranged	des/per/ate
de/men/ted	de/part/ure	der/el/ict	des/per/ation
dem/er/ara	de/pend	de/res/tric/ted	des/pic/able
demi/john	de/pend/able	de/ride	des/pise
de/mil/it/ar/ize	de/pend/ant	de/ris/ible	des/pite
de/mise	de/pend/ency	de/ris/ion	de/spoil
de/mister	de/pend/ent	de/ris/ive	des/pond/ency
de/mo/bil/ize	de/pict	de/ris/ory	des/pond/ent
de/moc/racy	de/pila/tory	de/riva/tive	des/pot
demo/crat	de/plete	de/rive	des/potic
demo/cratic	de/plor/able	der/ma/ti/tis	des/sert
demog/raphy	de/plore	de/roga/tory	des/tin/ation
de/mol/ish	de/ploy	der/rick	des/tine
demo/lition	de/popu/late	der/rin/ger	des/tiny
de/mon	de/port	des/cant	des/ti/tute
dem/on/strable	de/por/ta/tion	des/cend	

Hyphen

des/troy	de/vel/oper	di/ary	di/let/tante
des/troyer	de/vel/op/ment	di/as/tole	di/li/gence
de/struc/tion	de/viate	dia/tribe	di/li/gent
des/truc/tive	de/vice	di/chot/omy	di/lute
des/ul/tory	de/vil	di/coty/le/don	di/men/sion
de/tach	de/vil/ish	dic/tate	di/men/sional
de/tach/able	de/vi/ous	dic/ta/tor/ial	di/min/ish
de/tach/ment	de/vise	dic/ta/tor/ship	di/minu/endo
de/tail	de/void	dic/tion	dim/in/ution
de/tain	de/vol/ution	dic/tion/ary	dim/inu/tive
de/tainee	de/volve	di/dac/tic	dim/ness
de/tect	de/vote	did/dle	dim/ple
de/tec/tion	de/vo/tion	did/geri/doo	dingi/ness
de/tec/tive	de/vour	die/sel	din/ner
de/tec/tor	de/vout	dif/fer	di/no/saur
dE9/tente	dex/ter/ity	dif/fer/ence	dio/cese
de/ten/tion	dia/betes	dif/fer/ent	di/ode
de/ter	dia/betic	dif/fer/en/tial	di/ox/ide
de/ter/gent	dia/bol/ical	dif/fer/en/ti/ate	diph/theria
de/teri/or/ate	dia/dem	dif/fi/cult	diph/thong
de/teri/or/ation	di/ag/nose	dif/fi/dence	dip/loma
de/ter/min/ation	di/ag/nosis	dif/fi/dent	dip/lo/macy
de/ter/mine	di/ag/nos/tic	dif/frac/tion	dip/lo/matic
de/ter/rent	di/ag/onal	dif/fuse	dip/lo/ma/tist
de/test	dia/gram	di/gest	dip/so/mania
de/test/able	dia/gram/matic	dig/ger	dip/so/ma/niac
det/on/ate	dia/lect	dig/ging	di/rect
det/on/ation	dia/lec/tic	di/git	di/rection
det/on/ator	dial/ling	di/gi/talis	di/rectly
de/tour	dia/logue	dig/ni/fied	di/rect/ness
de/tract	dia/meter	dig/nit/ary	di/rec/tor
det/ri/ment	dia/met/ri/cally	dig/nity	di/rec/tory
det/ri/men/tal	dia/mond	di/gress	di/ri/gible
deu/ter/ium	di/an/thus	di/gres/sion	dis/ab/il/ity
de/valu/ation	dia/per (US)	di/hed/ral	dis/ad/van/tage
de/value	dia/phan/ous	di/lap/id/ated	dis/ad/van/ta/geous
de/vas/tate	dia/phragm	di/late	dis/af/fec/ted
de/vas/ta/tion	diar/rhoea diar/rhea (US)	dil/at/ory	dis/agree
de/velop		dil/emma	

Hyphen

dis/agree/able	dis/con/cert	dis/fran/chise	dis/miss
dis/agree/ment	dis/con/cer/ting	dis/gorge	dis/mount
dis/al/low	dis/con/nect	dis/grace	dis/obe/dience
dis/ap/pear	dis/con/so/late	dis/grace/ful	dis/obe/dient
dis/ap/pear/ance	dis/con/tent	dis/gruntled	dis/obey
dis/ap/point	dis/con/tinue	dis/guise	dis/order
dis/ap/point/ing	dis/con/tinu/ous	dis/gust	dis/or/gan/ize
dis/ap/point/ment	dis/cord	dis/gust/ing	dis/ori/en/tate
dis/ap/proval	dis/cor/dant	dis/har/mony	dis/own
dis/ap/prove	dis/co/thEsque	dish/cloth	dis/par/age
dis/ap/prov/ingly	dis/count	dis/hear/ten	dis/par/ate
dis/arm	dis/cour/age	dish/ev/elled	dis/pas/sion/ate
dis/arma/ment	dis/cour/age/ment	dis/hon/est	dis/patch
dis/arm/ing	dis/cour/ag/ing	dis/hon/our	dis/pel
dis/ar/range	dis/course	dis/honor (US)	dis/pen/sary
dis/ar/ray	dis/cour/teous	dis/hon/our/able	dis/pen/sation
dis/as/ter	dis/cour/tesy	dish/washer	dis/pense
dis/as/trous	dis/cover	dis/il/lu/sion	dis/perse
dis/band	dis/credit	dis/il/lu/sion/ment	dis/per/ser
dis/belief	dis/credit/able	dis/in/cen/tive	dis/pir/ited
dis/be/liever	dis/creet	dis/in/clin/ation	dis/place
dis/bud	dis/crep/ancy	dis/in/clined	dis/place/ment
dis/burse	dis/cre/tion	dis/in/fect	dis/play
dis/card	dis/crim/in/ate	dis/in/fec/tant	dis/please
dis/cern	dis/crim/in/ation	dis/in/gen/uous	dis/pleas/ure
dis/cern/ible	dis/cus	dis/in/herit	dis/pos/able
dis/charge	dis/cuss	dis/in/te/grate	dis/pose
dis/ciple	dis/cus/sion	dis/in/te/gration	dis/pos/sess
dis/cip/lin/arian	dis/dain	dis/in/ter	dis/pro/por/tion
dis/cip/lin/ary	dis/dain/ful	dis/in/ter/ested	dis/pro/por/tion/ate
dis/cip/line	dis/ease	dis/jointed	
dis/claim	dis/em/bark	dis/like	dis/prove
dis/claimer	dis/en/chan/ted	dis/lo/cate	dis/pute
dis/close	dis/en/chant/ment	dis/lo/cation	dis/qualify
dis/clos/ure	dis/en/gage	dis/lodge	dis/quiet
dis/col/our	dis/en/tangle	dis/loyal	dis/re/gard
dis/col/or (US)	dis/fav/our	dis/mal	dis/re/pair
dis/com/fit	dis/fav/or (US)	dis/mantle	dis/repu/table
dis/com/fort	dis/fig/ure	dis/may	dis/re/pute

Hyphen

dis/re/spect	dis/tri/bute	dog/gerel	doubt/less
dis/re/spect/ful	dis/tri/bu/tion	dog/ma	dough/nut
dis/rupt	dis/tribu/tive	dog/watch	dove/cote
dis/rup/tion	dis/tribu/tor	dol/drums	dove/tail
dis/sat/is/fac/tion	dis/trict	dole/ful	dow/ager
dis/sat/is/fied	dis/trust	dol/lar	dowel/ling
dis/sect	dis/turb	dol/lop	down/cast
dis/sem/in/ate	dis/use	dol/or/ous	down/fall
dis/sen/sion	dit/to	dol/phin	down/grade
dis/sent	dit/ty	dol/phin/ar/ium	down/hearted
dis/ser/ta/tion	di/ur/etic	do/main	down/hill
dis/ser/vice	di/van	dom/estic	down/pour
dis/si/dent	di/verge	do/mes/ti/cated	down/right
dis/simi/lar	di/ver/gence	dom/es/ti/city	down/stairs
dis/si/pate	di/verse	domi/ciled	down/stream
dis/si/pa/tion	di/ver/sity	dom/in/ant	down/town
dis/so/ci/ate	di/version	dom/in/ate	down/trodden
dis/so/lute	di/vide	dom/in/eer	down/wards
dis/solve	di/vi/dend	dom/in/ion	dra/co/nian
dis/suade	di/vine	dom/ino	drag/net
dis/tance	divin/ity	do/nate	dra/gon
dis/taste	di/vis/ible	don/key	dra/gon/fly
dis/taste/ful	di/vi/sion	do/nor	dra/goon
dis/tem/per	di/vis/ive	door/keeper	dra/matic
dis/tend	di/vorce	door/knob	drama/tist
dis/til	di/vor/cee	door/man	drama/tize
dis/til/lery	di/vulge	door/mat	dras/tic
dis/tinct	diz/zi/ness	door/step	drain/age
dis/tinc/tive	do/cile	door/way	drain/pipe
dis/tinctly	dock/yard	dor/mant	dres/sage
dis/tin/guish	doc/tor	dor/mer	dres/ser
dis/tin/guish/able	doc/tor/ate	dor/mit/ory	dress/maker
dis/tort	doc/trin/aire	dor/mouse	drift/wood
dis/tor/tion	doc/tri/nal	dor/sal	drink/able
dis/tract	doc/trine	do/sage	drip/ping
dis/trac/tion	docu/ment	doss/house	drom/ed/ary
dis/traught	docu/men/tary	dos/sier	drop/ping
dis/tress	dod/der	do/tage	drowsi/ness
dis/tres/sing	do/deca/he/dron	doubt/ful	drudg/ery

drug/gist	dy/namo	econ/omy	eight/een
drum/lin	dyn/asty	ec/stasy	eight/eenth
drum/mer	dys/en/tery	ec/to/plasm	eigh/ti/eth
drum/stick	dys/func/tion	ecu/men/ical	ei/stedd/fod
dry/ness	dys/lexia	ec/zema	ejacu/late
du/al/ism	dys/lexic	ed/ible	ejec/tor
dub/bin	dys/pep/sia	edi/fice	elab/or/ate
du/bi/ous	dys/pep/tic	edi/tor	elas/tic/ity
du/bious/ness	dys/trophy	edi/tor/ial	el/bow
duch/ess	ear/ache	edu/cate	el/der
duck/ling	ear/drum	edu/ca/tion	el/der/berry
duc/tile	ear/mark	edu/ca/tional	el/ect
duf/fel duf/fle	ear/phone	ef/face	elec/tion
dumb/bell	ear/ring	ef/fect	elec/toral
dumb/found	ear/shot	ef/fec/tive	elec/tor/ate
dump/ling	earn/est	ef/fem/in/ate	elec/tric
dun/ga/rees	earn/ings	ef/fer/vesce	elec/tri/cal
dun/geon	earth/en/ware	ef/fer/ves/cence	elec/tri/cian
duo/denal	earth/quake	ef/fi/ca/cious	elec/tri/city
duo/denum	ear/wig	ef/fi/ci/ency	elec/tri/fi/cation
du/plex (US)	east/bound	ef/ficient	elec/tro/cute
du/pli/cate	east/ern	ef/figy	elec/troly/sis
du/pli/ca/tion	east/wards	ef/flor/esce	elec/tron
du/pli/ca/tor	eat/ables	ef/flu/ent	elec/tronic
du/pli/city	eaves/drop	ef/fort	ele/gant
dur/able	ebul/li/ent	ef/front/ery	ele/giac
dur/ability	ec/cen/tric	ef/fus/ive	ele/ment
dura/tion	ec/cen/tri/city	egal/it/ar/ian	ele/men/tary
dur/ess	ec/cle/si/ast/ical	egg/cup	ele/phant
dur/ing	ech/elon	egg/plant	ele/vate
dust/bin	echo/lo/ca/tion	egg/shell	ele/va/tion
dust/man	ec/lamp/sia	egg/timer	ele/va/tor
dust/pan	ec/lec/tic	ego/cen/tric	el/even
duti/able	ec/lipse	ego/ism	eli/cit
duti/ful	eco/logi/cal	ego/ist	eli/gible
dy/ing	eco/logy	ego/tism	elim/in/ate
dy/nam/ic	econ/omic	ego/tist	elim/in/ation
dy/nam/ics	econ/om/ics	egre/gi/ous	el/lipse
dy/na/mite	econ/omize	eider/down	elo/cu/tion

Hyphen

Hyphen

elong/ate	em/ery	en/cour/age/ment	en/igma
elo/quence	emi/grant	en/croach	en/ig/matic
elo/quent	emi/grate	en/crust	en/joy
elu/ci/date	emi/nence	en/cyc/lical	en/joy/able
elu/sive	emi/nently	en/cyc/lo/pae/dia	en/joy/ment
ema/ci/ated	emol/li/ent	en/cyc/lo/pe/dia	en/large
em/an/ate	emolu/ment	en/dan/ger	en/large/ment
em/an/ci/pate	emo/tion	en/deav/our	en/lighten
em/an/ci/pa/tion	emo/tive	en/dev/or (US)	en/light/en/ment
em/balm	em/peror	en/demic	en/list
em/bank/ment	em/pha/sis	en/dive	en/mity
em/bar/go	em/pha/size	end/less	enor/mous
em/bark	em/phatic	en/dorse	en/quire
em/bar/ka/tion	em/pire	en/dow	en/rich
em/bar/rass	em/piri/cal	en/dow/ment	en/rol en/roll (US)
em/bar/rass/ment	em/ploy	en/dure	en/rol/ment
em/bassy	em/ploy/ment	end/ways	en/roll/ment (US)
em/bat/tled	em/por/ium	en/emy	en/semble
em/bed	em/power	en/er/getic	en/sign
em/bel/lish	em/press	en/er/geti/cally	en/slave
em/bers	emu/late	en/ergy	en/sue
em/bez/zle	emul/sion	en/er/vate	en/sure
em/bez/zle/ment	en/able	en/fil/ade	en/tab/la/ture
em/bit/tered	en/act	en/fold	en/tail
em/blem	en/amel	en/force	en/tangle
em/bodi/ment	en/am/oured	en/fran/chise	en/tangle/ment
em/body	en/camped	en/gage	en/ter
em/boss	en/camp/ment	en/gage/ment	en/ter/itis
em/brace	en/cap/su/late	en/gen/der	en/ter/prise
em/bro/ca/tion	en/case	en/gine	en/ter/tain
em/broi/der	en/ceph/al/itis	en/gin/eer	en/ter/tainer
em/bryo	en/chan/ting	Eng/land	en/ter/tain/ment
em/bry/onic	en/cir/cle	Eng/lish/man	en/thrall
emen/da/tion	en/clave	Eng/lish/woman	en/thral/ling
em/er/ald	en/close	en/grave	en/throne
emer/gency	en/com/pass	en/gra/ving	en/thuse
emer/gent	en/core	en/grossed	en/thu/si/asm
emer/itus	en/coun/ter	en/gulf	en/thusi/ast
emer/sion	en/cour/age	en/hance	en/thusi/astic

Hyphen

en/tice	epi/lep/tic	es/cal/ate	eu/logy
en/tire	epi/logue	es/cal/ator	eu/logize
en/tirety	epis/copal	es/cap/ade	eu/nuch
en/title	epis/co/pa/lian	es/cape	eu/phem/ism
en/tity	epi/sode	es/capee	eu/phoria
en/to/mol/ogy	epi/taph	es/cape/ment	eu/reka
en/tour/age	epi/thet	es/carp/ment	Eur/ope
en/trails	epit/ome	es/cort	Euro/pean
en/trance	epit/om/ize	Es/kimo	eu/than/asia
en/tranc/ing	equ/able	eso/phagus (US)	evacu/ate
en/trant	equal/ity	eso/teric	evacu/ation
en/treat	equal/ize	es/pal/ier	cvalu/ate
en/treat/ing	equan/im/ity	es/pec/ial	evalu/ation
en/trench	equa/tor/ial	es/pion/age	evan/es/cent
en/tre/pre/neur	eques/trian	es/plan/ade	evan/gel/ical
en/tre/pren/eur/ial	equi/dis/tant	es/presso	evan/gel/ist
en/trust	equi/lat/eral	es/say	evap/or/ate
en/twine	equi/lib/rium	es/sence	evap/or/ation
enu/mer/ate	equi/noc/tial	es/sen/tial	eva/sion
enun/ci/ate	equi/nox	es/tab/lish	evas/ive
en/velop	equip/ment	es/tab/lish/ment	even/ing
en/vel/ope	equi/table	es/tate	even/song
en/vi/able	equi/val/ent	es/teem	event/ful
en/vi/ous	equivo/cal	es/tim/able	even/tual
en/viron/ment	equi/vo/cate	es/tim/ate	eventu/al/ity
en/vi/rons	erad/ic/ate	es/tim/ation	ever/green
en/vis/age	erect/ile	es/trange	ever/lasting
en/voy	erec/tion	es/tu/ary	every/body
en/zyme	er/go/nomics	et/cet/eras	every/day
epaul/ette	er/mine	eter/nal	every/one
eph/em/eral	erog/en/ous	eter/nity	every/thing
epi/carp	er/rand	eth/er/eal	every/where
epi/centre	er/ratic	eth/ics	evic/tion
epi/cure	er/rati/cally	eth/nic	evi/dence
epi/demic	er/ratum	eth/nol/ogy	evi/dently
epi/der/mis	er/ron/eous	eti/quette	evis/cer/ate
epi/glot/tis	eru/dite	ety/mol/ogy	evoc/a/tive
epi/gram	eru/di/tion	eu/cal/yptus	evo/lu/tion
epi/lepsy	erup/tion	euch/ar/ist	ex/acer/bate

Hyphen

ex/acer/ba/tion	ex/cre/ment	ex/on/er/ate	ex/pli/cit
ex/acti/tude	ex/cres/cence	ex/on/er/ation	ex/plode
ex/ag/ger/ate	ex/creta	ex/or/bit/ant	ex/ploit
ex/ag/ger/ation	ex/crete	ex/or/cism	ex/ploi/ta/tion
ex/al/ta/tion	ex/cru/ci/at/ing	ex/or/cize	ex/plore
ex/alted	ex/cur/sion	ex/otic	ex/plora/tion
ex/amine	ex/cus/able	ex/pand	ex/plora/tory
ex/am/inee	ex/cuse	ex/panse	ex/plo/sion
ex/ample	ex-di/rec/tory	ex/pan/sion	ex/plo/sive
ex/as/per/ate	ex/ecrable	ex/pan/sive	ex/po/nent
ex/as/per/ation	ex/ecrate	ex/pa/ti/ate	ex/port
ex/cav/ate	ex/ecute	ex/pat/ri/ate	ex/pose
ex/ca/vation	ex/ecu/tion	ex/pect	ex/posE9
ex/ca/va/tor	ex/ecu/tioner	ex/pec/tancy	ex/pos/tu/late
ex/ceed	exec/u/tive	ex/pec/tant	ex/po/sure
ex/cel	exec/u/tor	ex/pec/ta/tion	ex/pound
ex/cel/lence	ex/ec/u/trix	ex/pect/or/ant	ex/press
ex/cept	ex/em/plary	ex/pe/di/ency	ex/pres/sion
ex/cep/tion/able	ex/emp/lify	ex/pe/di/ent	ex/pres/sive
ex/cep/tional	ex/empt	ex/pe/dite	ex/pressly
ex/cerpt	ex/emp/tion	ex/pedi/tion	ex/press/way
ex/cess	ex/er/cise	ex/pedi/tious	ex/pro/pri/ate
ex/ces/sive	ex/ert	ex/pel	ex/pro/pri/ation
ex/change	ex/er/tion	ex/pend/able	ex/pul/sion
ex/chequer	ex/hale	ex/pend/it/ure	ex/pur/gate
ex/cise	ex/haust	ex/pense	ex/quis/ite
ex/cis/ion	ex/hibit	ex/pen/sive	ex/tant
ex/cit/ability	ex/hibi/tion	ex/peri/ence	ex/tem/pore
ex/cit/able	ex/hibi/tion/ist	ex/peri/ment	ex/tem/por/ize
ex/cite/ment	ex/hil/ar/ate	ex/peri/men/tal	ex/ten/sion
ex/claim	ex/hil/ar/ation	ex/pert	ex/ten/sive
ex/clam/ation	ex/hort	ex/per/tise	ex/tent
ex/clude	ex/hume	ex/pire	ex/tenu/at/ing
ex/clu/sion	ex/hu/ma/tion	ex/piry	ex/ter/ior
ex/clu/sive	ex/ile	ex/plain	ex/term/in/ate
ex/com/muni/cate	ex/ist	ex/plan/ation	ex/ter/min/ation
ex/com/muni/ cation	ex/ist/ence	ex/plana/tory	ex/ter/nal
	ex/odus	ex/pletive	ex/tinct
	ex of/fi/cio	ex/plic/able	ex/tinc/tion
			ex/tin/guish

ex/tol	eye/strain	fal/si/fy	fau/cet (US)
ex/tort	eye/wash	fa/mil/iar	fault/less
ex/tor/tion	eye/wit/ness	fam/ili/ar/ity	fa/vour
ex/tor/tion/ate	fab/ric	fam/ili/ar/ize	fa/vor (US)
ex/tra	fab/ri/cate	fam/ily	fa/vour/able
ex/tract	fab/ri/ca/tion	fam/ine	fav/or/able (US)
ex/trac/tion	fa/bu/lous	fam/ished	fa/vour/ite
ex/tra/dite	face/cloth	fam/ous	fav/or/ite (US)
ex/tra/di/tion	face/lift	fan/atic	fear/ful
ex/tran/eous	fa/ce/tious	fan/at/ical	fear/less
ex/tra/ord/in/arily	fa/cial	fan/cier	fear/some
ex/tra/ord/in/ary	fa/cile	fan/dan/go	feas/ible
ex/trap/o/late	fa/cili/tate	fan/fare	feasi/bility
ex/trap/ol/ation	fa/cil/ity	fan/light	feath/er/weight
ex/tra/va/gance	fac/sim/ile	fan/tas/tic	fea/ture
ex/trava/gant	fac/tion	fan/tasy	feb/rile
ex/trava/ganza	fac/tor	far/away	Feb/ru/ary
ex/treme	fac/tory	far/ci/cal	feck/less
ex/trem/ist	fac/tual	fare/well	fec/und
ex/trem/ity	fac/ulty	farm/house	fed/eral
ex/tri/cate	fad/dist	farm/ing	fed/era/tion
ex/tro/vert	fag/got	farm/yard	feeble/ness
ex/trude	Fah/ren/heit	far/rea/ching	feed/back
ex/uber/ance	fail/ure	far/thest	feel/ing
ex/uber/ant	fair/ground	fas/cia	fe/licity
ex/ude	fair/ness	fas/cin/ate	fe/line
ex/ult	fairy/land	fas/cina/tion	fel/low
ex/ult/ant	faith/ful	fas/cism	fel/low/ship
eye/ball	faith/less	fas/cist	fe/male
eye/bath	fal/con	fash/ion	fem/in/ine
eye/brow	fal/la/cious	fash/ion/able	fem/in/in/ity
eye/ful	fal/lacy	fas/tidi/ous	fem/in/ist
eye/lash	fal/len	fa/tal/ism	fe/mur
eye/lid	fal/lible	fat/al/ity	fenc/ing
eye/liner	fall/out	fate/ful	fen/der
eye/piece	fal/low	fa/tigue	fen/nel
eye/shade	false/hood	fat/ten	fer/ment
eye/sight	fal/setto	fat/ten/ing	fer/men/ta/tion
eye/sore	fal/ter	fat/uous	fe/ro/cious

Hyphen

fer/ret	fila/ment	fish/bone	flat/ten
fer/rous	fil/bert	fish/cake	flat/ter
fer/rule	fili/buster	fisher/man	flatu/lence
fer/ry	fili/gree	fish/ery	flat/worm
fer/ry/man	fil/ler	fish/monger	flaut/ist
fer/tile	fil/let	fis/sion	fla/vour fla/vor
fer/til/ity	fil/ter	fis/si/ped	(US)
fer/til/ize	fi/nal	fis/sure	flaw/less
fer/til/izer	fi/nal/ist	fis/tula	fledg/ling
fer/vent	fi/nal/ity	fit/ful	fleet/ing
fer/vour fer/vor	fi/nal/ize	fit/ment	flex/ible
(US)	fi/nale	fit/ness	flexi/bility
fes/ter	fi/nance	fit/ting	flint/lock
fest/ival	fin/an/cial	fix/ation	flip/pant
fes/tive	fin/an/cier	fixa/tive	flip/per
fes/toon	find/ings	fiz/zle out	flir/ta/tion
fet/ish	fin/esse	flab/ber/gast	floc/cose
fet/lock	fin/ger	flac/cid	flood/gate
fet/ter	fin/ger/nail	fla/geo/let	flood/light
feud/al/ism	fin/ger/print	flag/gel/ate	floor/board
fe/ver/ish	fin/ger/tip	flag/pole	floor/cloth
fi/asco	fin/icky	flag/rant	floor/show
fibre/glass	fin/ish	flag/ship	flor/es/cence
fib/ula	fin/ite	flag/stone	flo/ri/bunda
fic/tion	Fin/land	flam/boy/ant	flo/rist
fic/tit/ious	fire/arm	flame/proof	flo/ta/tion
fid/dle	fire/fly	flam/ingo	flo/tilla
fid/el/ity	fire/guard	flam/mable	flot/sam
fid/get	fire/light	flan/nel	flour/ish
field/mouse	fire/man	flap/ping	flour/mill
fields/man	fire/place	flash/back	flower/bed
field/work	fire/proof	flash/bulb	flower/pot
fiend/ish	fire/side	flash/cube	fluc/tu/ate
fierce/ness	fire/war/den	flasg/gun	fluc/tu/ation
fif/teen	fire/wood	flash/gun	flu/ency
fif/ti/eth	fire/work	flash/light	flu/ent
fig/ment	fir/ma/ment	flash/point	fluor/es/cence
fig/ure	first/hand	flat/fish	fluor/escent
fig/ure/head	fis/cal	flat/let	fluor/ide

Hyphen

fluor/ine	for/bade	for/feit	four/some
flus/ter	for/bear/ance	for/gave	four/teen
flu/tist	for/bid	forg/ery	fox/glove
flut/ter	for/bid/ding	for/get	fox/hound
flyi/ng	force/ful	for/get/ful	fox/trot
fly/leaf	force/meat	for/give	frac/tion
fly/over	for/ceps	for/go	frac/tious
fly/past	for/cible	for/got	frac/ture
fly/sheet	fore/arm	for/lorn	fra/gile
fly/weight	fore/bear	form/al	fra/gil/ity
fly/wheel	fore/bo/ding	for/mal/de/hyde	frag/ment
fod/der	fore/cast	for/mat	fra/grance
foe/tus	fore/castle	for/mer	fra/grant
fog/horn	fore/close	for/mid/able	frame/work
fog/lamp	fore/father	for/mula	fran/chise
fo/li/age	fore/fin/ger	for/mu/late	frank/furter
fol/low	fore/front	for/sake	fran/tic
fol/ly	fore/go	for/sythia	fran/ti/cally
fo/ment	fore/gone	forth/coming	fra/ter/nal
fon/dant	fore/ground	forth/right	fra/ter/nity
fond/ness	fore/hand	forth/with	frat/er/nize
fon/due	fore/head	for/ti/fi/cation	frat/ri/cide
food/stuff	fore/leg	for/tify	fraudu/lent
fool/hardy	fore/man	for/ti/tude	freak/ish
fool/ish/ness	fore/most	fort/night	free/hand
fool/proof	fore/noon	fort/ress	free/hold
fools/cap	for/en/sic	for/tu/it/ous	free/lance
foot/ball	fore/runner	for/tu/nate	free/loader
foot/brake	fore/see	for/ti/eth	free/mason
foot/hills	fore/shadow	for/tune	free/way
foot/hold	fore/sight	for/ward	free/wheel
foot/ing	fore/skin	fos/sick	fre/quent
foot/lights	for/est	fos/sil	fre/quency
foot/man	fore/stall	fos/sil/ized	fresh/man
foot/note	fore/taste	fos/ter	fresh/ness
foot/path	fore/tell	foun/da/tion	fresh/water
foot/plate	fore/thought	found/ries	fret/ful
foot/print	for/ever	foun/tain	fret/saw
for/age	fore/word	four/poster	fret/work

Hyphen

fric/tion	fun/gus	gall/stone	gar/ment
Fri/day	fu/nicu/lar	Gal/lup poll	gar/ner
friend/li/ness	fun/nel	ga/lore	gar/net
friend/ship	fun/nily	ga/loshes	gar/nish
frig/ate	fur/nace	ga/lumph	gar/ret
fright/en/ing	furn/ish	gal/van/ize	gar/ri/son
fri/gid	fur/ni/ture	gal/va/nometer	gar/rul/ous
fri/gid/ity	fur/ore	gam/bit	gar/ter
friski/ness	fur/rier	gam/ble	gas/eous
frit/ter	fur/row	gam/bol	gas/ket
fri/vol/ity	fur/ther	game/keeper	gas/mask
friv/ol/ous	fur/ther/more	games/man/ship	gaso/line
friz/zle	fur/ther/most	gam/ma rays	gaso/meter
frog/man	fur/tive	gam/mon	gas/works
frog/march	fusel/age	gam/my	gas/tric
front/age	fu/sil/ier	ga/mut	gas/tro/en/ter/it/is
fron/tier	fu/sil/lade	gan/der	gas/tro/nome
front/is/piece	fu/sion	gang/ling	gas/tro/pod
frost/bite	fu/tile	gang/lion	gat/eau
frost/ily	fu/ture	gang/plank	gate/crash
fru/gal	gab/ar/dine	gan/grene	gate/post
fruit/cake	gad/about	gan/gren/ous	gate/way
fruit/ful	gaf/fer	gang/ster	gather/ing
frump/ish	gain/ful	gang/way	gaunt/let
frus/trate	gain/say	gan/net	gaz/ebo
fuch/sia	ga/lac/tic	gaol/bird	ga/zelle
fuel/ling	gal/axy	gar/age	gaz/et/teer
fu/git/ive	gal/lant	gar/bage	ga/zump
ful/crum	gal/lan/try	gar/ble	gear/box
ful/fil	gal/leon	gar/den	gear/lever
ful/fil/ment	gal/lery	gar/denia	gear/stick
full/ness	gal/ley	gar/den/ing	gear/shift (US)
ful/some	Gal/lic	garde/robe	gear/wheel
fu/mi/gate	gal/li/cism	gar/gan/tuan	gel/at/in(e)
func/tion	gal/ling	gar/goyle	gel/at/in/ous
fun/da/men/tal	gal/li/vant	gar/ish	gel/ding
fun/er/al	gal/lon	gar/land	gel/ig/nite
fun/fair	gal/lop	gar/lic	Gem/ini
fun/gi/cide	gal/lows		gem/stone

gen/darme	ge/ri/at/rics	(US)	god/send
gen/der	ger/mane	glam/or/ize	god/son
genea/lo/gical	Ger/many	glam/or/ous	gog/gle
gen/eal/ogist	ger/mi/cide	glan/du/lar	gold/finch
gen/eal/ogy	ger/min/ate	glass/house	gold/fish
gen/eral	ge/ron/to/logy	glass/ware	gold/smith
gen/er/alis/simo	ger/und	glau/coma	gol/li/wog
gen/er/al/iz/ation	ges/ta/tion	gla/zier	gon/dola
gen/er/ate	ges/ticu/late	glee/ful	good/bye
gen/er/ation	ges/ture	glen/garry	good/ness
gen/er/ator	get/away	glim/mer	good/night
gen/eric	get-to/gether	glis/ten	good/will
gen/er/ous	gey/ser	glit/ter	goose/berry
gen/er/os/ity	gher/kin	glob/ate	gor/geous
gen/esis	gib/ber/ish	globe/trot/ter	gor/illa
gen/et/ics	gib/bet	globu/lar	gorm/less
ge/nial	gib/bon	glob/ule	gos/hawk
gen/ital	gib/lets	glori/ous	gos/ling
gen/it/ive	gid/di/ness	glos/sary	gos/pel
ge/nius	gi/gan/tic	glu/cose	gos/sa/mer
geno/cide	gig/gle	glu/ten	gos/sip
gen/teel	gim/bals	glu/tin/ous	got/ten (US)
gen/til/ity	gim/let	glut/ton	gou/ache
gen/tile	gim/mick	glot/ton/ous	gou/lash
gentle/man	gin/ger	gly/cer/in(e)	gour/mand
gentle/ness	gin/ger/bread	goal/keeper	gour/met
gen/tri/fi/cation	ging/ham	goal/mouth	gov/ern
genu/flect	gin/giv/itis	goal/post	gov/ernor
genu/ine	gin/seng	gob/ble/de/gook	grace/ful
geo/detic	gir/affe	go-/be/tween	grace/ful/ness
geo/graphi/cal	gir/der	gob/let	gra/cious
geo/graphy	girl/friend	gob/lin	gra/di/ent
geo/logi/cal	giz/zard	god/child/ren	grad/ual
geo/logy	gla/cial	god-daugh/ter	grad/uate
geo/met/ri/cal	gla/cier	god/dess	gradu/ation
geo/metry	gla/di/ator	god/father	graf/fiti
ge/ran/ium	gla/di/olus	god/for/saken	gram/mar
ger/bil	glad/ness	god/mother	gram/mati/cal
geria/tri/cian	glam/our glam/or	god/par/ents	gramo/phone

Hyphen

gran/ary	green/grocer	guide/lines	hail/stone
gran/dad	green/house	guile/less	hail/storm
grand/child	green/ish	guil/lot/ine	hair/brush
grand/daugh/ter	greet/ings	gui/tar	hair/cut
gran/deur	greg/arious	gul/let	hair/dres/ser
grand/father	gren/ade	gull/ible	hair/less
grand/par/ents	grey/hound	gul/li/bility	hair/net
grand/son	grey/lag	gum/boot	hair/raising
grand/stand	grid/iron	gump/tion	hair/spring
gran/ite	griev/ance	gurg/ling	hair/style
granu/lar	griev/ous	gus/set	hal/cyon
granu/late	grim/ace	gut/ter	half/wit
gran/ule	grind/ing	gut/tural	hali/but
grape/fruit	grind/stone	guy/rope	hali/tosis
grape/vine	gro/cery	gym/khana	hall/mark
graphi/cal	gro/tesque	gym/nas/ium	hal/low
graph/ite	ground/less	gym/nast	hal/lu/cin/ate
graph/ol/ogy	ground/nut	gym/nas/tics	hal/lu/cin/ation
grass/hopper	ground/sel	gyn/ae/co/logi/cal	hal/lu/cin/atory
grass/land	ground/sheet	gyn/ae/col/ogy	hal/lu/cino/gen
grass/roots	grounds/man	gy/rate	halo/gen
grass/widow	ground/work	gy/ro/scope	hal/ter
grate/ful	growl/ing	hab/eas cor/pus	ham/burger
grati/fi/cation	grub/bi/ness	hab/er/dash/ery	ham/let
grat/ify	grudg/ing	hab/it/able	ham/mer
grat/it/ude	gru/el/ling	habi/tat	ham/mock
gra/tu/itous	grue/some	habi/ta/tion	ham/per
gra/tu/ity	grump/ily	hab/it/ual	hamp/ster
grave/digger	guar/an/tee	hab/itu/ate	ham/string
grave/stone	guar/an/tor	hack/neyed	ham/strung
grave/yard	guar/dian	hack/saw	hand/bag
grav/it/ate	guard/room	had/dock	hand/ball
grav/ity	guards/man	hae/mo/globin	hand/clap
grease/paint	guer(r)/illa	hae/mo/philia	hand/cuff
grease/proof	guess/work	haem/or/rhage	hand/ful
green/ery	guest/house	haem/or/rhoids	han/di/cap
green/finch	guf/faw	hag/gard	handi/craft
green/fly	guid/ance	hag/gis	handi/work
green/gage	guide/book	hag/gle	hand/ker/chief

Hyphen

handle/bar	harm/less	head/light	heir/loom
hand/ler	har/mon/ica	head/line	he/li/an/thus
hand/made	har/mo/nium	head/long	heli/cop/ter
hand/out	har/mony	head/mas/ter	he/lio/trope
hand/rail	har/ness	head/mis/tress	heli/pad
hand/shake	har/poon	head/phones	heli/port
hand/some	harp/si/chord	head/quar/ters	he/lium
hand/spring	har/rier	head/rest	hel/le/bore
hand/stand	har/row	head/room	hel/met
hand/wri/ting	harsh/ness	head/scarf	helms/man
handy/man	har/vest	head/set	help/ful
hang/man	hash/ish	head/ship	help/less
hang/nail	has/sle	head/stone	hemi/sphere
hang/over	has/sock	head/strong	hemi/spheri/cal
han/ker	has/tily	head/way	hem/line
hanky/panky	has/ti/ness	head/wind	hem/lock
han/som	hatch/back	health/ily	hen/bane
hap/haz/ard	hatch/ery	hear/say	hence/forth
hap/less	hat/chet	heart/beat	hench/man
hap/pen	hate/ful	heart/burn	hen/house
hap/pily	haugh/tily	heart/felt	hen/pecked
hap/pi/ness	haul/age	heart/less	hepa/ti/tis
har/angue	haul/ier	heart/search/ing	hep/ta/gon
har/ass	hav/er/sack	hearth/rug	her/ald
har/bin/ger	haw/ker	heat/wave	her/aldic
har/bour	haw/ser	hea/venly	herb/aceous
har/bor (US)	haw/thorn	hea/vi/ness	her/bi/vore
hard/back	hay/fever	heavy/weight	her/biv/or/ous
hard/board	hay/maker	Heb/rew	here/abouts
hard/core	hay/making	hec/tare	here/after
hard/ener	hay/stack	hec/tic	here/with
hard/liner	hay/wire	hec/tor	her/edi/tary
hard/ness	haz/ard	hedge/hog	her/ed/ity
hard/ship	haz/ard/ous	hedge/row	her/esy
hard/work	hazel/nut	hed/on/ist	here/tic
hard/wor/king	head/ache	heed/less	her/itage
hare/bell	head/board	he/gem/ony	her/maph/ro/dite
hari/cot	head/dress	hein/ous	her/meti/cally
har/le/quin	head/land	heir/ess	her/mit/age

Hyphen

her/nia	hind/sight	hom/og/en/ize	hor/ti/cul/ture
hero/ine	hin/ter/land	hom/ol/o/gate	hos/pit/able
hero/ism	hip/pie	homo/sexual	hos/pital
her/pes	hip/po/drome	hom/un/cu/lus	hos/pit/al/ity
her/ring	hip/po/pota/mus	hon/est	hos/tage
her/self	hip/sters	honey/comb	hos/tel
hesi/tant	hire/ling	honey/moon	host/ess
hes/it/ate	hir/sute	honey/suckle	hos/tile
hes/sian	his/tol/ogy	hon/or/ary	hos/til/ity
het/ero/gen/eous	his/torian	hon/our	hot/bed
het/ero/sex/ual	his/tori/cal	hon/our/able	hotch/potch
hex/agon	his/tory	hon/or/able (US)	ho/tel
hey/day	his/tri/onic	hood/lum	hot/house
hi/atus	hoard/ing	hood/wink	hot/plate
hi/ber/nate	hoar/frost	hoo/li/gan	hour/glass
hic/cup hic/cough	hoarse/ness	hope/ful	house/boat
hid/den	hob/nailed	hope/less	house/breaker
hide/bound	hob/nob	hop/field	house/coat
hid/eous	hog/manay	hop/per	house/ful
hier/archi/cal	hogs/head	hop/scotch	house/hold
hier/archy	hold/all	ho/ri/zon	house/keeper
hiero/glyphics	holi/day	ho/ri/zontal	house/maid
high/ball	holi/ness	hor/mone	house/man
high/brow	Hol/land	horn/beam	house/master
high/lands	hol/low	hor/net	house/mistress
high/light	hol/ly	horo/scope	house/room
high/ness	hol/ly/hock	hor/rible	house/warming
high/road	holo/caust	hor/rific	house/wife
high/way	hol/ster	hor/ror	house/work
high/way/man	hom/age	horse/back	hov/er/craft
hi/jack	hom/burg	horse/box	how/ever
hil/ari/ous	home/less	horse/hair	hub/bub
hil/arity	home/sick/ness	horse/man	hulk/ing
hill/billy	home/work	horse/play	hul/la/ba/loo
hill/lock	hom/icide	horse/power	hu/man
hill/side	hom/ily	horse/radish	hu/mane
hin/der	hom/oe/opathy	horae/rider	hu/man/ism
hin/drance	hom/eopathy (US)	horse/shoe	hu/man/it/ar/ian
hind/most	homo/geneous	horse/woman	hu/man/ity

Hyphen

hum/ble/ness	hy/dro/phobia	ideal/istic	im/agin/a/tive
hum/bug	hy/dro/plane	ideal/ize	ima/gine
hum/drum	hy/dro/pon/ics	ident/ical	im/bal/ance
hu/merus	hy/dro/ther/apy	identi/fica/tion	im/be/cile
hu/mid	hy/giene	iden/tify	im/bibe
hu/midi/fier	hy/grom/eter	identi/kit	im/bue
hu/mili/ate	hym/nal	iden/tity	im/it/ate
hum/ming/bird	hy/per/bole	ideo/logi/cal	imi/tat/ive
hu/mour hu/mor (US)	hy/per/crit/ical	ideol/ogy	imi/ta/tor
hump/backed	hy/per/mar/ket	ideo/matic	im/macu/late
hu/mus	hy/per/sen/sit/ive	idio/syn/crasy	im/ma/nent
hunch/back	hy/per/ten/sion	idi/otic	im/ma/ter/ial
hun/dred	hy/phen/ate	idle/ness	im/ma/ture
hun/dred/weight	hyp/no/sis	id/ol/atry	im/meas/ur/able
Hun/gar/ian	hyp/notic	ig/loo	im/me/di/ate
hun/ger	hyp/no/tism	ig/neous	im/me/morial
hun/grily	hyp/no/tize	ig/nite	im/mense
hunts/man	hy/po/chon/dria	ig/noble	im/men/sity
hur/rah hur/ray	hy/po/crisy	ig/no/mi/ni/ous	im/merse
hur/ri/cane	hypo/crite	ig/nora/mus	im/mi/grate
hur/riedly	hy/po/der/mic	ig/nor/ance	im/mi/grant
hurt/ful	hy/po/ten/sion	ig/nor/ant	im/mi/nent
hus/band	hy/pot/en/use	ig/nore	im/mob/ile
hus/bandry	hy/po/ther/mia	il/legal	im/mobility
husk/ily	hy/pothe/sis	il/leg/ible	im/mobilize
huski/ness	hy/po/theti/cal	il/le/git/imate	im/mod/er/ate
hust/ings	hys/ter/ec/tomy	il/li/cit	im/moral
hust/ler	hys/teria	il/lit/er/acy	im/mor/tal
hy/acinth	hys/teri/cal	il/lit/er/ate	im/mor/tal/ity
hy/brid	hys/terics	ill/ness	im/mor/tal/ize
hy/dran/gea	ice/berg	il/lo/gical	im/mov/able
hy/drant	ice/box	il/lu/min/ate	im/mune
hy/draulic	ice/cap	il/lusion	im/mun/ize
hy/dro/elec/tric	ice/field	il/lus/trate	im/mut/able
hy/dro/foil	ice/house	il/lus/tra/tive	im/pact
hy/dro/gen	ici/ness	il/lus/tri/ous	im/pair
hy/drog/ra/pher	icono/clast	im/age	im/pale
hy/droly/sis	ideal/ism	ima/gery	im/pal/pable
	ideal/ist	im/agin/ary	im/part

Hyphen

im/par/tial	im/plant	im/proper	in/can/des/cent
im/pass/able	im/ple/ment	im/pro/pri/ety	in/cap/able
im/passe	im/pli/cate	im/prove	in/ca/paci/tate
im/pas/sioned	im/pli/cit	im/prov/i/dent	in/ca/pa/city
im/pass/ive	im/plore	im/pro/vis/ation	in/car/cer/ate
im/pa/tient	im/ply	im/pro/vise	in/car/nate
im/peach	im/pol/ite	im/pu/dence	in/cau/tious
im/peach/ment	im/poli/tic	im/pru/dent	in/cen/di/ary
im/pec/cable	im/pon/der/ables	im/pu/dent	in/cense
im/pe/cu/ni/ous	im/port	im/pugn	in/cen/tive
im/ped/ance	im/port/ance	im/pulse	in/cep/tion
im/pedi/ment	im/port/ant	im/pu/nity	in/cess/ant
im/pede	im/por/tu/nate	im/pure	in/cest
im/pel	im/por/tune	im/pute	in/ces/tu/ous
im/pend/ing	im/pose	in/ab/il/ity	in/ci/dent
im/pen/et/rable	im/po/sition	in/ac/cess/ible	in/ci/den/tal
im/peni/tant	im/poss/ible	in/ac/cur/acy	in/cin/er/ate
im/per/at/ive	im/pos/tor	in/ac/cur/ate	in/cipi/ent
im/per/cep/tible	im/pos/ture	in/ac/tive	in/cision
im/per/fect	im/po/tence	in/ade/quate	in/cis/ive
im/per/ial	im/po/tent	in/ad/miss/ible	in/cisor
im/per/ial/ist	im/pound	in/ad/ver/tent	in/cite
im/peril	im/pov/er/ish	in/ad/vis/able	in/civ/il/ity
im/peri/ous	im/prac/tic/able	in/alien/able	in/clem/ent
im/per/ma/nent	im/prac/tical	in/ane	in/clin/ation
im/per/me/able	im/pre/cation	in/an/im/ate	in/cline
im/per/son/al	im/pre/cise	in/ap/plic/able	in/clude
im/per/son/ate	im/preg/nable	in/ap/pro/pri/ate	in/clu/sion
im/per/son/ator	im/preg/nate	in/ap/ti/tude	in/cog/nito
im/per/tin/ence	im/pre/sario	in/ar/ticu/late	in/co/her/ent
im/per/ti/nent	im/press	in/ar/tis/tic	in/come
im/per/turb/able	im/pres/sion	in/at/ten/tion	in/coming
im/per/vious	im/pres/sion/ism	in/at/ten/tive	in/com/mu/ni/cado
im/pe/tigo	im/pres/sive	in/aud/ible	in/com/par/able
im/petu/osity	im/prim/atur	in/aug/ur/ate	in/com/pat/ible
im/petu/ous	im/print	in/aus/pic/ious	in/com/pet/ent
im/petus	im/prison	in/born	in/com/plete
im/pinge	im/prob/able	in/bred	in/com/pre/hen/sible
im/plac/able	im/promptu	in/cal/cul/able	

Hyphen

in/con/ceiv/able	in/de/fen/sible	in/dub/it/able	in/fan/tile
in/con/clus/ive	in/de/fin/able	in/duce	in/fan/try
in/con/gru/ous	in/def/in/ite	in/duc/tion	in/fatu/ated
in/con/se/quen/tial	in/del/ible	in/dulge	in/fect
in/con/sid/er/able	in/del/ic/ate	in/dus/try	in/fec/tious
in/con/sid/er/ate	in/dem/nify	in/eb/ri/ate	in/fer
in/con/sis/tent	in/dent	in/ed/ible	in/fer/ence
in/con/sol/able	in/den/tures	in/ef/fable	in/ferior
in/con/spicu/ous	in/de/pen/dent	in/ef/fec/tive	in/feri/or/ity
in/con/stancy	in/des/crib/able	in/ef/fec/tual	in/fer/nal
in/con/stant	in/des/truc/tible	in/ef/fi/cient	in/ferno
in/con/ti/nent	in/de/term/in/able	in/ele/gant	in/fer/tile
in/con/tro/vert/ible	in/de/term/in/ate	in/el/igible	in/fest
in/con/veni/ence	in/dex	in/ept	in/fi/del/ity
in/cor/por/ate	in/di/cate	in/ep/ti/tude	in/fighting
in/cor/rect	in/dict	in/equal/ity	in/fil/trate
in/cor/rig/ible	in/dif/fer/ent	in/equit/able	in/fin/ite
in/cor/rupt/ible	in/di/gen/ous	in/eradi/cable	in/fin/it/esi/mal
in/crease	in/di/gent	in/ert	in/fini/tive
in/cred/ible	in/di/ges/tion	in/ertia	in/firm
in/credu/lous	in/dig/nant	in/es/cap/able	in/firm/ary
in/cre/ment	in/dig/nity	in/es/sen/tial	in/flame
in/crim/in/ate	in/digo	in/es/tim/able	in/flate
in/cu/bate	in/dir/ect	in/ev/it/able	in/fla/tion
in/cu/bus	in/dis/creet	in/ex/act	in/flex/ible
in/cul/cate	in/dis/cretion	in/ex/cus/able	in/flict
in/cum/bent	in/dis/crim/in/ate	in/ex/haust/ible	in/flow
in/cur	in/dis/pen/sable	in/ex/or/able	in/flu/ence
in/cur/able	in/dis/posed	in/ex/pen/sive	in/flu/enza
in/cur/ious	in/dis/put/able	in/ex/peri/enced	in/flux
in/cur/sion	in/dis/sol/uble	in/ex/pert	in/form
in/debted	in/dis/tinct	in/ex/plic/able	in/for/mal
in/de/cent	in/dis/tin/guish/able	in/ex/press/ible	in/form/ant
in/de/ci/pher/able	in/di/vid/ual	in/ex/tric/able	in/for/ma/tion
in/de/cision	in/di/vis/ible	in/fal/lible	in/for/ma/tive
in/de/ci/sive	in/doc/trin/ate	in/fal/li/bility	in/fra/struc/ture
in/dec/or/ous	in/do/lence	in/fam/ous	in/fre/quent
in/deed	in/dom/it/able	in/fant	in/fringe
in/de/fati/gable	in/door	in/fan/ti/cide	in/furi/ate

Hyphen

in/fuse	in/nards	in/set	in/sub/stan/tial
in/geni/ous	in/nate	in/shore	in/suf/fer/able
in/genu/ity	in/ner	in/side	in/suf/fi/cient
in/genu/ous	in/nings	in/si/di/ous	in/su/lar
in/got	in/no/cence	in/sight	in/su/lar/ity
in/grained	in/no/cent	in/sig/nia	in/su/late
in/gra/ti/ate	in/nocu/ous	in/sig/ni/fi/cant	in/su/lin
in/grati/tude	in/nov/ate	in/sin/cere	in/sult
in/gred/ient	in/no/va/tive	in/sin/cerity	in/su/per/able
in/grow/ing	in/no/vator	in/sinu/ate	in/sure
in/habit	in/nu/endo	in/sipid	in/sur/gent
in/hale	in/nu/mer/able	in/sist	in/sur/mount/able
in/her/ent	in/ocu/late	in/sol/ent	in/sur/rec/tion
in/herit	in/of/fen/sive	in/sol/uble	in/tact
in/habit	in/op/er/able	in/sol/vent	in/take
in/hi/bi/tion	in/op/er/ative	in/som/nia	in/tan/gible
in/hos/pit/able	in/op/por/tune	in/spect	in/teger
in/human	in/or/din/ate	in/spec/tor/ate	in/teg/ral
in/hu/man/ity	in/or/ganic	in/spire	in/te/grate
in/im/ical	in/put	in/stab/il/ity	in/teg/rity
in/im/it/able	in/quest	in/stall	in/tel/lect
in/iqui/tous	in/quire	in/stal/ment	in/tel/lec/tual
in/iquity	in/quisi/tive	in/stall/ment (US)	in/tel/li/gence
ini/tial	in/roads	in/stance	in/tel/li/gent/sia
ini/ti/ate	in/rush	in/stant	in/tel/li/gible
ini/ti/at/ive	in/sane	in/stan/ta/neous	in/tem/per/ate
in/ject	in/san/it/ary	in/stead	in/tend
in/ju/di/cious	in/san/ity	in/step	in/tense
in/junc/tion	in/sa/ti/able	in/sti/gate	in/ten/sify
in/jure	in/scribe	in/stil	in/ten/sity
in/just/ice	in/scrut/able	in/stinct	in/ten/sive
ink/ling	in/sect	in/sti/tute	in/tent
ink/well	in/sec/ti/cide	in/sti/tu/tional	in/ten/tion
in/laid	in/se/cure	in/struct	in/ten/tional
in/land	in/sem/in/ation	in/struc/tive	in/ter
in/lay	in/sens/ible	in/struc/tor	in/ter/act
in/let	in/sens/it/ive	in/stru/ment	in/ter/cede
in/mate	in/sep/ar/able	in/stru/men/tal	in/ter/cept
in/most	in/sert	in/sub/ord/in/ate	in/ter/cep/tion

Hyphen

in/ter/ces/sion	in/ter/sperse	in/vali/date	ir/ate
in/ter/change	in/ter/stel/lar	in/valu/able	Ire/land
in/ter/com	in/ter/twine	in/vari/able	iri/des/cent
in/ter/con/tin/ental	in/ter/val	in/vasion	irk/some
in/ter/course	in/ter/vene	in/vec/tive	ironi/cal
in/ter/est	in/ter/view	in/veigle	ir/radi/ate
in/ter/face	in/ter/viewee	in/vent	ir/ra/tional
in/ter/fere	in/ter/weave	in/ven/tive	ir/rec/on/cil/able
in/ter/fer/ence	in/tes/tate	in/ven/tor	ir/re/deem/able
in/ter/im	in/tes/ti/nal	in/ven/tory	ir/re/fut/able
in/ter/ior	in/tes/tine	in/verse	ir/regu/lar
in/ter/ject	in/ti/macy	in/ver/sion	ir/rele/vant
in/ter/lock	in/ti/mate	in/vert	ir/re/li/gious
in/ter/loper	in/tim/id/ate	in/ver/te/brate	ir/rep/ar/able
in/ter/lude	in/tol/er/able	in/vest	ir/re/place/able
in/ter/marry	in/tol/er/ant	in/ves/ti/gate	ir/re/press/ible
in/ter/me/di/ary	in/ton/ation	in/ves/ti/ga/tor	ir/re/proach/able
in/ter/me/di/ate	in/tone	in/ves/ti/ture	ir/re/sist/ible
in/term/in/able	in/toxi/cate	in/vest/ment	ir/res/ol/ute
in/ter/mingle	in/tran/si/gence	in/ves/tor	ir/re/spec/tive
in/ter/mis/sion	in/tran/si/gent	in/vet/er/ate	ir/re/spon/sible
in/ter/mit/tent	in/tran/si/tive	in/vidi/ous	ir/re/triev/able
in/tern	in/tra/venous	in/vi/gil/ate	ir/rev/er/ent
in/ter/nal	in/trepid	in/vig/or/ate	ir/re/ver/sible
in/ter/na/tional	in/tri/cacy	in/vin/cible	ir/re/vo/cable
in/ter/nee	in/tri/cate	in/vis/ible	ir/ri/gate
in/tern/ment	in/trigue	in/vi/ta/tion	ir/ri/tant
in/ter/phone	in/trin/sic	in/vite	ir/ri/tate
in/ter/planetary	in/tro/duce	in/vo/ca/tion	ir/rup/tion
in/ter/play	in/tro/spec/tive	in/voice	iso/bar
in/ter/po/late	in/tro/vert	in/voke	iso/late
in/ter/pose	in/trude	in/vol/un/tary	iso/la/tion
in/ter/pret	in/tru/sion	in/volve	iso/sceles
in/ter/pre/ter	in/tu/ition	in/vul/ner/able	iso/therm
in/ter/reg/num	in/tui/tive	in/ward	iso/tope
in/ter/ro/gate	in/un/date	iod/ine	Is/rael
in/ter/ro/ga/tive	in/ure	ion/ize	is/sue
in/ter/rupt	in/vade	iono/sphere	isth/mus
in/ter/sect	in/valid	iras/cible	it/alic

Hyphen

item/ize
it/in/er/ant
it/in/er/ary
it/self
jab/ber
jack/ass
jack/boot
jack/daw
jack/eted
jack/pot
ja/cuzzi
jag/uar
jail/bird
ja/lopy
jam/boree
jam/ming
jan/itor
Janu/ary
ja/pon/ica
jar/gon
jas/mine
jaun/dice
jav/elin
jaw/bone
jay/walker
jeal/ousy
jeal/ously
jelly/bean
jelly/fish
jeop/ard/ize
jeo/pardy
jer/boa
je/re/miad
jer/kin
jer/sey
jes/ter
jet/sam
jet/ti/son
jew/el/ler

jig/saw
jin/go/ism
jit/ter/bug
jit/ters
job/ber
joc/ular
jocu/lar/ity
joc/und
jodh/purs
jog/ging
jog/trot
join/ery
jol/lity
jot/tings
jour/nal
jour/nal/ese
jour/nal/ism
jour/ney
jov/ial
jovi/ality
joy/ful
joy/less
joy/ride
joy/stick
ju/bil/ant
ju/bilee
judge/ment
ju/di/ca/ture
ju/di/cial
ju/di/ciary
ju/di/cious
jug/ger/naut
jug/gler
jug/ular
juici/ness
juke/box
junc/tion
junc/ture
ju/nior

ju/ni/per
jun/ket
juri/di/cal
jur/is/dic/tion
jur/is/pru/dence
jur/ist
jury/man
just/ice
justi/fi/able
just/ify
just/ness
ju/ven/ile
jux/ta/pose
jux/ta/posi/tion
kal/eido/scope
kami/kaze
kan/garoo
kao/lin
ka/pok
ka/put
kar/ate
katy/did
ke/bab
ked/geree
keep/ing
keep/sake
kel/vin
ken/nel
kerb/stone
curb/stone (US)
ker/chief
ker/nel
kero/sene
kes/trel
ket/chup
ket/tle
ket/tle/drum
key/board
key/hole

key/note
kick/back
kid/nap
kid/nap/ping
kid/ney
kil/ling
kill/joy
kilo/cycle
kilo/gram
kilo/metre
kilo/meter (US)
kilo/watt
ki/mono
kin/der/gar/ten
kin/dle
kind/ness
kin/etic
king/dom
king/cup
king/fisher
king/pin
kin/ka/jou
kin/ship
kip/per
kit/bag
kit/chen
kitch/en/ette
kit/ten
kit/ti/wake
klep/to/mania
knap/sack
knee/cap
knick/er/bock/ers
knick/ers
knight/hood
knit/ting
knit/ware
knob/ker/rie
knock/out

Hyphen

know/ingly	lamp/shade	laugh/ter	leg/ate
know/ledge	land/fall	laun/d(e)rette	lega/tee
ko/ala	land/lady	laun/dro/mat	leg/ation
koo/ka/burra	land/lord	laun/dry	le/gend
ku/dos	land/lubber	laur/eate	leg/gings
Ku/wait	land/mark	lav/at/ory	leg/gy
la/bel	land/owner	lav/en/der	le/gible
la/bor/at/ory	land/scape	lav/ish	le/gib/il/ity
la/bori/ous	land/slide	law/ful	le/gion
la/bour	lan/guage	law/less	le/gis/late
la/bor (US)	lan/guid	law/suit	le/gis/la/ture
lab/ra/dor	lan/guish	law/yer	le/git/im/acy
la/bur/num	lan/guor	lawn/mower	le/git/im/ize
laby/rinth	lan/olin	lax/at/ive	leg/ume
la/cer/ate	lan/tern	lay/about	leis/ure
la/cer/ation	lan/yard	lay/man	lem/on/ade
lach/ry/mose	lap/dog	lay/out	le/mur
lacka/dais/ical	lap/wing	lazi/ness	length/ily
lack/lustre	lar/ceny	lazy/bones	lengthi/ness
lack/luster (US)	lar/der	leader/ship	length/ways
lac/onic	lar/gesse	leafi/ness	le/ni/ency
lac/quer	lar/yn/gi/tis	leaf/let	len/ten
la/crosse	lar/ynx	leak/age	len/til
lac/tate	las/ci/vi/ous	lean/ing	leo/pard
lac/tif/er/ous	lash/ing	lean/ness	leo/tard
lad/der	lassi/tude	leap/frog	lepi/dop/ter/ist
lady/bird	latch/key	learn/ing	lep/rosy
lady/bug (US)	late/comer	lease/hold	les/bian
lady/killer	late/ness	leath/ery	les/see
lady/like	la/tent	Leb/anon	les/sen
lady/ship	lat/eral	lech/er/ous	les/son
la/goon	la/tex	lec/tern	let/down
lam/bast	lati/tude	lec/ture	leth/argy
lamb/skin	lat/rine	led/ger	let/out
la/ment	lat/ter	lee/ward	let/ter
la/ment/able	lat/tice	lee/way	let/ter/box
lam/in/ated	laud/able	left/overs	let/ter/head
lamp/light	lau/da/num	leg/acy	let/ter/press
lam/poon	laugh/able	leg/al/ity	let/tuce

Hyphen

leu/kae/mia	light/ning	li/quor/ice	log/ar/ithm
leu/ke/mia (US)	light/weight	lis/ten	log/book
lever/age	like/able	list/less	log/ger/heads
lev/eret	like/li/hood	lit/any	logi/cal
lev/it/ate	like/ness	lit/er/acy	lo/gis/tics
lev/ity	like/wise	lit/eral	loin/cloth
lexi/co/grapher	li/lac	li/ter/ary	loi/ter
lexi/co/graphy	lim/ber	lit/er/ate	lol/li/pop
lex/icon	lime/light	lit/er/at/ure	lone/li/ness
li/able	lim/er/ick	li/tho/graph	lon/gev/ity
li/aison	lime/stone	li/ti/gant	lon/gi/tude
li/ba/tion	lim/ous/ine	li/ti/gate	long/shore/man
li/bel	limi/ta/tion	li/tig/ious	long/stand/ing
libel/lous	lim/pet	lit/mus	loo/fah
lib/eral	lim/pid	lit/ter	look/out
lib/er/al/ism	limp/ness	lit/tle	loop/hole
lib/er/ate	linc/tus	lit/toral	loose/leaf
li/bido	lin/ear	lit/urgy	lo/qua/cious
lib/rary	lines/man	live/li/hood	lo/quacity
lib/retto	lin/ger	live/li/ness	lord/li/ness
li/cence	lin/gerie	liv/ery	lord/ship
li/cense	lin/guist	live/stock	lo/tion
li/cen/ti/ate	lini/ment	liz/ard	lot/tery
li/cen/ti/ous	lin/ing	loath/some	loud/ness
li/chen	link/age	lob/ster	loud/speaker
lic/orice (US)	link/man	lo/cale	lour/ing
lieu/te/nant	lin/net	lo/cal/ity	lov/able
life/belt	li/no/leum	lo/cate	love/li/ness
life/boat	lin/seed	lock/out	love/sick
life/guard	lin/tel	lock/smith	low/brow
life/jacket	lion/ess	lock/up	low/down
life/less	lip/stick	lo/co/mo/tion	lower/ing
life/like	lique/fac/tion	lo/co/mo/tive	low/land
life/long	li/quefy	lo/cust	loy/ally
life/time	li/queur	lode/stone	loy/alty
liga/ment	li/quid	lodg/ing	loz/enge
liga/ture	li/qui/date	lo/ess	lub/ri/cant
light/house	li/quid/ity	lofti/ness	lub/ri/cate
light/ness	li/qui/dizer	lo/gan/berry	lu/cerne

Hyphen

lu/cid	mad/house	main/ten/ance	mana/gerial
luc/ra/tive	mad/man	mais/on/ette	man/da/rin
lu/di/crous	mad/ness	ma/jes/tic	man/date
lug/gage	ma/donna	ma/jesty	man/dible
lug/hole	mad/ri/gal	ma/jor/ette	man/do/lin
lu/gu/bri/ous	mael/strom	ma/jor/ity	man/fully
luke/warm	maes/tro	make/shift	man/gan/ese
lul/laby	mag/a/zine	make/weight	man/ger
lum/bago	ma/genta	mala/chite	man/grove
lum/ber	mag/got	mal/ad/jus/ted	man/handle
lum/ber/jack	ma/gic	mal/adroit	man/hole
lum/in/ous	ma/gis/ter/ial	mal/ady	man/hood
lun/acy	ma/gis/trate	mal/aise	mani/cure
lun/cheon	mag/nan/im/ity	mal/a/prop/ism	mani/curist
lunch/time	mag/nani/mous	mal/aria	mani/fest
lu/pin	mag/nate	Ma/lay/sia	mani/fes/ta/tion
lus/cious	mag/nes/ium	mal/ed/ic/tion	mani/festo
lus/trous	mag/net	mal/ev/ol/ence	mani/fold
lux/uri/ance	mag/net/ism	mal/for/ma/tion	man/ipu/late
lux/uri/ate	mag/net/ize	mal/func/tion	man/li/ness
lux/uri/ously	mag/neto	mal/ice	man/ne/quin
lux/ury	mag/ni/fi/cation	ma/lign	man/ner
lyri/cism	mag/ni/fi/cent	ma/lig/nancy	man/nish
ma/cabre	mag/nify	ma/lin/ger	man/oeuvre
ma/car/oni	mag/ni/tude	mal/lard	man/euver (US)
ma/car/oon	mag/nolia	mal/le/able	man/power
ma/caw	mag/num	mal/let	man/sard
ma/cerate	mag/pie	mal/low	man/slaugh/ter
ma/chete	ma/hog/any	mal/nu/tri/tion	man/sion
mach/in/ation	mai/den	mal/odor/ous	man/tel/piece
ma/chine	mai/den/hair	mal/prac/tice	man/tle
ma/chin/ery	mail/bag	mal/treat	man/ual
ma/chin/ist	mail/box	mam/mal	man/u/fac/ture
mack/erel	mail/man	mam/mary gland	man/ure
mack/in/tosh	main/land	mam/moth	man/u/script
mac/ro/bio/tic	main/spring	man/acle	map/ping
mad/cap	main/stay	man/age	mara/thon
mad/den	main/stream	man/age/ment	mar/aud
ma/deira	main/tain	man/ager/ess	mar/auder

Hyphen

mar/ble	mar/vel	ma/ter/nal	meas/ure/ment
mar/chion/ess	mar/vel/lous	ma/ter/nity	meas/ure
mar/gar/ine	mar/zi/pan	math/ema/tician	mech/anic
mar/gin	mas/cara	math/e/matics	mech/an/ics
mar/ginal	mas/cot	mat/inée	mech/an/ism
mar/guer/ite	mas/cu/line	mat/ins	mech/an/ize
mari/gold	maso/chism	mat/ri/arch	med/al/lion
mari/juana	maso/chist	mat/ri/cide	med/dle
mar/ina	ma/son	mat/ricu/late	me/dia
mar/in/ade	mas/onic	mat/ri/mo/nial	me/di/ate
mar/ine	mas/onry	mat/ri/mony	me/di/ator
mar/ion/ette	mas/quer/ade	mat/rix	med/ical
mar/ital	mas/sacre	mat/ron	me/di/cated
mari/time	mas/sage	mat/ter	me/di/cinal
mar/joram	mas/sif	mat/ting	me/di/cine
mark/edly	mas/sive	mat/tress	me/di/eval
mar/ket	mas/tec/tomy	ma/ture	me/di/ocre
mar/ket/able	mas/ter	maud/lin	me/di/oc/rity
marks/man	mas/ter/ful	maun/der	me/di/tate
mar/ma/lade	mas/terly	mau/so/leum	me/dium
mar/mo/set	mas/ter/mind	mav/er/ick	med/lar
mar/mot	mas/ter/piece	mawk/ish	med/ley
mar/oon	mas/ter/stroke	maxi/mize	meek/ness
mar/quee	mast/head	max/imum	meet/ing
mar/quetry	mas/ti/cate	may/day	me/ga/cycle
mar/riage	mas/tiff	may/hem	me/ga/lith
mar/riage/able	mas/titis	may/on/naise	me/ga/lo/mania
mar/row	mas/toid	may/oress	me/ga/phone
mar/ry	mas/tur/bate	may/pole	mega/ton
mar/shal	mata/dor	mea/dow	mel/an/choly
marsh/mallow	match/box	meagre/ness	mel/low
mar/su/pial	match/less	meager/ness (US)	mel/low/ness
mar/ten	match/maker	me/an/der	mel/odic
mar/tial	match/stalk (US)	mean/ing/ful	melo/drama
mar/tin	match/stick	mean/ing/less	melo/dra/matic
mar/tinet	match/wood	mean/ness	mel/odious
mar/tin/gale	ma/ter/ial	mean/time	mel/ody
mar/tini	ma/ter/ial/ist	mean/while	melt/ing
mar/tyr	ma/ter/ial/ize	meas/ur/able	mem/ber

Hyphen

mem/brane
me/men/to
mem/oir
mem/or/able
mem/or/an/dum
mem/or/ial
mem/ory
men/ace
men/ag/erie
men/da/cious
men/da/city
men/di/cant
men/folk
me/nial
men/in/gitis
meno/pause
men/strual
men/stru/ate
mens/wear
men/tal
men/tal/ity
men/tion
men/tor
mer/can/tile
mer/cen/ary
mer/cer
mer/chan/dise
mer/chant
mer/chant/man
merci/ful
mer/ci/less
mer/cury
mere/tri/cious
mer/gan/ser
mer/id/ia<?>
me/ringue
me/rino
mer/it
mer/maid

mer/ri/ment
mer/ry
merry/maker
mes/mer/ize
mes/sage
mes/sen/ger
meta/bolic
met/ab/olism
meta/carpus
me/tal/lic
me/tal/lur/gist
me/tal/work
meta/mor/phose
meta/mor/pho/sis
meta/phor
meta/phori/cal
meta/phy/sics
meta/tarsus
met/eor
met/eoric
met/eor/ite
met/eor/ology
me/thane
met/eor/olo/gist
methy/lated spi/rits
meth/odi/cal
met/icu/lous
met/ri/cal
met/ri/cate
met/ro/nome
met/rop/olis
met/ro/poli/tan
met/tle
Mex/ico
mez/zan/ine floor
mi/asma
Mich/ael/mas
daisy
mi/crobe

mi/cro/cosm
mi/cro/fiche
mi/cro/film
mi/cro/light
mi/cron
mi/cro/phone
mi/cro/scope
mi/cro/wave
mid/day
mid/dle
mid/dle/weight
mid/dling
mid/get
mid/land
mid/night
mid/riff
mid/ship/man
mid/stream
mid/sum/mer
mid/way
mid/wife
mid/winter
mi/graine
mi/grant
mi/grate
mi/gra/tion
mil/dew
mild/ness
mile/age
mile/stone
mi/li/tant
mi/li/tancy
mi/li/tar/ism
mi/li/tary
mi/li/tate
mi/litia
milk/man
mill/pond
mill/stone

mil/len/nium
mil/let
mil/li/gram
mil/li/metre
mil/li/meter (US)
mil/liner
mil/lion
mil/li/pede
mim/icry
mim/osa
min/aret
mince/meat
min/cing
mind/ful
mind/less
mine/field
mine/layer
min/eral
min/er/al/ogist
min/es/trone
mine/sweeper
min/ia/ture
mini/bus
min/im/ize
min/imum
min/ion
mini/skirt
min/ister
min/is/ter/ial
min/is/ter/ing
min/is/try
min/now
min/ster
min/strel
min/uet
min/us/cule
mi/nute (adj)
mi/nute (n)
mi/nute/ness

Hyphen

mi/nu/tiae	mis/giv/ing	mis/un/der/stand	mo/ment
mir/acle	mis/guided	mis/use	mo/men/tary
mir/acu/lous	mis/hap	miti/gate	mo/men/tous
mir/age	mis/in/form	mit/ten	mo/men/tum
mir/ror	mis/in/ter/pret	mix/ture	mon/arch
mis/ad/ven/ture	mis/judge	mne/monic	mon/ar/chic
mis/an/thrope	mis/lay	mo/bile	mon/archy
mis/an/thropic	mis/lead	mo/bil/ity	mon/as/tery
mis/apply	mis/man/age	mo/bil/iz/ation	mon/as/tic
mis/ap/pre/hend	mis/nomer	mo/bil/ize	Mon/day
mis/ap/pre/hen/sion	mis/ogy/nist	moc/casins	mone/tar/ist
mis/ap/pro/pri/ate	mis/place	mock/ery	mone/tary
mis/be/have	mis/print	mock/ing	money/box
mis/be/hav/iour	mis/pro/nounce	mock/ing/bird	money/lender
mis/cal/cu/late	mis/pro/nun/ci/ation	mod/er/ate	mon/gol
mis/car/riage		mod/er/ation	mon/gol/ism
mis/carry	mis/quo/ta/tion	mod/er/ator	mon/goose
mis/cast	mis/quote	mod/ern	mon/grel
mis/cel/lan/eous	mis/read	mod/er/nity	mon/itor
mis/chance	mis/rep/re/sent	mod/ern/ize	mon/key
mis/chief	mis/sal	mod/est	mono/chrome
mis/chiev/ous	mis/sel	mod/icum	mon/ocle
mis/con/cep/tion	mis/shapen	mod/ify	mon/ocu/lar
mis/con/duct	mis/sile	mod/ish	mon/og/amous
mis/con/struc/tion	mis/sing	mod/ulate	mon/og/amy
mis/con/strue	mis/sion	modu/lar	mono/gram
mis/count	mis/sion/ary	mod/ule	mono/graph
mis/creant	mis/sive	mo/hair	mono/lith
mis/cue	mis/spell	moist/ness	mono/logue
mis/deed	mis/state/ment	moist/ure	mono/mania
mis/de/mean/our	mis/sus	mo/lar	mono/nu/cle/osis
mis/de/meanor (US)	mis/take	mo/las/ses	mono/phonic
mis/di/rect	mis/taken	mole/cule	mon/op/ol/ize
mis/er/able	mis/ter	mole/skin	mon/op/oly
mi/ser/li/ness	mis/time	mo/lest	mono/rail
mis/ery	mis/tle/toe	mol/lify	mono/syl/lable
mis/fire	mis/took	mol/lusc	mono/tone
mis/fit	mis/tress	mol/lusk (US)	mon/ot/on/ous
mis/for/tune	mis/trust	mol/ly/coddle	mon/ot/ony

mon/ox/ide	mort/ga/gor	mouth/wash	mu/seum
mon/soon	mor/tice	mouth/water/ing	mush/room
mon/ster	mor/tic/ian	mov/able	mu/sician
mon/stro/sity	mor/tify	move/ment	Mus/lim
mon/strous	mor/tise	mu/cus	mus/lin
mon/tage	mor/tuary	mud/dle	mus/quash
monu/ment	mo/saic	mud/flat	mus/sel
moodi/ness	Mos/lem	mud/guard	mus/tang
moon/beam	mos/quito	muf/fin	mus/tard
moon/light	mo/tel	muf/fle	mus/ter
moon/lit	moth/balls	mug/ging	musti/nes<?>
moon/stone	moth/eaten	mu/latto	mu/tate
moor/ing	moth/er	mul/berry	mu/ti/late
moor/land	moth/er/hood	mule/teer	mu/tin/eer
mo/ped	moth/er/less	mul/let	mu/tin/ous
mor/aine	mo/tif	mul/lion	mu/tiny
mor/ale	mo/tion	mul/ti/col/oured	mut/ter
mor/al/ist	mo/ti/vate	mul/ti/far/ious	mut/ton
mor/al/ity	mo/tive	mul/ti/na/tional	mu/tual
mor/al/ize	mot/ley	mul/tiple	muz/zle
mor/ass	mo/tor	mul/ti/pli/cation	my/opia
mora/tor/ium	motor/bike	mul/ti/pli/city	my/self
mor/bid	motor/boat	mul/ti/ply	mys/teri/ous
mor/bid/ity	motor/cade	mul/ti/racial	mys/tery
mor/dant	motor/car	mul/ti/storey	mys/tic
mori/bund	motor/cycle	mul/ti/tude	mys/ti/cism
morn/ing	motor/ist	mul/ti/tu/din/ous	mys/tify
mo/rocco	motor/ize	mun/dane	mys/tique
mor/ose	motor/way	mu/nici/pal	myth/ol/ogy
mor/phia	mot/tled	mu/nici/pal/ity	myxo/ma/to/sis
mor/phine	mouldi/ness	mu/ni/fi/cence	na/celle
mor/phol/ogy	mould/ing	mu/ni/tions	nag/ging
mor/ris dance	moun/tain	mur/der	nail/brush
mor/sel	mouse/trap	mur/derer	nail-bit/ing
mor/tal	mous/tache	mur/der/ess	naked/ness
mor/tal/ity	mus/tache (US)	mur/der/ous	name/less
mor/tar	mouth/ful	mur/ki/ness	name/sake
mort/gage	mouth/organ	mur/mur	na/palm
mort/ga/gee	mouth/piece	mus/cle	naph/tha

Hyphen

Hyphen

nap/kin	neb/ula	neu/ral/gia	night/shade
nap/ping	nebu/lous	neur/ol/ogist	nim/ble
nar/cis/sus	ne/ces/sary	neur/ol/ogy	nim/bus
nar/cotic	ne/ces/sit/ate	neu/ro/sis	nin/com/poop
nar/rate	ne/ces/sit/ous	neur/otic	nine/pins
nar/ra/tion	ne/ces/sity	neu/ter	nine/teen
nar/ra/tive	neck/band	neu/tral	nine/ti/eth
nar/ra/tor	neck/lace	neu/tral/ity	nip/per
nar/row	neck/tie	neu/tra/lize	nip/ple
na/sal	nec/ro/mancy	neu/tron	ni/trate
nas/ti/ness	nec/tar	never/more	ni/tro/gen
nas/tur/tium	nec/tar/ine	never/the/less	nit/wit
na/tion	needle/point	new/born	nob/ble
na/tion/al/ist	need/less	new/comer	no/bil/ity
na/tion/al/ity	needle/woman	new/fangled	no/ble
na/tion/wide	needle/work	new/ness	noble/man
na/tive	ne/far/ious	news/agent	no/body
na/tiv/ity	ne/gate	news/caster	noc/tur/nal
nat/ter	nega/tive	news/letter	noc/turne
nat/ural	neg/lect	news/man	nod/ule
nat/ur/al/ism	neg/lect/ful	news/paper	noise/less
nat/ur/al/ist	neg/li/gence	news/print	nois/ily
nat/ur/ally	neg/li/gible	news/reel	no/mad
nat/ure	ne/go/ti/ate	news/worthy	no/men/cla/ture
nat/ur/ism	ne/gro	new/ton	nom/inal
nat/ur/ist	neigh/bour	nib/ble	nom/in/ate
naugh/ti/ness	neigh/bor (US)	nice/ness	nom/inee
nau/sea	nei/ther	ni/cety	non/a/gen/arian
nau/seate	neo/lithic	nick/name	non-ag/gres/sion
nau/seous	nep/ot/ism	ni/co/tine	non-al/co/holic
nau/tical	nerve/less/ness	Ni/geria	non/align/ment
nau/ti/lus	nest/ling	nig/gardly	non/chal/ance
navi/gable	net/ball	nig/gle	non/chal/ant
navi/gate	Nether/lands	nig/gling	non/com/bat/ant
navi/gation	nether/most	night/cap	non-com/mis/sioned
navi/gator	net/ting	night/clothes	non-com/mit/tal
Nea/pol/itan	net/tle	night/dress	non-con/form/ist
near/ness	net/work	night/in/gale	non/de/script
neat/ness		night/mare	

Hyphen

non/en/tity	no/tor/iety	nut/shell	ob/ser/va/tory
non/ex/ist/ent	no/tor/ious	nu/tri/ent	ob/serve
non-fic/tion	not/with/standing	nu/tri/ment	ob/ser/ver
non-pay/ment	nour/ish	nu/tri/tious	ob/sess
non/plussed	nour/ish/ment	nu/tri/tive	ob/ses/ive
non-re/fund/able	nov/elty	nuz/zle	ob/so/les/cent
non-resi/dent	No/vem/ber	ny/lon	ob/so/lete
non-re/turn/able	nov/ice	nym/pho/mania	ob/stacle
non/sense	now/a/days	nym/pho/maniac	ob/stet/ric
non/sen/si/cal	no/where	oaf/ish	ob/stet/rician
non-smo/ker	nox/ious	oast/house	ob/stin/ate
non-star/ter	noz/zle	oat/cake	ob/strep/er/ous
non-vio/lence	nu/bile	oat/meal	ob/struct
nor/mal	nu/clear	ob/dur/acy	ob/struc/tive
nor/mal/ity	nu/cleus	ob/dur/ate	ob/tain
north/bound	nu/dism	obedi/ence	ob/trude
north/ern	nu/dist	obedi/ent	ob/tru/sive
north/ward	nu/ga/tory	ob/el/isk	ob/tuse
Nor/way	nug/get	ob/fus/cate	ob/verse
nose/bag	nuis/ance	obit/uary	ob/vi/ate
nose/bleed	nul/lify	ob/ject	ob/vi/ous
nose/dive	num/ber	ob/jec/tion	oc/ca/sion
nose/gay	num/ber/less	ob/jec/tive	oc/cas/ional
nos/tal/gia	numb/ness	ob/jec/tor	oc/ci/dent
nos/tril	numb/skull	ob/late	oc/cult
not/ab/il/ity	num/er/acy	ob/lig/at/ory	oc/cu/pant
not/able	nu/me/ral	ob/lige	oc/cu/pation
not/ary	nu/meri/cal	ob/lig/ing	oc/cupy
no/ta/tion	nu/mer/ous	ob/lique	oc/cur
note/book	nu/mis/mat/ics	ob/lit/er/ate	oc/cur/rence
note/case	nu/mis/ma/tist	ob/liv/ion	ocean/ography
note/paper	nup/tial	ob/long	oc/ta/gon
note/worthy	nurse/maid	ob/nox/ious	oc/tane
noth/ing	nur/sery	obo/ist	oc/tave
noth/ing/ness	nur/sery/man	ob/scene	oc/tavo
no/tice	nur/ture	ob/scure	oc/tet
no/tice/able	nut/case	ob/scur/ity	Oc/to/ber
no/ti/fi/able	nut/crack/ers	ob/sequi/ous	oc/to/gen/ar/ian
no/tify	nut/meg	ob/serv/ance	oc/to/pus

oc/u/lar	om/ni/bus	op/tim/ism	ori/ginal
odd/ment	om/ni/po/tence	op/ti/mist	ori/gin/ate
odi/ous	om/nis/cient	op/ti/mum	ori/gin/ator
odo/meter	om/niv/or/ous	op/tion	ori/ole
odor/ous	on/coming	op/to/metrist (US)	or/na/ment
odour/less	on/er/ous	opu/lence	or/nate
Oed/ipus com/plex	one/self	or/acle	orn/ith/ol/ogist
oeso/phagus	one-up/man/ship	or/ange	orn/ith/ology
of/fal	on/ion	orange/ade	or/phan
off/cut	on/looker	or/ang-ut/ang	or/phan/age
off/fence	on/rush	ora/tion	or/tho/dox
off/fen/sive	on/set	ora/tori/cal	or/tho/graphy
of/fer	on/slaught	ora/torio	or/tho/paedic
of/fice	on/ward	or/bit	os/cil/late
of/fi/cial	opa/city	or/chard	os/ier
of/ficial/ese	opal/es/cent	or/ches/tra	os/mo/sis
of/fi/cious	open/cast	or/ches/trate	os/prey
of/fing	open/ing	or/chid	os/sify
off-li/cence	open/ness	or/chis	os/ten/sible
off/set	op/era	or/dain	os/ten/ta/tious
off/shore	oper/able	or/deal	os/teo/arth/ritis
off/side	oper/ate	or/der	os/teo/path
off/spring	oper/atic	or/der/li/ness	os/tra/cism
off/stage	oper/ative	or/di/nal	os/tra/cize
of/ten	oper/ator	or/di/nance	os/trich
oil/field	oph/thal/mic	or/din/ary	other/wise
oil/rig	oph/thal/mol/ogist	or/din/ation	other/worldly
oil/skin	op/in/ion	ord/nance	ot/ter
oil/slick	op/os/sum	or/gan	ot/to/man
oil/tan/ker	op/po/nent	or/gan/ism	our/selves
oint/ment	op/por/tune	or/gan/ist	out/back
old-fash/ioned	op/por/tun/ist	or/gan/ize	out/bid
ol/fac/tory	op/pose	or/gasm	out/board
oli/garchy	op/po/site	ori/ent	out/break
ol/ive	op/press	ori/ental	out/build/ings
Olym/pic	op/pres/sor	ori/en/tate	out/burst
om/buds/man	op/pro/brium	ori/en/teer/ing	out/cast
om/elette	op/ti/cal	ori/fice	out/cry
om/in/ous	op/tic/ian	ori/gin	out/dated

Hyphen

out/doors	out/wit	over/ride	pa/ci/fism
out/er/most	ova/tion	over/rule	paci/fist
out/fit	over/all	over/run	pa/cify
out/going	over/awe	over/seas	pack/age
out/grow	over/bal/ance	over/seer	pack/ing
out/ing	over/bear/ing	over/shadow	pad/ding
out/land/ish	over/board	over/shoes	pad/dle
out/last	over/cast	over/shoot	pad/dock
out/law	over/charge	over/sight	pad/dy field
out/lay	over/coat	over/sleep	pad/lock
out/line	over/come	over/spend	pae/dia/tri/cian
out/live	over/crowded	over/state	pa/gan
out/look	over/dose	over/step	pag/eant
out/lying	over/draft	over/stuffed	pag/in/ate
out/man/oeuvre	over/draw	over/sub/scribed	pa/goda
out/man/euver (US)	over/eat	over/take	pain/ful
out/moded	over/es/ti/mate	over/tax	pain/kil/ler
out/number	over/ex/posed	over/throw	pain/less
out/patient	over/fed	over/time	pains/taking
out/post	over/flow	over/tones	paint/work
out/pour/ings	over/grown	over/ture	pa/jamas (US)
out/put	over/hang/ing	over/turn	Pak/istan
out/rage	over/haul	over/view	pal/ace
out/ra/geous	over/head	over/ween/ing	pal/at/able
out/rider	over/heat	over/weight	pal/ate
out/right	over/joyed	over/whelm	pa/la/tial
out/set	over/land	over/work	pal/at/ine
out/shine	over/lap	over/wrought	pal/aver
out/side	over/leaf	ovu/late	pale/ness
out/size	over/load	own/er/ship	pal/eo/lithic
out/skirts	over/look	ox/ide	Pal/es/tine
out/smart	over/night	ox/id/ize	pal/ette
out/spo/ken	over/pass	oxy/acet/yl/ene	pal/in/drome
out/stand/ing	over/play	oxy/gen	pal/ing(s)
out/stay	over/power	oy/ster	pal/is/ade
out/vote	over/pro/duc/tion	pace/ma/ker	pall/bearer
out/ward	over/rate	pace/set/ter	pal/let
out/weigh	over/reach	pachy/derm	pal/li/ate
	over/re/act	pa/ci/fier	pal/lia/tive

Hyphen

pal/lid	par/able	par/ish/ioner	pas/sage
pal/lor	para/bola	par/ity	pass/book
pal/mate	para/bolic	par/lance	pas/sen/ger
pal/mis/try	para/chute	par/ley	pas/sion
pal/pable	par/ade	par/lia/ment	pas/sion/ate
pal/pi/tate	para/dise	par/lia/men/tar/ian	pas/sive
pal/try	para/dox	par/lour	pas/siv/ity
pam/pas	par/af/fin	par/lor (US)	pass/over
pam/per	para/gon	pa/ro/chial	pass/port
pamph/let	para/graph	par/ody	pass/word
pana/cea	para/keet	par/ole	pas/tel
pan/ache	par/al/lax	par/oxysm	pas/teur/ize
pan/cake	par/al/lel	par/quet	pas/tiche
pan/chro/matic	par/al/lel/ogram	par/ri/cide	pas/tille
pan/creas	para/lyse	par/rot	pas/time
pan/demic	par/alytic	par/ry	pas/tor
pan/de/mo/nium	para/meter	par/sec	pas/try
pan/der	para/military	par/si/mony	pas/ture
pan/egyric	para/mount	pars/ley	patch/work
pan/el/list	para/noia	pars/nip	pa/tent
pan/nier	par/an/oiac	par/son	pa/ten/tee
pan/oply	par/an/oid	par/take	pa/ter/nal
pan/or/ama	para/pet	par/ting	pa/ter/nity
pan/ta/loons	para/pher/na/lia	par/terre	pa/thetic
pan/theism	para/phrase	par/tial	path/fin/der
pan/ther	para/plegia	par/ti/ci/pant	path/ogen
pan/ties	para/site	par/ti/ci/pate	path/ol/ogy
pan/to/graph	para/sol	par/ti/ci/pa/tory	pa/thos
pan/to/mime	para/trooper	par/ti/ciple	path/way
pan/try	par/boil	par/ticle	pa/tience
pa/pacy	par/cel	par/ti/col/oured	pa/tient
pa/per	parch/ment	par/tic/ular	pat/ina
paper/back	par/don	par/ti/san	pa/tis/serie
paper/chase	par/ent	par/ti/tion	pat/ois
paper/clip	par/en/tage	part/ner	pat/rial
paper/knife	par/en/the/sis	part/ner/ship	pat/ri/arch
paper/weight	pa/ri/ah	part/ridge	pat/ri/cian
pap/rika	pa/ri/etal	par/tur/ition	pat/ri/cide
pa/py/rus	par/ish	pass/able	pat/ri/mony

Hyphen

pat/riot	ped/es/trian	pen/ul/tim/ate	per/jure
pat/riot/ism	pe/dia/trician	pen/um/bra	per/ma/nency
pat/rol	pedi/cure	pen/ury	per/ma/nent
pat/rol/man	pedi/gree	pe/ony	per/man/gan/ate
pat/ron	ped/lar	pep/per	per/me/able
pat/ron/age	peel/ings	pep/per/corn	per/me/ate
pat/ron/ize	peep/hole	pep/per/mill	per/miss/ible
pat/ter	peer/age	pep/per/mint	per/mis/sion
pat/tern	pee/wit	pep/tic	per/mit
pau/city	pej/ora/tive	per/am/bu/lator	per/mu/ta/tion
pau/per	pel/ican	per/ceive	per/ni/cious
pave/ment	pel/let	per/cen/tile	per/nick/ety
pav/il/ion	pel/met	per/cep/tible	per/ox/ide
pay/able	pe/nal	per/cep/tive	per/pen/dic/ular
pay/check	pe/nal/ize	per/co/late	per/pe/trate
pay/load	pen/alty	per/cus/sion	per/pet/ual
pay/master	pen/ance	pere/grine	per/petu/ate
pay/ment	pen/chant	per/emp/tory	per/petu/ity
pay/roll	pen/cil	per/en/nial	per/plex
peace/able	pen/dant	per/fect	per/quis/ite
peace/ful	pen/ding	per/fec/tion	per/se/cute
peace/maker	pen/du/lum	per/fidy	per/se/vere
pea/cock	pen/etrate	per/for/ate	per/sist
pea/nut	pen/etra/tion	per/form	per/sis/tent
pea/sant	pen/guin	per/form/ance	per/son
peb/ble	pe/ni/cil/lin	per/fume	per/son/able
pec/ca/dillo	pen/in/sula	per/func/tory	per/sonal
peck/ish	pen/in/sular	per/haps	per/son/al/ity
pec/tin	peni/tent	peri/lous	per/soni/fi/cation
pec/toral	peni/ten/tiary	peri/meter	per/son/nel
pecu/late	pen/knife	peri/odic	per/spec/tive
pe/cu/liar	pen/ni/less	peri/pat/etic	per/spex
pe/cu/li/arity	penny/worth	peri/pheral	per/spic/acious
pe/cu/ni/ary	pen/sion	peri/phery	per/spic/acity
peda/gogi/cal	pen/sive	peri/scope	per/spi/cu/ity
ped/ant	pen/ta/gon	per/ish	per/spire
ped/an/tic	pen/tag/onal	per/ish/ables	per/suade
ped/dle	pen/tath/lon	peri/ton/itis	per/suas/ive
ped/es/tal	pent/house	peri/winkle	per/tain

Hyphen

per/ti/na/cious	phil/at/ely	pic/colo	pin/afore
per/tin/ent	phil/har/monic	pick/axe	pin/ball
per/turb	Phil/ip/pines	pick/pocket	pin/cers
per/use	phil/is/tine	pic/nic	pin/cush/ion
per/vade	phil/lum/en/ist	pic/to/graph	pine/apple
per/vas/ive	philo/logical	pic/tor/ial	pin/ion
per/verse	philo/logy	pic/ture	pink/eye
per/vert	philo/soph/ical	pictur/esque	pin/nace
pes/sary	philo/sophy	pid/gin	pin/nacle
pes/si/mism	phle/bi/tis	pie/bald	pin/nate
pes/ti/cide	pho/bia	piece/meal	pin/point
pes/til/ence	pho/netic	piece/work	pin/prick
pe/tard	pho/ney	pi/geon	pin/stripe
pe/tite	pho/no/graph	pi/geon/hole	pi/on/eer
pe/ti/tion	phos/phate	piggy/back	pipe/line
pet/rel	phos/phor	piggy/bank	pi/per
pet/rify	phos/phor/es/cence	pig/let	pip/ette
pet/ro/chem/ical	phos/phorus	pig/ment	pi/ping
pet/ro/dollar	photo/copy	pig/skin	pi/quant
pet/rol	photo/elec/tric	pig/sty	pi/ranha
pet/ro/leum	photo/genic	pig/tail	pi/rate
pet/ti/coat	photo/graph	pike/man	pi/rati/cal
pet/ti/ness	photo/stat	pil/as/ter	pir/ou/ette
pet/u/lant	phras/eology	pil/chard	Pis/ces
pe/tunia	phren/ol/ogy	pile/driver	pis/tachio
pew/ter	phys/ical	pil/fer	pis/til
phal/anx	phys/ician	pil/grim	pis/tol
phal/lus	phys/ics	pil/grim/age	pis/ton
phan/tom	physi/og/nomy	pil/lage	pit/cher
phar/ma/ceu/ti/cal	physi/ology	pil/lar	pitch/fork
phar/ma/cist	physio/ther/apy	pill/box	pit/eous
phar/ma/co/poeia	phys/ique	pil/lion	pit/fall
phar/macy	pian/ist	pil/low	pit/head
phar/yn/gitis	pi/ano	pil/low/case	piti/able
phar/ynx	piano/forte	pil/low/slip	pit/iful
phea/sant	pian/ola	pi/lot	piti/less
phe/nom/enon	pi/azza	pim/ento pim/iento	pit/tance
phil/an/thro/pist	pic/ar/esque	(US)	pit/ter/pat/ter
phil/an/thropy	pic/ca/lilli	pim/ple	pi/tu/it/ary

Hyphen

plac/ard	pleas/ure	pole/axe	pon/cho
pla/cid/ity	pleb/is/cite	pole/cat	pon/der
pla/cate	plec/trum	po/lemic	pon/tiff
pla/cebo	plen/ary	po/lice	pon/tifi/cate
pla/centa	ple/ni/po/ten/ti/ary	po/lice/man	pon/toon
pla/cid	pleni/tude	po/lice/woman	pony/tail
pla/gi/ar/ism	plen/teous	pol/icy	poor/ness
pla/gi/ar/ize	plen/ti/ful	po/lio/my/el/itis	pop/lar
plain/clothes	pleth/ora	pol/ish	pop/lin
plain/ness	pleur/isy	Pol/ish	popu/lace
plain/tiff	pli/able	pol/ite	popu/lar
plain/tive	pli/ant	pol/ite/ness	popu/lar/ity
plan/et/ar/ium	pli/ers	pol/iti/cal	popu/late
plank/ton	plim/solls	pol/it/ician	por/cel/ain
plan/ning	plough/man	pol/it/ics	por/cu/pine
plan/tain	plug/hole	pol/len	por/no/graphic
plan/ta/tion	plu/mage	pol/lin/ate	por/nog/raphy
plas/ter	plumb/line	pol/ling	por/ous
plas/tic	plum/met	pol/lute	por/poise
plat/eau	plun/der	pol/ter/geist	por/ridge
plate/layer	plu/ral	poly/an/thus	port/able
plate/let	plu/to/crat	poly/ester	por/tal
plat/form	plu/to/nium	poly/gam/ist	port/cul/lis
plat/inum	ply/wood	poly/gam/ous	por/tent
plat/it/ude	pneu/matic	poly/gamy	por/ter
pla/toon	pneu/monia	poly/glot	port/fo/lio
plat/ter	pocket/ful	poly/gon	port/hole
platy/pus	pod/ium	poly/mer	por/tico
plau/dits	poe/tic	poly/sty/rene	por/tion
plaus/ible	pog/rom	poly/syl/lable	por/trait
play/boy	poign/ancy	poly/tech/nic	por/trait/ure
play/ful	poign/ant	poly/thene	por/tray
play/ground	poin/set/tia	poly/un/sat/ur/ated	Por/tu/gal
play/group	point/edly	poly/ure/thane	pos/eur
play/thing	point/less	po/man/der	po/si/tion
play/time	poi/son	pome/gran/ate	pos/it/ive
play/wright	poi/son/ous	pom/mel	pos/sess
pleas/ant	Pol/and	pom/pom	pos/ses/sive
pleas/antry	po/lar	pom/pous	pos/sib/il/ity

Hyphen

pos/sible	prac/ti/cality	pre/dom/in/ate	pre/pos/ter/ous
post/age	prac/tice	pre-emi/nent	pre/requis/ite
post/box	prac/tise	pre-emp/tive	pre/rog/at/ive
post/code	prac/ti/tioner	pre/fab/ri/cated	pres/cient
post/date	prag/matic	pre/face	pre/scribe
pos/ter/ior	praise/worthy	pre/fect	pre/scrip/tion
pos/ter/ity	pre/amble	pre/fer	pre/sence
post/gradu/ate	pre/bend/ary	pre/fer/able	pre/sent
post/hum/ous	pre/car/ious	pre/fer/en/tial	pre/sen/ti/ment
post/man	pre/cau/tion	pre/fer/ment	pre/ser/va/tive
post/mark	pre/cede	pre/fix	pre/serve
post/mas/ter	pre/ce/dent	preg/nancy	pre/side
post/mis/tress	pre/cept	preg/nant	presi/dent
post/pone	pre/cinct	pre/hen/sile	pres/id/ium
post/pone/ment	pre/cious	pre/his/tory	pres/sure
post/script	pre/ci/pice	pre/judge	pres/tige
pos/tu/late	pre/cipi/tate	pre/judice	pre/sume
pos/ture	pre/cipi/tous	pre/ju/dicial	pre/sump/tuous
post/war	prE9/cis	pre/late	pre/sup/pose
pot/ash	pre/cise	pre/lim/in/ary	pre/tence
pot/as/sium	pre/clude	pre/lude	pre/tend
po/tato	pre/co/cious	prem/ature	pre/ten/sion
po/tency	pre/co/city	pre/med/it/ate	pre/ten/tious
po/ten/tate	pre/con/ceive	prem/ier	pre/text
po/ten/tial	pre/con/cep/tion	prem/iE8re	pret/tily
po/ten/ti/ometer	pre/cur/sor	pre/mise	pret/tiness
po/tion	pre/date	pre/mises	pret/zel
pot/shot	pre/dator	pre/miss	pre/vail
pot/ter	pre/de/cease	pre/mium	preva/lent
poul/tice	pre/de/ces/sor	pre/molar	pre/vari/cate
poul/try	pre/des/tine	pre/mon/ition	pre/vent
pound/age	pre/de/ter/mine	pre/natal	pre/ven/tive
pov/erty	pre/dica/ment	pre/oc/cu/pa/tion	pre/view
pow/der	pre/dict	pre/para/tory	pre/vi/ous
power/ful	pre/dict/able	pre/pare	priest/hood
power/less	pre/di/lec/tion	pre/pay	prima bal/ler/ina
pow/wow	pre/dis/pose	pre/pon/der/ance	pri/mar/ily
prac/tic/able	pre/dis/po/si/tion	prep/osition	pri/mary
prac/tical	pre/dom/in/ant	pre/pos/ses/sing	pri/mate

Hyphen

prim/eval	pro/fane	pro/motion	pros/trate
prim/it/ive	pro/fess	prom/ul/gate	pro/tag/on/ist
prim/rose	pro/fes/sion	pro/noun	pro/tect
prim/ula	pro/fes/sor	pro/nounce	pro/tégé
prin/cipal	pro/fi/cient	pro/nun/ci/ation	pro/tein
prin/ci/pal/ity	pro/file	pro/pa/ganda	pro/test
prin/ciple	profit/able	pro/pa/gate	Prot/es/tant
print/ing	pro/fit/eer	pro/pane	pro/to/col
prior/ess	prof/li/gate	pro/pel	pro/ton
pri/or/ity	pro/forma	pro/pel/ler	pro/to/plasm
pris/matic	pro/found	pro/pen/sity	pro/to/type
pri/son	pro/fund/ity	prop/erly	pro/trac/ted
pris/tine	pro/fuse	prop/erty	pro/trude
pri/vacy	pro/geny	proph/ecy	pro/tub/er/ance
pri/vate	pro/ges/ter/one	pro/phetic	prov/en/ance
pri/vation	prog/nos/ti/cate	pro/phy/lac/tic	prov/erb
privi/lege	pro/gramme	pro/phy/laxis	pro/vide
prob/able	pro/gram	pro/pi/ti/ate	provi/dence
pro/bate	pro/gress	pro/por/tion	provi/den/tial
pro/ba/tion	pro/gres/sive	pro/por/tion/ate	prov/ince
prob/lem	pro/hibit	pro/pose	prov/in/cial
prob/le/mat/ical	pro/hib/ition	pro/pound	pro/vis/ion
pro/bos/cis	pro/ject	pro/prie/tary	pro/viso
pro/ceed	pro/jec/tile	pro/pri/etor	pro/voca/tive
pro/ceeds	pro/jec/tor	pro/pri/ety	pro/voke
pro/cess	pro/lapse	pro/pul/sion	prow/ess
pro/claim	pro/le/tar/iat	pro/rogue	prox/im/ity
proc/la/ma/tion	pro/lific	pro/saic	pru/dence
pro/cliv/ity	pro/lix	pro/scen/ium	prud/ery
pro/cras/tin/ate	pro/logue	pro/scribe	pru/dish/ness
pro/cre/ate	pro/long	pro/sec/ute	pseph/ology
pro/cur/ator	pro/lon/gation	pro/sec/utor	pseu/do/nym
pro/cure	prom/en/ade	pro/sody	psy/che/delic
prod/igal	prom/in/ence	pros/pect	psy/chia/trist
pro/dig/ious	pro/mis/cu/ous	pros/pec/tus	psy/chi/atry
prod/igy	pro/mise	pros/per	psy/chic
prod/uce (*n*)	prom/is/sory	pros/per/ity	psy/cho/ana/lysis
pro/duce (*v*)	prom/on/tory	pros/tate	psy/chol/ogy
pro/duc/tive	pro/mote	pros/ti/tute	psy/cho/path

Hyphen

psy/cho/sis	pur/ga/tory	quan/dary	rac/coon
psy/cho/som/atic	pur/ify	quan/gos	race/course
pu/berty	pur/itan	quan/tify	race/horse
pu/bic	pur/port	quan/tity	race/track
pub/lic	pur/pose	quan/tum	ra/cial/ism
pub/li/can	pur/ser	quar/an/tine	ra/cism
pub/li/cation	pur/sue	quar/rel	rack/et/eer
pub/li/cist	pur/suit	quar/ry	rac/quet
pub/lish	pur/veyor	quar/ter	ra/dar
pud/ding	push/bike	quar/ter/light	ra/dial
pud/dle	push/chair	quar/tet(te)	ra/di/ance
puer/ile	push/ing	quar/to	ra/di/ate
puf/fin	push/over	quat/rain	ra/di/ator
pug/il/ist	pu/sil/lan/im/ous	qua/ver	rad/ical
pug/nac/ious	pussy/cat	quay/side	ra/dio
pul/let	pu/ta/tive	queer/ness	radio/ac/tive
pul/ley	pu/trefy	queru/lous	radi/ogra/pher
pull/man	pu/trid	ques/tion	radi/ology
pull/over	put/ter	ques/tion/able	radio/ther/apy
pul/pit	puz/zle	ques/tion/naire	rad/ish
pul/sar	py/jamas	quib/ble	rad/ium
pul/ver/ize	py/lon	quick/lime	rad/ius
pum/ice (stone)	pyr/amid	quick/sand	raf/fia
pum/mel	pyr/ites	quick/silver	raf/fish
pump/kin	pyro/ma/niac	qui/es/cent	raf/fle
punc/tili/ous	pyro/tech/nics	quiet/ness	raf/ter
punc/tual	py/thon	quin/ine	ra/ga/muf/fin
punc/tu/ate	quad/rangle	quin/tes/sence	rag/lan
punc/ture	quad/rant	quin/tet(te)	rag/out
pun/dit	quad/ra/phonic	quin/tuple	rail/ings
pun/gent	quad/ri/lat/eral	quin/tu/plets	rail/road (US)
pun/ish	quad/ru/ped	quix/otic	rail/way
pun/net	quad/ruple	quiz/master	rail/way/man
pun/ter	quad/ru/pli/cate	quiz/zical	rai/ment
pu/pate	quag/mire	quo/ta/tion	rain/bow
pu/pil	quali/fi/ca/tion	quo/tient	rain/coat
pup/pet	qual/ify	rab/bini/cal	rain/drop
pup/pet/eer	quan/ti/ta/tive	rab/bit	rain/fall
pur/chase	qual/ity	rab/ble	rain/water

rai/sin	rau/cous	re/cap/itu/late	re/con/sti/tute
ram/ble	rav/age	re/cap/ture	re/con/struct
rame/kin	rav/en/ous	re/cast	rec/ord (*n*)
ra/mi/fica/tion	ra/vine	re/cede	re/cord (*v*)
ram/page	ra/vi/oli	re/ceipt	re/count
ram/pant	rav/ish	re/ceive	re/coup
ram/part	raw/hide	re/cent	re/course
ram/shackle	razz/ma/tazz	re/cept/acle	re/cover
ran/cid	re/act	re/cep/tion	rec/re/ation
ran/cour	re/ac/ti/vate	re/cep/tion/ist	re/crim/ina/tion
ran/cor/ous	read/able	re/cep/tive	re/cru/des/cence
ran/dom	re/ad/dress	re/cess	re/cruit
ran/sack	readi/ness	re/ces/sion	rec/tal
ran/som	re/ad/just	re/cid/iv/ist	rect/angle
ra/pa/cious	re/agent	re/cipe	rec/tan/gu/lar
ra/pa/city	re/align	re/cipi/ent	rec/tify
ra/pier	real/is/tic	re/cip/ro/cate	rec/ti/tude
rap/ist	real/ize	reci/pro/city	rec/tor
rap/port	real/tor (US)	re/ci/tal	rec/tory
rap/ture	re/an/im/ate	re/cita/tive	rec/tum
rap/tur/ous	re/ap/pear	re/cite	re/cum/bent
rare/bit	rear/guard	reck/less	re/cu/per/ate
rare/fied	re/arm	re/claim	re/cur
rar/ing	re/ar/ma/ment	re/cline	re/cur/rent
ras/cal	re/ar/range	re/cluse	re/cycle
rasp/berry	rea/son	rec/og/ni/tion	red/cur/rant
rat/chet (wheel)	reas/on/able	rec/og/nize	re/dec/or/ate
rate/able	re/as/semble	rec/og/niz/ance	re/deem
rate/payer	re/as/sure	re/coil	re/demp/tion
ra/ther	re/bate	re/col/lect	re/deploy
rat/ify	re/bel/lion	re/com/mend	red/head
ra/tio	re/bound	re/com/pense	red/ol/ent
ra/tion	re/buff	re/com/pose	re/double
ra/tional	re/build	re/con/cile	re/doubt/able
ra/tion/ale	re/buke	re/con/dite	re/dound
ration/al/ize	re/but	re/con/di/tion	re/dress
rat/tan	re/cal/ci/trant	re/con/nais/sance	re/duce
rat/tle	re/call	re/con/noitre	re/dun/dant
rat/tle/snake	re/cant	re/con/sider	red/wood

Hyphen

re/elect	ré/gime	rel/ev/ant	ren/net
re/enter	re/gi/ment	re/li/ance	re/nounce
re/fect/ory	re/gion	re/li/able	ren/ov/ate
re/fer	reg/is/ter	rel/ict	re/nown
re/fer/ral	reg/is/trar	re/lief	re/nun/ci/ation
ref/er/en/dum	reg/is/try	re/li/gion	re/open
re/fill	re/gress	re/lin/quish	re/or/gan/ize
re/fine	re/gres/sion	re/lish	re/ori/en/tate
re/fin/ery	re/gret	re/lo/cate	re/paid
re/fit	re/gret/table	re/luc/tant	re/pair
re/flate	regu/lar	re/main	re/par/ation
re/flect	regu/lar/ity	re/mand	re/par/tee
re/flec/tor	regu/late	re/mark	re/pat/ri/ate
re/flex	re/gur/gi/tate	re/mark/able	re/pay
re/flex/ive	re/hab/il/it/ate	re/med/ial	re/peal
re/float	re/hash	rem/edy	re/peat
re/form	re/hearse	re/mem/ber	re/pe/chage
re/for/ma/tory	re/im/burse	re/mem/brance	re/pel
re/frac/tion	re/in/car/na/tion	re/mind	re/pel/lent
re/fract/ory	rein/deer	rem/in/is/cence	re/pent
re/frain	re/in/force	re/miss	re/per/cus/sion
re/fresh	re/in/state	re/mis/sion	rep/er/toire
re/fri/ger/ator	re/it/er/ate	re/mit	rep/er/tory
re/fuel	re/ject	re/mit/tance	re/pe/ti/tion
re/fuge	re/joice	rem/nant	re/phrase
re/fu/gee	re/join	re/mon/strate	re/place
re/fund	re/join/der	re/morse	re/play
re/furbish	re/ju/ven/ate	re/mote	re/plen/ish
re/fuse	re/kindle	re/mount	re/plete
re/fute	re/lapse	re/mov/able	rep/lica
re/gain	re/late	re/move	rep/li/cate
re/gal	re/la/tion	re/mun/er/ate	re/ply
re/gale	rel/at/ive	re/nais/sance	re/port
re/galia	re/lat/iv/ity	ren/der	re/pose
re/gard	re/lax	ren/dez/vous	re/posi/tory
re/gard/less	re/lay	ren/di/tion	re/pos/sess
re/gatta	re/lease	ren/eg/ade	rep/re/hen/sible
re/gen/er/ate	re/leg/ate	renege	rep/re/sent
re/gent	re/lent	re/new	rep/re/sen/ta/tive

re/press	re/sign	re/sur/gent	re/ver/ence
re/prieve	resig/na/tion	re/sur/rect	rev/er/end
rep/ri/mand	re/si/li/ent	re/sus/ci/tate	rev/erie
re/print	re/sist	re/tail	re/ver/sal
re/pri/sal	re/sis/tor	re/tain	re/verse
re/prise	re/sit	re/tali/ate	re/vers/ible
re/proach	res/ol/ute	re/tard	re/vert
rep/ro/bate	re/solve	re/ten/tion	re/view
re/pro/duce	res/on/ant	re/think	re/vile
re/pro/graphics	re/sorb	re/ti/cent	re/vise
re/proof	re/sort	re/ti/cu/late	re/vis/ion/ism
re/prove	re/sound	ret/ina	re/visit
rep/tile	re/source	ret/inue	re/viv/al/ist
re/pub/lic	re/spect	re/tire	re/vive
re/pu/di/ate	re/spect/able	re/tort	re/voke
re/pug/nant	re/spect/ful	re/touch	re/volt
re/pulse	re/spect/ive	re/trace	re/volu/tion
re/pul/sive	res/pira/tion	re/tract	re/volve
repu/table	re/spire	re/tread	re/vue
re/pute	re/spite	re/treat	re/vul/sion
repu/tedly	re/splen/dent	re/trench	re/ward
re/quest	re/spond	re/trial	rhap/sody
re/quiem	re/spon/dent	re/tri/bu/tion	rheo/stat
re/quire	re/spon/sib/il/ity	re/trieve	rhe/sus
re/quis/ite	re/spon/sible	re/tro/act/ive	rhet/oric
re/quisi/tion	rest/aurant	re/tro/grade	rheum/at/ism
re/run	res/ti/tu/tion	re/tro/spect	rheu/ma/toid
res/cind	res/tive	re/turn	rhine/stone
res/cue	rest/less	re/unify	rhi/no/ceros
re/search	res/tora/tive	re/union	rho/do/den/dron
re/semble	re/store	re/value	rhom/bus
re/sent	re/strain	re/vamp	rhu/barb
re/serve	re/straint	re/veal	ri/bald
re/ser/vist	re/strict	re/veille	rib/bon
res/er/voir	rest/room	rev/el/ler	rich/ness
re/shuf/fle	re/sult	re/venge	rick/ets
re/side	re/sume	rev/enue	rick/shaw
res/id/en/tial	ré/sumé	re/ver/be/rate	ri/co/chet
res/idue	re/sur/face	re/vere	↑id/dance

Hyphen

Hyphen

rid/dle	ro/dent	rub/ber	sac/ri/fice
rider/less	roent/gen	rub/bish	sac/ri/fi/cial
ri/di/cule	roguish/ness	rub/ble	sac/ri/lege
ri/di/cu/lous	roll/call	ru/bella	sac/ri/le/gious
riff/raff	roll/mop	ru/bi/cund	sac/ris/tan
rig/ging	Ro/man	rub/ric	sac/risty
right/eous	ro/mance	ruck/sack	sac/ro/sanct
right/ful	Ro/man/esque	ruc/tions	sad/den
right/ness	Ro/mania	rud/der	sad/dle
ri/gid/ity	ro/man/tic	rudi/ments	sad/dle/bag
rig/mar/ole	ro/man/ti/cize	ruf/fian	sa/dism
rig/our	Ro/many	ruf/fle	sa/dis/tic
rim/less	rook/ery	rug/ged	saf/ari
ring/leader	room/mate	rug/ger	safe/guard
ring/let	ro/sary	ruin/ous	saf/fron
ring/mas/ter	ros/eate	ru/min/ant	sa/ga/cious
ring/side	rose/mary	ru/min/ate	sa/ga/city
ring/worm	ros/ette	rum/mage	Sa/git/tar/ius
ri/ot/ous	ros/ter	ru/mour	sail/boat
ri/par/ian	ros/trum	rum/pus	sail/cloth
rip/cord	ro/tate	run/away	saint/li/ness
ri/poste	ro/tor	run/down	sa/la/cious
rip/ple	rot/ten	run/way	sa/lami
ris/ible	rot/ter	rup/ture	sal/ary
ri/sotto	ro/tund	rus/set	sale/able
ris/sole	ro/tunda	Rus/sia	sale/room
ri/val	rough/age	rus/tic	sales/man
river/side	rough/ness	rust/ling	sales/woman
road/block	rough/shod	ru/ta/baga	sa/li/ent
road/hog	roul/ette	ruth/less	sa/line
road/side	round/about	Sab/bath	sa/liva
road/way	roun/del	sab/bat/ical	sa/li/vate
road/works	round/house	sab/otage	sal/low
road/worthy	roust/about	sab/oteur	sal/ly
rob/ber	rou/tine	sac/charin	sal/mon
ro/bot	rov/ing	sack/ing	sal/mon/ella
ro/bust	row/lock	sack/cloth	sa/loon
rock/ery	roy/al/ist	sac/ra/ment	sal/sify
rock/ing	roy/alty	sac/red	salt/petre

salt/peter (US)	sar/casm	sca/bi/ous	school/girl
sa/lu/bri/ous	sar/cas/tic	scaf/fold	school/chil/dren
sa/luki	sar/coma	scal/lion	school/mas/ter
sal/u/tary	sar/co/phagus	scal/lop	school/mis/tress
sa/lute	sar/dine	scal/ly/wag	school/tea/cher
sal/vage	sar/donic	scal/pel	sci/at/ica
sal/va/tion	sa/rong	scam/per	sci/ence
sal/ver	sar/tor/ial	scan/dal	sci/en/ti/fic
Sam/ari/tan	Sas/sen/ach	scan/dal/mon/ger	scin/til/late
samo/var	sat/chel	scan/dal/ous	scis/sors
sam/pan	sat/el/lite	scan/ner	scler/osis
sam/phire	sa/ti/ate	Scan/din/avia	scof/fing
samp/ler	sat/ire	scan/sion	scorch/ing
sam/urai	sat/ir/ical	scan/tily	score/board
san/at/or/ium	sat/is/fac/tion	scape/goat	scorn/ful
san/it/ar/ium (US)	sat/isfy	scap/ula	Scor/pio
sanc/tify	sat/suma	scar/city	scor/pion
sanc/ti/mon/ious	sat/ur/ate	scare/crow	Scot/land
sanc/tion	Sat/ur/day	scare/mon/ger	scoun/drel
sanc/tity	sat/ur/nine	scar/ify	scout/master
sanc/tu/ary	sauce/pan	scar/let	scrap/book
sanc/tum	sau/cer	scath/ing	scream/ing
san/dal	sauer/kraut	scat/ter	screen/play
san/dal/wood	saun/ter	scat/ter/brain	screen/wri/ter
sand/bag	saus/age	sca/venge	screw/driver
sand/bank	sav/age	scav/en/ger	scrib/ble
sand/paper	sav/ag/ery	scen/ario	scrim/mage
sand/piper	sav/eloy	sce/nery	scrip/ture
sand/stone	sav/ings	scep/tic	scro/tum
sand/wich	sav/iour	skep/tic (US)	scrub/bing
san/guin/ary	sav/ior (US)	sched/ule	scrump/tious
san/guine	sav/our	sche/matic	scru/pu/lous
san/it/ary	sav/or (US)	schis/ma/tic	scru/tin/ize
san/ita/tion	sa/voy	schizo/phre/nia	scuf/fle
sap/ling	saw/dust	schnit/zel	scul/lery
sap/per	saw/mill	schol/arly	sculp/tor
sap/phire	saxo/phone	scholar/ship	sculp/ture
sap/wood	saxo/phon/ist	schol/astic	scup/per
sara/band	scab/bard	school/book	scur/ril/ous

Hyphen

scut/tle	se/dan	sem/inary	se/rene
sea/board	se/date	Sem/itic	ser/geant
sea/farer	se/da/tion	se/mo/lina	ser/ial
sea/food	sed/a/tive	sen/ate	ser/ious
sea/gull	sed/en/tary	sena/tor	ser/mon
seal/ant	sedi/ment	se/nile	ser/pent
seal/skin	se/di/tion	se/nior	ser/rated
sea/man	se/duce	se/ni/or/ity	ser/vant
seam/less	se/duc/tion	sen/sa/tion	ser/vice
seam/stress	seed/bed	sense/less	ser/vice/man
sé/ance	seed/ling	sens/ible	ser/vi/ette
sea/port	seeds/man	sen/sit/ive	ser/vile
search/ing	seem/ing	sen/sit/iv/ity	ser/vi/tude
search/light	seep/age	sen/sor	ses/sion
sea/shore	see/saw	sen/sual	set/back
sea/sick	seg/ment	sen/su/ous	set/tee
sea/side	seg/re/gate	sen/tence	set/ter
sea/son	seis/mic	sen/ten/tious	set/ting
sea/weed	seis/mo/graph	sen/ti/ment	set/tle
sea/worthy	seis/mol/ogy	sen/ti/nel	set/tle/ment
se/ca/teurs	seiz/ure	sen/try	set/tler
se/cede	sel/dom	se/pal	sev/en/teen
se/ces/sion	sel/ect	sep/ar/ate	sev/enty
se/clu/ded	sel/en/ium	sep/ar/at/ism	sev/eral
sec/ond	self/fish	se/pia	sev/er/ance
sec/ond/ary	self/less	sep/sis	se/vere
se/cond/hand	sel/lo/tape	Sep/tem/ber	se/ver/ity
se/cond/ment	sel/vedge	sep/tet	sew/age
sec/recy	se/man/tic	sep/tic	sex/ist
sec/ret	sema/phore	sep/ti/caemia	sex/tant
sec/re/tary	sem/blance	sep/tua/gen/arian	sex/tet
se/cre/tive	se/men	sep/tup/let	sex/ton
se/crete	se/mes/ter	se/pul/chre	sex/tup/let
sec/tar/ian	semi/breve	se/pul/cher (US)	sex/ual
sec/tion	semi/circle	se/quel	shab/bi/ness
sec/tor	semi/conductor	se/quence	shadi/ness
secu/lar	semi/tone	se/quin	sha/king
se/cure	sem/inal	se/quoia	shal/lot
se/cur/ity	sem/inar	ser/en/ade	shal/low

Hyphen

shame/faced	shoe/horn	shuf/fle	sil/icon
shame/ful	shoe/lace	shut/eye	sil/ic/one
shame/less	shoe/maker	shut/ter	sil/ic/osis
sham/poo	shoe/string	shut/tle	silk/screen
sham/rock	shoot/ing	shut/tle/cock	silk/worm
shape/less	shop/floor	shy/ness	sil/li/ness
share/holder	shop/keeper	sib/il/ant	sil/ver
sharp/ener	shop/lif/ter	sick/bay	sil/ver/side
sharp/ness	shop/ping	sick/ness	sil/ver/smith
sharp/shooter	shop/walker	side/board	sil/ver/ware
shat/ter	short/age	side/burns	sim/ilar
sha/ving	short/bread	side/car	sim/ile
sheep/dog	short/cake	side/light	sim/mer
sheep/ish	short/coming	side/line	simp/li/fy
sheep/shank	short/en/ing	side/long	simu/late
sheep/skin	short/fall	side/show	sim/ul/tan//eous
sheikh/dom	short/hand	side/step	sin/cere
shel/lac	short/horn	side/track	sine/cure
shell/fish	shot/gun	side/walk (US)	sin/ful
shel/ter	shoul/der	side/ways	sin/gle/breasted
shep/herd	shoul/der/blade	si/enna	sin/gle/decker
shep/herd/ess	shovel/ful	si/esta	sin/gle/handed
sher/bet	show/boat	sif/ter	sing/let
sher/iff	show/case	sight/less	sing/song
shifti/ness	showi/ness	sight/screen	sin/gu/lar
shift/less	show/man	sight/seeing	sin/is/ter
shim/mer	show/man/ship	sight/seer	sin/ner
shin/ing	show/piece	sig/nal	sinu/ous
ship/builder	show/room	sig/nal/man	si/nus
ship/mate	shower/proof	sig/na/ture	si/nu/si/tis
ship/ment	show/ery	sign/board	si/phon
ship/owner	shrap/nel	sig/net	si/ren
ship/ping	shred/der	sig/ni/fi/cance	sir/loin
ship/shape	shrew/ish	sig/nify	sis/ter
ship/wreck	shrewd/ness	sign/post	sit/ter
ship/yard	shrink/age	sil/age	situ/ate
shirt/sleeves	shrub/bery	si/lence	six/pence
shock/ing	shrun/ken	sil/hou/ette	si/lence
shod/di/ness	shud/der	sil/ica	six/teen
			six/ti/eth

Hyphen 214

skate/board	slip/case	snow/plough	some/how
ske/dad/dle	slip/pery	snuf/fle	some/one
skel/eton	slip/stream	snug/gle	som/er/sault
sketch/ing	slip/way	soak/ing	some/thing
sketch/pad	slob/ber	soap/suds	some/time
skew/bald	slo/gan	sober/ness	some/times
ski/boots	slog/ger	sob/ri/ety	some/where
skil/ful	slop/pily	soc/cer	som/nam/bu/lism
skill/ful (US)	slov/enly	so/ci/able	som/no/lence
skil/let (US)	slow/coach	so/cial	son/ata
skin/diver	slow/worm	so/ci/ety	song/ster
skin/flint	slug/gish	so/ci/ol/ogy	son/net
skip/per	slum/ber	sod/den	son/or/ous
skir/mish	slum/ber/wear	so/dium	soph/ist/icate
skirt/ing	sly/ness	so/journ	soph/omore (US)
skit/tish	small/holder	sol/ace	sop/or/ific
skull/cap	small/pox	sol/der	sop/rano
sky/div/ing	smat/ter/ing	sol/dier	sor/bet
sky/lark	smelt/ing	sol/emn	sor/cery
sky/line	smith/er/eens	sol/em/nity	sor/did
sky/scraper	smoke/less	sol/en/oid	sor/ghum
slack/ness	smoke/screen	so/li/cit	sor/or/ity (US)
sla/lom	smoul/der	sol/ici/tor	sor/rel
slan/der	smug/gler	sol/ici/tous	sor/row
slant/ing	snack/bar	soli/dar/ity	sor/row/ful
slant/wise	snap/dragon	sol/id/ity	sor/ter
slap/dash	snap/shot	sol/id/ify	sor/tie
slap/stick	snea/kers (US)	soli/dus	sort/ing
slaugh/ter	snig/ger	so/li/lo/quy	soul/ful
slaugh/ter/house	snip/pet	so/li/taire	soul/less
sla/vish	snob/bery	sol/it/ary	sound/ing
sledge/ham/mer	snob/bish	solo/ist	sound/less
sleepi/ness	snor/kel	sol/stice	sound/ness
sleep/ing	snow/ball	sol/uble	sound/proof
sleep/less	snow/bound	sol/u/tion	sound/track
sleep/walk	snow/drift	sol/vency	south/bound
slen/der	snow/drop	sol/vent	south/erner
slight/ingly	snow/fall	som/brero	south/paw
sling/shot	snow/flake	some/body	south/wards

sou/venir	speed/ometer	spor/ran	stale/mate
sov/er/eign	speed/way	spor/ting	stale/ness
space/craft	spe/le/ology	sports/man	stall/holder
space/man	spell/bound	sports/man/ship	stal/lion
space/sav/ing	spel/ling	sports/wear	stal/wart
space/ship	spend/thrift	spot/less	sta/men
space/suit	sphag/num	spot/light	stam/ina
spa/cious/ness	spheri/cal	spread/eagled	stam/mer
spa/ghetti	spi/der	spring/board	stam/pede
Span/iard	spil/lage	spring/bok	stamp/ing
span/iel	spina bif/ida	spring/clean	stan/chion
Span/ish	spin/ach	springi/ness	stan/dard
span/ner	spin/dle	spring/like	stand/offish
spar/ing	spin/drift	spring/time	stand/pipe
spark/ing	spine/less	sprink/ler	stand/point
spark/ler	spin/na/ker	spuri/ous	stand/still
spar/row	spin/ner	sput/ter	sta/phy/lo/coc/cus
spar/row/hawk	spin/neret	spu/tum	star/board
spar/tan	spin/ney	squad/ron	star/dom
spas/modic	spin/ster	squan/der	star/fish
spas/tic	spi/ral	squat/ter	star/gazer
spa/tial	spiri/tual	squeam/ish	star/light
spat/ter	spiri/tual/ism	squee/gee	star/ling
spat/ula	spite/ful	squir/rel	star/va/tion
spear/head	splen/did	sta/bil/ize	state/less
spear/mint	splen/dour	stac/cato	state/ment
spe/cial	splin/ter	sta/dium	state/side (US)
spe/cies	splut/ter	stage/coach	states/man
spe/ci/fi/ca/tion	spo/ken	stage/craft	sta/tion
spe/cify	spoil/sport	stage/hand	sta/tioner
spe/ci/men	spoke/shave	stag/ger	sta/tion/mas/ter
spe/cious	spokes/man	stag/fla/tion	sta/tis/ti/cal
spec/tacle	spo/li/ation	stag/nant	sta/tis/tics
spec/tacu/lar	sponge/bag	stag/nate	statu/ary
spec/ta/tor	spon/sor	stain/less	statu/esque
spec/trum	spon/tan/eous	stair/car/pet	stat/ure
spec/ulate	spoon/feed	stair/case	sta/tus
speech/less	spoon/ful	stal/ac/tite	stat/ute
speed/boat	spor/adic	stal/ag/mite	stead/fast

Hyphen

Hyphen

stead/ily	stickle/back	stop/per/age	strong/hold
steak/house	stick/ler	store/house	stron/tium
steal/thy	stif/fen	store/keeper	struc/ture
steam/boat	stiff/ness	story/line	strug/gling
steam/roller	stig/mata	story/teller	strych/nine
steam/ship	stil/etto	stout/ness	stub/ble
steel/works	still/born	stove/pipe	stub/born
steeple/chase	still/ness	stow/away	stu/dent
steeple/jack	stimu/lant	strad/dler	stu/dio
steer/ing	stimu/late	strag/gler	stu/di/ous
stel/lar	stimu/lus	straight/for/ward	stuf/fing
sten/cil	sting/ray	strait/jacket	stuf/fi/ness
sten/gun	stingi/ness	strait/laced	stul/tify
steno/grapher	sti/pend	strange/ness	stun/ning
sten/torian	sti/pen/di/ary	stran/gu/la/tion	stu/pe/fac/tion
step/brother	stip/ple	strap/less	stu/pefy
step/child	stipu/late	strap/ping	stu/pen/dous
step/daughter	stir/ring	stra/ta/gem	stu/pid
step/father	stir/rup	stra/tegic	stur/geon
step/ladder	stock/ade	stra/tegi/cal	stut/ter
step/mother	stock/broker	strat/ify	sty/lish
step/sister	stock/car	stra/to/sphere	sty/lis/tics
step/son	stock/ing	straw/berry	sty/lize
ste/reo	stock/ist	stream/line	sty/lus
ste/reo/phonic	stock/man	stream/lining	sty/mie
ste/reo/scope	stock/pile	street/cat	styp/tic
ste/reo/type	stock/pot	strenu/ous	sub/al/tern
ster/ile	stock/tak/ing	strep/to/coc/cus	sub/aqua
ster/il/ize	stoi/cism	strep/to/my/cin	sub/com/mit/tee
ster/ling	sto/len	stric/ture	sub/con/scious
stern/ness	stom/ach	strike/breaker	sub/con/ti/nent
stern/wheeler	stone/crop	strik/ing	sub/con/tract
ster/num	stone/mason	stri/dent	sub/cu/ta/ne/ous
ster/oid	stone/wall	strin/gent	sub/div/ide
stetho/scope	stone/ware	strip/ing	sub/due
steve/dore	stop/cock	strip/per	sub/edit
stew/ard	stop/gap	strip/tease	sub/head/ing
stew/ard/ess	stop/over	stro/bo/scope	sub/ject
sticki/ness	stop/page	strol/ler	sub/ju/dice

sub/junc/tive	sub/urb	sump/tu/ous	su/per/man
sub/lease	sub/urbia	sun/bathe	su/per/mar/ket
sub/let	sub/ven/tion	sun/beam	su/per/nat/ur/al
sub/lieu/ten/ant	sub/ver/sion	sun/burn	su/per/nova
sub/lim/ate	sub/way	sun/dae	su/per/num/er/ary
sub/lime	sub/zero	Sun/day	su/per/power
sub/lim/in/al	suc/ceed	sun/deck	su/per/sede
sub/mach/ine gun	suc/cess	sun/dial	su/per/son/ic
sub/mar/ine	suc/cinct	sun/down	su/per/sti/tion
sub/merge	suc/cour	sun/drenched	su/per/struc/ture
sub/mer/sion	suc/cu/lent	sun/dry	su/per/tan/ker
sub/mis/sion	suc/cumb	sun/flower	su/per/vene
sub/mit	such/like	sun/glasses	su/per/vise
sub/nor/mal	sud/den	sun/lamp	su/per/woman
sub/ord/in/ate	suf/fer	sun/less	su/pine
sub/poena	suf/fice	sun/light	sup/per
sub/scribe	suf/fi/cient	sun/rise	sup/per/time
sub/scrip/tion	suf/fix	sun/set	sup/plant
sub/se/quent	suf/fo/cate	sun/shade	sup/ple
sub/ser/vient	suf/frage	sun/shine	sup/ple/ment
sub/side	sug/gest	sun/spot	sup/pli/ca/tion
sub/sid/iary	sug/ges/tible	sun/stroke	sup/ply
sub/si/dize	sui/cide	sun/tan	sup/port
sub/sidy	suit/ability	sun/trap	sup/pose
sub/sist	suit/case	su/per	sup/pos/edly
sub/soil	sul/len	su/per/abund/ance	sup/pos/it/ory
sub/stance	sul/phur	su/per/an/nu/ated	sup/press
sub/stan/dard	sul/fur (US)	su/perb	sup/pres/sor
sub/stan/tial	sul/tan	su/per/charged	su/pra/na/tional
sub/stan/ti/ate	sul/try	su/per/cili/ous	su/prem/acy
sub/stant/ive	sum/mar/ize	su/per/fi/cial	su/preme
sub/sta/tion	sum/mary	su/per/fine	su/premo
sub/sti/tute	sum/mar/ily	su/per/flu/ous	sur/charge
sub/stra/tum	sum/mer	su/per/high/way (US)	sure/ness
sub/ten/ant	sum/mer/house	su/per/hu/man	sur/face
sub/ter/fuge	sum/mer/time	su/per/im/pose	surf/board
sub/ter/ra/nean	sum/mery	su/per/in/tend	surf/boat
sub/title	sum/mit	su/per/ior	sur/feit
sub/tract	sum/mon	su/per/lat/ive	sur/geon

Hyphen

sur/gi/cal	swel/ter	syn/thesis	tam-o'shan/ter
sur/li/ness	swift/ness	syn/thetic	tam/per
sur/mise	swim/ming	syph/ilis	tam/pon
sur/mount	swim/suit	syr/inge	tan/dem
sur/name	swinge/ing	sys/tem	tan/gent
sur/pass	swing/ing	sys/te/matic	tan/gen/tial
sur/plice	switch/back	sys/temic	tan/ger/ine
sur/plus	switch/board	tab/er/nacle	tan/gible
sur/prise	Swit/zer/land	tab/leau	tank/ard
sur/real/ism	swol/len	table/cloth	tan/nery
sur/ren/der	sword/fish	table/land	tan/nin
sur/rep/ti/tious	swords/man	table/spoon	tan/tal/ize
sur/round	sword/stick	tab/let	tan/ta/mount
sur/tax	sy/ca/more	tab/loid	tan/trum
sur/veil/lance	sy/co/phant	ta/boo	tap/es/try
sur/vey	syl/labic	tabu/lar	ta/pi/oca
sur/vive	syl/lable	tabu/la/tor	ta/pir
sus/cept/ible	syl/la/bub	tacho/graph	tap/pet
sus/pect	syl/la/bus	ta/cit	tap/ping
sus/pend	sym/bi/osis	taci/turn	ta/ran/tula
sus/pen/ders	sym/bol	tact/ful	tar/get
sus/pen/sion	sym/metry	tact/less	tar/iff
sus/pi/cion	sym/pa/thize	tac/ti/cian	tar/mac
sus/pi/sious	sym/pathy	tac/tics	tar/nish
sus/tain	sym/phony	tac/tile	tar/pau/lin
sus/ten/ance	sym/po/sium	tad/pole	tar/ra/gon
su/ture	symp/tom	taf/feta/back	tar/sus
swag/ger	symp/to/matic	tail/board	tar/tan
swal/low	syn/agogue	tail/gate	tar/tar
swash/buck/ling	syn/chro/mesh	tail/less	tar/tare sauce
swas/tika	syn/chro/nize	take/away	tart/ness
sweat/shirt	syn/co/pate	take/over	task/mas/ter
Swe/den	syn/di/cate	tal/ent	tas/sel
sweep/ing	syn/drome	tal/is/man	taste/ful
sweep/stake	sy/nod	talk/ative	taste/less
sweet/bread	syn/onym	talk/ing	tat/ters
sweet/heart	syn/ony/mous	tall/boy	tat/ting
sweet/ness	syn/op/sis	tam/bour/ine	tat/tle
sweet/shop	syn/tax	tame/ness	tat/too

Hyphen

tat/ty	tel/eph/on/ist	ter/cen/ten/ary	theor/eti/cal
Tau/rus	tele/photo lens	ter/mi/nal	the/ory
tau/tol/ogy	tele/printer	ter/min/ate	thera/peu/tic
tav/ern	tele/scope	ter/min/ology	thera/pist
taw/dry	tele/vision	ter/minus	ther/apy
tax/able	tel/ling	ter/mite	there/after
taxi/dermy	tell/tale	ter/race	there/upon
tax/man	te/mer/ity	ter/ra/cot/ta	ther/mi/onic
taxi/meter	tem/per	ter/rain	ther/mo/dy/nam/ics
tax/payer	tem/pera	ter/ra/pin	ther/mo/meter
tea/bag	tem/pera/ment	ter/rest/rial	ther/mo/nu/clear
tea/cake	tem/per/ance	ter/rible	Ther/mos (flask)
tea/cloth	tem/per/ate	ter/rier	ther/mo/stat
tea/cup	tem/pest	ter/ri/fic	the/sau/rus
tea/leaf	tem/pes/tuous	ter/rit/ory	thick/set
tea/pot	tem/plate	ter/ror	thim/ble/ful
tea/room	tem/poral	ter/ror/ism	thin/ness
tea/spoon	tem/por/ary	ter/tiary	thin/nings
tea/time	temp/ta/tion	Tery/lene	thinga/ma/jig
team/ster	ten/able	testa/ment	think/ing
team/work	ten/acious	test/icle	thir/teen
tear/ful	ten/acity	test/ify	thir/ti/eth
tea/sel	ten/ant	tes/ti/mony	this/tle/down
tech/nical	ten/den/tious	tet/anus	thor/acic
tech/nique	ten/der	tet/ra/hed/ron	thor/ough
tech/no/crat	ten/der/hearted	text/book	thor/ough/bred
tech/no/logi/cal	ten/der/loin	text/ual	thor/ough/fare
te/di/ous	ten/don	tex/tile	thor/ough/going
teen/age	ten/dril	tex/ture	thor/ough/ness
tee/ter	tene/ment	Thai/land	thought/ful
tee/ter-tot/ter (US)	ten/fold/nis	thank/ful	thought/less
tee/total	ten/sion	thank/less	thou/sand
tele/cast	ten/sile	thanks/giving	thrash/ing
tele/com/mu/ni/ca/tions	tent/acle	theat/ri/cal	thread/bare
tele/gram	tent/at/ive	them/selves	thread/like
tele/graph	ten/ter/hooks	theo/do/lite	thread/worm
tel/egra/phist	tenu/ous	theo/lo/gian	three/fold
tele/pathy	ten/ure	theo/logy	three/some
tele/phone	te/pee	the/orem	thresh/old

Hyphen

throm/bo/sis	tim/pani	tom/tom	touch/down
through/out	tinc/ture	tongue/twister	touchi/ness
through/put	tin/der	to/night	touch/paper
through/way	tin/ker	ton/nage	touch/stone
throw/away	tin/sel	ton/sil	tough/ness
throw/back	tip/ple	ton/sil/litis	tou/pee
thumb/nail	tip/ster	ton/sure	tour/na/ment
thumb/tack	tip/toe	tooth/ache	tour/ni/quet
thun/der	tir/ade	tooth/brush	to/wards
thun/der/ous	tired/ness	tooth/comb	tow/el/ling
thun/der/struck	tire/less	tooth/less	tow/path
Thurs/day	tire/some	tooth/paste	towns/folk
thy/roid (gland)	tis/sue	tooth/pick	town/ship
ti/ara	ti/tanic	to/paz	towns/man
tick/er/tape	tit/bit tid/bit (US)	to/pi/ary	towns/woman
tick/ing	tit/il/late	top/less	towns/people
tick/lish	tit/iv/ate	to/po/graphy	tox/aemia
tid/dler	ti/tra/tion	to/po/logy	tox/emia (US)
tid/dly	tit/ter	top/side	toxi/col/ogy
tide/mark	tit/tle tat/tle	top/soil	tra/chea
tide/way	titu/lar	torch/light	tra/cheot/omy
tid/ings	toad/stool	tor/ment/men/tor	track/less
tidi/ness	toast/mas/ter	tor/nado	tract/able
tie/pin	toast/rack	tor/pedo	trac/tion
tif/fin	to/bacco	tor/pid	trac/tor
ti/ger	to/bog/gan	tor/rent	trade/mark
ti/gress	to/day	tor/ren/tial	trades/man
tight/fit/ting	toe/nail	tor/rid	trades/people/wind
tight/rope	tof/fee	tor/sion	tra/di/tion
til/ler	to/gether	tor/toise	traf/fic
tim/ber	toi/let	tor/toise/shell	traf/fi/cator
tim/ber/yard	tol/er/able	tor/tu/ous	trag/edy
time/keeper	tol/er/ate	tor/ture	train/ing
time/lag	toma/hawk	to/tal/it/arian	trai/tor
time/less	to/mato	to/tal/ity	tra/ject/ory
time/piece	tom/bola	to/tal/iz/ator	tram/car
time/server	tom/boy	to/tem pole	tram/way
time/table	tom/fool	tot/ter	tram/po/line
tim/or/ous	to/mor/row	tou/can	tran/quil

Hyphen

tran/quil/lizer	trap/pings	tri/logy	Tues/day
trans/act	trau/matic	tri/maran	tug/boat
trans/at/lan/tic	tra/vel/lator	trim/ming	tu/ition
tran/scend	tra/vel/ler	trin/ity	tum/ble/down
trans/con/tin/ental	tra/verse	trin/ket	tum/my/ache
trans/scribe	trav/esty	tri/par/tite	tu/mour tu/mor
trans/script	treach/ery	tri/pod	(US)
tran/sept	tread/mill	trip/per	tu/mult
trans/fer	trea/son	trip/tych	tu/mu/lus
trans/figure	treas/ure	tri/umph	tun/dra
trans/fix	treat/ment	tri/um/phant	tung/sten
trans/form	treat/ise	tri/um/vir/ate	tu/nic
trans/fuse	tree/creeper	triv/ial	Tu/nisia
tran/ship	tree/less	trog/lo/dyte	tun/nel
tran/si/ence	tree/top	Tro/jan	tur/ban
tran/sis/tor	tre/foil	trol/ley	tur/bid
tran/sit	trel/lis	trom/bone	tur/bine
trans/it/ive	tre/mend/ous	tro/phies	tur/bot
trans/it/ory	tremu/lous	trop/ical	tur/bu/lent
trans/late	tren/chant	trouble/maker	tur/een
trans/lit/er/ate	tre/pan	trouble/shooter	tur/gid
trans/lu/cent	tre/phine	trouble/some	Tur/key
trans/mis/sion	trep/ida/tion	trouble/spot	tur/meric
trans/mit	tres/pass	trous/seau	tur/moil
trans/mute	tres/ses	tru/ant	turn/coat
tran/som	tri/angle	truck/load	turn/over
trans/parency	tri/an/gular	truc/ulence	turn/pike
trans/par/ent	tribes/man	tru/ism	turn/stile
tran/spire	tri/bunal	trum/pet	turn/table
trans/plant	tri/bu/tary	trun/cated	tur/nip
trans/port	trib/ute	trun/cheon	tur/pen/tine
trans/pose	trick/ster	trus/tee	tur/quoise
trans/ship	tri/col/our	trust/ful	tur/ret
trans/ur/anic	tri/cycle	trust/worthy	tur/tle
trans/verse	tri/dent	truth/ful	tur/tle/dove/sock
trans/vest/ite	tri/en/nial	tu/ber/cu/lar	tu/tor
tra/peze	trig/ger	tuber/cu/losis	tux/edo
tra/pez/ium	tri/go/no/metry	tube/less	twen/ti/eth
trap/per	tril/lion	tu/bu/lar	twi/light

Hyphen 222

twit/ter	un/ac/count/able	un/break/able	un/cork
two/penny	un/ac/cus/tomed	un/bridled	un/cor/rec/ted
twp/some	un/ac/quain/ted	un/broken	un/cor/rob/or/ated
ty/coon	un/adop/ted	un/burden	un/couth
tym/panum	un/adul/ter/ated	un/busi/ness/like	un/cover
type/setter	un/af/fec/ted	un/but/ton	un/crossed
type/writer	un/aided	un/called for	un/crush/able
typ/ist	un/al/loyed	un/canny	unc/tion
ty/po/graphy	un/al/ter/able	un/cared for	un/cul/tiv/ated
ty/phoid	un/am/bigu/ous	un/ceas/ing	un/cut
ty/phoon	un/an/im/ous	un/cere/mo/ni/ous	un/dam/aged
ty/phus	una/nim/ity	un/cer/tain	un/daun/ted
typ/ical	un/an/nounced	un/chal/lenged	un/de/cided
tyr/anny	un/answer/able	un/change/able	un/de/fen/ded
tyr/an/nical	un/ap/pet/izing	un/char/it/able	un/demo/cratic
tyr/an/nous	un/ap/proach/able	un/checked	un/deni/able
ty/rant	un/armed	un/civ/il/ized	un/der/achieve
ubi/quit/ous	un/ash/amed	un/claimed	un/der/arm
ud/der	un/asked	un/clas/si/fied	un/der/car/riage
ug/li/ness	un/as/sum/ing	un/clean	un/der/charge
ul/cer	un/at/tached	un/clut/tered	un/der/clothes
ul/cer/ous	un/at/tain/able	un/coil	un/der/coat
ul/ter/ior	un/at/ten/ded	un/com/fort/able	un/der/cover
ul/ti/mate	un/at/trac/tive	un/com/mit/ted	un/der/cur/rent
ul/ti/matum	un/au/thor/ized	un/com/mon	un/der/cut
ul/tra/marine	un/avoid/able	un/com/mu/nic/at/ive	un/der/de/vel/oped
ultra/vio/let	un/aware	uncom/pli/ment/ary	un/der/dog
um/ber	un/awares	un/com/prom/ising	un/der/done
um/bil/ical	un/bal/anced	un/con/cealed	un/der/es/tim/ate
um/brage	un/bear/able	un/con/cerned	un/der/ex/posed
um/brella	un/beat/able	un/con/ditional	un/der/fed
um/pire	un/be/known	un/con/nected	un/der/felt
ump/teen	un/be/liev/able	un/con/scious	un/der/foot
un/abated	un/bend	un/con/scion/able	un/der/gar/ment
un/able	un/biased	un/con/trol/lable	un/der/go
un/abridged	un/bleached	un/con/ven/tional	un/der/gradu/ate
un/ac/cept/able	un/bolt	un/cooked	un/der/ground
un/ac/coun/ted for	un/bosom	un/co/op/er/ative	un/der/growth
un/ac/com/pan/ied	un/boun/ded		un/der/hand(ed)

Hyphen

un/der/lay	un/detec/ted	un/fail/ing	uni/fica/tion
un/der/lie	un/de/vel/oped	un/fair	uni/form
un/der/line	un/did	un/faith/ful	uni/lat/eral
un/der/ling	un/dies	un/fa/mil/iar	un/im/por/tant
un/der/manned	un/dig/ni/fied	un/fasten	un/in/formed
under/men/tioned	un/di/lu/ted	un/fa/vour/able	un/in/hab/it/able
un/der/mine	un/dis/charged	un/feel/ing	un/in/hib/ited
un/der/neath	un/dis/tin/guished	un/fit	un/ini/ti/ated
un/der/nour/ished	un/di/vided	un/flin/chingly	un/in/tel/lig/ible
un/der/paid	un/doubted	un/fold	un/in/ter/rup/ted
un/der/pants	un/dreamt of	un/fore/seen	un/in/vited
un/der/pass	un/dress	un/for/get/table	union/ist
un/der/priv/ileged	un/drink/able	un/for/tu/nate	uni/sex
un/der/rate	un/due	un/foun/ded	uni/son
un/der/seal	un/du/late	un/freeze	uni/valve
un/der/sell	un/dy/ing	un/fre/quented	uni/ver/sal
un/der/shirt	un/earned	un/friendly	uni/verse
un/der/side	un/earth	un/furl	uni/ver/sity
un/der/signed	un/easi/ness	un/fur/nished	un/just
un/der/sized	un/easy	un/gainly	un/jus/ti/fied
un/der/slung	un/eat/able	un/get/at/able	un/kempt
un/der/staffed	un/eco/nom/ic(al)	un/godly	un/kind
un/der/stand	un/edu/cated	un/gracious	un/known
un/der/state	un/em/ployed	un/grate/ful	un/laden
un/der/stood	un/end/ing	un/guar/ded	un/lady/like
un/der/study	un/en/light/ened	un/gu/late	un/law/ful
un/der/take	un/en/vi/able	un/happy	un/leash
un/der/taker	un/equal	un/harmed	un/leavened
un/der/tone	un/equi/vocal	un/healthy	un/less
un/der/tow	un/er/ring	un/heard of	un/like
un/der/value	un/eth/ical	un/help/ful	un/lim/ited
un/der/water	un/even	un/her/al/ded	un/load
un/der/wear	un/event/ful	un/hinged	un/lock
un/der/weight	un/ex/cep/tion/able	un/holy	un/looked for
un/der/went	un/excep/tional	un/hook	un/lucky
un/der/world	un/ex/pected	un/hoped for	un/man/age/able
un/der/write	un/ex/plored	un/hurt	un/manned
un/de/served	un/ex/posed	uni/corn	un/mar/ried
un/desir/able	un/ex/pur/gated	un/iden/ti/fied	un/mask

un/men/tion/able	un/pro/fes/sional	un/seat	un/used
un/mis/tak(e)/able	un/pro/fit/able	un/seen	un/us/ual
un/mit/ig/ated	un/pro/nounce/able	un/sel/fish	un/varn/ished
un/moved	un/pro/tec/ted	un/set/tle	un/veil
un/musi/cal	un/pro/voked	un/sightly	un/wary
un/nat/ural	un/quali/fied	un/skilled	un/well
un/ne/ces/sary	un/quest/ion/able	un/soci/able	un/whole/some
un/nerve	un/quote/ravel	un/soc/ial	un/wieldy
un/no/ticed	un/real	un/so/licited	un/wil/ling
un/num/bered	un/reas/on/able	un/solved	un/wind
un/ob/ser/vant	un/rec/og/niz/able	un/soph/is/ti/cated	un/wise
un/ob/struc/ted	un/re/corded	un/sound	un/wit/tingly
un/ob/tain/able	un/re/fined	un/spar/ing	un/won/ted
un/ob/tru/sive	un/re/lated	un/speak/able	un/work/able
un/oc/cu/pied	un/re/li/able	un/spoilt	un/wor/thy
un/of/ficial	un/re/lieved	un/stable	un/wound
un/op/posed	un/re/mit/ting	un/steady	un/wrap
un/or/tho/dox	un/re/quited	un/stick	un/writ/ten
un/pack	un/re/served	un/stop/pable	un/zip
un/paid	un/res/er/vedly	un/suc/ces/sful	up/braid
un/pal/at/able	un/rest	un/suit/able	up/bring/ing
un/par/al/leled	un/rivalled	un/sure	up/date
un/par/don/able	un/roll	un/sus/pec/ted	up/end
un/pat/ri/otic	un/ruf/fled	un/swerv/ing	up/grade
un/person	un/ruly	un/sym/pa/thetic	up/heaval
un/pick	un/safe	un/tapped	up/hill
un/placed	un/said	un/ten/able	up/hold
un/pleasant	un/sal/ted	un/think/able	up/hol/ster
un/popu/lar	un/sat/is/fac/tory	un/tidi/ness	up/keep
un/pre/ce/den/ted	un/sat/is/fied	un/tidy	up/land
un/pre/ju/diced	un/sav/oury	un/tie	up/lift
un/pre/med/it/ated	un/sav/ory (US)	un/til	up/per
un/pre/pared	un/scathed	un/timely	up/per/most
un/pre/pos/ses/sing	un/scien/ti/fic	un/told	up/pity
un/pre/ten/tious	un/scramble	un/to/ward	up/right
un/prin/cipled	un/screw	un/true	up/rising
un/print/able	un/scru/pu/lous	un/trust/worthy	up/roar
un/pro/duc/tive	un/sealed	un/truth/ful	up/root
		un/us/able	up/set

Hyphen

up/shot	vac/cine	ve/he/mence	ver/mouth
up/side down	va/cil/late	ve/hicle	ver/na/cu/lar
up/stage	vac/uous	vel/lum	ver/ruca
up/stairs	vac/uum	ve/lo/city	ver/sa/tile
up/stan/ding	vaga/bond	ve/lour	ver/si/fi/ca/tion
up/start	vag/ar/ies	vel/vet	ver/sion
up/stream	va/gina	ve/nal	ver/so
up/take	vag/rant	ven/detta	ver/sus
up/tight	vague/ness	vend/ing	ver/te/bra
up/turn	val/en/tine	ven/eer	ver/te/brate
up/ward	vali/ant	ven/er/able	ver/tex
ur/anium	vali/date	ven/er/ate	ver/ti/cal
ur/ban	val/ley	ven/er/eal	ver/tices
ur/bane	val/our	ve/ne/tian blind	ver/tigo
ur/chin	valu/able	ven/geance	ves/icle
ur/eter	value/less	ven/ial	ves/pers
ur/ethra	val/vu/lar	ven/ison	ves/sel
ur/gent	vam/pire	ven/om	ves/ti/bule
ur/inal	van/dal	ven/ous	ves/tige
urin/ate	van/guard	ven/ti/late	ves/ti/gial
ur/ine	va/nilla	ven/tral	vest/ments
us/able	van/ish	ven/tricle	ves/try
us/age	van/ity	ven/tri/lo/quist	vet/eran
use/ful	van/quish	ven/ture	vet/er/in/ary
use/less	van/tage point	ver/acious	vex/ation
ush/er/ette	va/por/ize	ver/anda(h)	vi/able
us/urer	vari/ability	ver/bally	via/duct
uten/sil	vari/ance	ver/batim	vi/brate
util/ity	vari/cose vein	ver/bena	vi/bur/num
util/ize	varie/gated	ver/biage	vic/ar/age
ut/most	vari/ety	ver/bose	vi/cari/ous
uto/pia	vari/ous	ver/dict	vice/re/gal
ut/ter	var/nish	ver/di/gris	vice/roy
ut/ter/ance	vas/ec/tomy	ver/ger/fi/able	vi/cini/ty
ut/ter/most	vat/man	ver/it/able	vi/cious
uxori/ous	vec/tor	ver/mi/celli	vi/cis/si/tude
va/cancy	ve/gan	ver/mil/ion	vic/tim
va/cate	ve/get/able	ver/min	vic/tor
vac/cin/ate	ve/ge/tar/ian		vic/tor/ious

Hyphen

vid/eo/cas/sette	vis/ual	vul/ner/able	war/rant
vid/eo/tape	vi/tal	vul/ture	war/ring
view/fin/der	vit/amin	wad/ding	war/rior
view/point	viti/ate	waf/fle	war/ship
vi/gil/ant	vit/reous	wag/gon	wart/hog
vig/our	vit/rify	wag/tail	war/time
vil/ify	vit/riol	wains/cot	wash/able
vil/lage	vi/tup/era/tion	waist/line	wash/basin
vil/lain	vi/va/cious	wait/ing	wash/bowl
vin/di/cate	viv/id/ness	wait/ress	wash/cloth
vin/dic/tive	vi/vi/par/ous	wake/ful	wash/day
vin/egar	vi/vi/sec/tion	walk/about	wash/down
vine/yard	vo/cabu/lary	walk/out	washer/woman
vin/tage	vo/cal	walk/over	wash/ing
vi/nyl	vo/ca/tion	walk/way	wash/leather
vi/ola	vo/ci/fer/ate	wal/laby	wash/out
vi/ol/ate	vo/cif/er/ous	wal/let	wash/room
vi/ol/ence	voice/less	wall/flower	wash/stand
vi/olet	vol/at/ile	wal/lop	wasp/ish
vi/olin	vol/cano	wal/low	wast/age
vi/ol/on/cello	vo/li/tion	wall/pa/per	waste/ful
vi/per	vol/ley	wal/nut	was/trel
vir/gin	vol/ley/ball	wal/rus	watch/dog
vir/ginia creeper	vol/tage	wan/der	watch/ful
vir/ile	vol/uble	wan/der/lust	watch/ing
viro/logy	vol/ume	want/ing	watch/ma/ker
vir/tual	vol/un/tary	wan/ton	watch/man
vir/tue	vol/un/teer	ward/ress	watch/word
vir/tu/oso	vol/up/tu/ous	ward/robe	water/colour
viru/lence	voo/doo	ward/room	water/course
vis/cera	vo/ra/cious	ware/house	water/cress
vis/cos/ity	vor/tex	war/fare	water/fall
vis/cous	vo/tary	war/head	water/fowl
vis/count	vo/tive	war/horse	water/front
vise/like (Am)	vouch/safe	war/like	water/less/level
vis/ible	voy/age	war/mon/ger	water/logged
vi/sion	vul/can/ize	warn/ing	water/mark
visi/ta/tion	vul/can/ology	war/paint	water/proof
vi/sor	vul/gar	war/path	water/shed

water/side	west/bound	whole/sale	win/some
water/spout	west/ern/ize	whole/some	wire/less
water/tight	west/bound	whop/per	wis/dom
water/way	wet/ness	wick/ed/ness	wise/crack
water/works	wet/ting	wick/er/work	wish/bone
wave/band	whale/boat	wicket/kee/per	wish/ful
wave/length	whale/bone	wide/spread	wis/atria wis/teria
wa/ver/ing	what/so/ever	wid/ow/hood	wist/ful
wax/works	wheat/sheaf	wig/wam	witch/craft
way/farer	wheelbar/row	wil/der/ness	with/draw
way/lay	wheel/base	wild/fire	with/ers
way/side	wheel/chair	wild/fowl	with/hold
way/ward	wheel/wright	wild/life	with/out
weak/en/ing	where/abouts	wil/ful	with/stand
weak/ling	where/fore	wil/lies	wit/ness
weak/ness	wher/ever	wil/ling	wiz/ard
wea/pon	where/upon	wil/low	wiz/ened
wea/sel	where/withal	wil/low herb	woe/be/gone
wea/ther/cock	whet/stone	will/power	woman/hood
wea/ther/man	whim/per	wind/bag	women/folk
wea/ther/proof	whim/si/cal	wind/break	won/der
web/footed	whip/hand	wind/burn	wood/car/ving
wed/ding	whip/lash	wind/cheater	wood/craft
Wed/nes/day	whip/pet	wind/fall	wood/land
weed/kil/ler	whip/ping	wind/lass	wood/pecker
week/day	whirl/pool	wind/mill	wood.shed
week/end	whirl/wind	win/dow	woods/man
wee/vil	whis/ker	wind/pipe	wood/wind
weigh/bridge	whis/key (US)	wind/screen	wood/work
weight/ing	whis/per	wind/shield	wood/worm
weight/less	whistle/stop tour	wind/sock	wool/len
weight/lifter	white/bait	wind/swept	work/able
wel/come	white/wash	wind/ward	work/force
weld/ing	white/wood	win/dow/ledge	work/ing
wel/fare	whit/ing	win/dow/sill	work/man
well/being	whit/low	wine/glass	work/man/ship
wel/ling/ton boots	Whit/sun	wing/less	work/out
wel/ter	whole/hearted	wing/span	work/room
wel/ter/weight	whole/meal	win/now	work/shop

Hyphen

wor/ri/some	xeno/phobe	yes/ter/year	zeal/ous
wor/ship	xylo/phone	Yid/dish	zen/ith
wor/sted	yard/age	yo/del	zig/zag
wrap/ping	yard/arm	yog/hurt yog/urt	Zim/babwe
wreck/age	yard/stick	yon/der	zip/per
wrest/ler	yawn/ing	York/shire pud/ding	zir/con/ium
wrest/ling	year/book	your/self	zod/iac
writ/ing	year/ling	Yugo/slavia	zom/bie
wrong/doer	yel/low	Yule/tide	zoo/logy
wrong/doing	yel/low/ham/mer	yum/yum	zuc/chini
wrong/ful	yel/low/ish	Zam/bia	zwie/back (US)
	yes/ter/day		

Glossary

One cannot make an omelette without breaking eggs, and by the same token one cannot explain punctuation without introducing a few grammatical terms. We have tried to keep these to a minimum, and usually they are explained at their first appearance. However, to get around the necessity of the reader hunting for that first appearance, we have collected the most important terms in this brief glossary. Please note that this is far from being a complete list of terms used in grammar.

absolute construction a phrase that is independent of or isolated from the syntax of the main clause of a sentence. Such constructions often contain a present participle. In the sentence 'The time of the next meeting having been agreed, the committee adjourned its proceedings', the words 'the time of the next meeting having been agreed' form an absolute construction.

adjectival subordinate clause a subordinate clause that functions grammatically as an adjective. Relative clauses are typical adjectival clauses. In the sentence 'Jane is the girl who lives next door', the words *who lives next door* describe the kind of girl Jane is, in the same way as the word *favourite* does in the sentence 'Jane is my favourite girl.'

adjective one of a class of words in a language that denote a certain characteristic or attribute of a noun or pronoun. Adjectives are describing words and can be placed before the noun or pronoun they describe or can be linked to it by certain verbs. The word 'sick' is an adjective in these two sentences: 'Bonzo is a sick dog' and 'My dog Bonzo is sick.'

See also **attributive**. (Note that certain adjectives may be placed directly after the noun they belong to: e.g. 'everlasting' in the sentence 'Through Jesus we may attain life everlasting.'

adverb any of a class of words that restrict or specify the action denoted by a verb or the attribute specified by an adjective. Adverbs can also modify (that is, qualify the effects of) other adverbs or even whole sentences. Examples of adverbs are 'obviously', 'fast', 'very', 'easily', in the sentence 'Obviously, because she was fit, she could run fast very easily.'

adverbial clause a subordinate clause that functions as an adverb within a sentence: for example. in the sentence 'You cannot remain within this society, because you do not wholeheartedly share its views', the last eight words represent an adverbial phrase modifying the rest of the sentence.

adverbial phrase a group of words that lacks a finite verb and functions as an adverb within a sentence. Such phrases often contain a preposition, as in 'down the street' in the sentence 'She ran naked down the street', or as in 'in that case' in the sentence 'In that case, I'll have beans on toast.'

Glossary

affix a combination of letters added to a word or root to make a derived word or an inflected form. For example, the letters *-ly* form an affix that can be added to certain adjectives to produce the corresponding adverbs: e.g. *beautiful* plus the affix *-ly* gives the adverb *beautifully*. The affix *de-* placed in front of a verb or noun produces a word of opposite meaning: e.g. demobilize, de-icer. An affix added to the end of a word is a suffix; one added to the beginning of a word is a prefix.

affix boundary the point in a word between an affix and the word or root that precedes or follows it. In end-of-line hyphenation, one of the principles is that the hyphen should be placed at an affix boundary, as it is for example in the hyphenated words *quick-ly* or *de-mobilize*.

agent person or thing that is the doer of the action specified by the verb in a clause or sentence. In both of the following sentences, the words *my wife Helen* function as an agent: 'My wife Helen bought a new car yesterday'; 'This new Audi was bought yesterday by my wife Helen.'

agent-noun any of a class of nouns formed from words, often verbs, by the addition of a suffix such as *-er, -or, -ist*, etc. Typical agent-nouns are *worker, actor, therapist*, etc.

apposition a grammatical construction in which a noun or a phrase functioning as a noun is placed directly after another noun in order to explain or modify its meaning. In the following sentence, the words 'Britain's prime minister' are said to be in apposition to 'Mrs Thatcher': 'On 14 July, Mrs Thatcher, Britain's prime minister, visited Paris.'

appositional comma a comma, usually one of a pair, that marks off the words that are in apposition to a preceding noun. Note the appositional commas around 'Britain's prime minister' in the example in the previous entry.

attributive (of an adjective or its position in a sentence or clause) directly preceding the noun that the adjective is modifying. In the sentence 'She wore a revealing dress', the adjective 'revealing' is in attributive position.

clause a group of words that consists of a subject, a finite verb, and (usually) a predicate but is not necessarily a complete sentence. The two chief types of clause are the main clause (or *co-ordinate clause*) and the **subordinate clause**.

close punctuation a type of punctuation marked by liberal use of punctuation marks, especially commas. Close punctuation can lead to excessive use of such stops as the comma and is now generally regarded as unhelpful and old-fashioned. *See also* **open punctuation**.

comma fault a punctuation error noted by some writers in the United States in which a comma is used to link two independent clauses in a sentence instead of a semicolon. *See* the chapter on Comma.

comma of address a comma (often one of a pair) used to mark off the name of a person being addressed from the rest of the sentence; for example, in the sentence 'Come in, John, and meet the other guests', the commas around 'John' are commas of address. Also called a vocative comma.

common collocation a phrase or group of words that follows a set pattern or word order and is in common use but is not normally classed as an idiom. Typical common collocations are 'fish and chips' and 'in abeyance'. *See* **idiom**.

compound word a word made up from two or more existing words, e.g. *bloodstream* (from *blood* and *stream*). Compound words may or may not be written with a hyphen. *See* the chapter on Hyphen.

conjunction any of a class of words that serve to connect two or more words, phrases or clauses. *See* **co-ordinating conjunction; subordinating conjunction**.

conjunctive adverb an adverb or adverbial phrase that functions like a conjunction in that it connects what has gone before with the following clause or sentence. Typical conjunctive adverbs are however, moreover, in addition, in that case, etc. *See* the chapter on Semicolon.

co-ordinate clause one of two or more clauses in a sentence that share the same level of importance within the sentence and are connected by co-ordinating conjunctions. *See* **co-ordinating conjunction**.

co-ordinating conjunction a type of conjunction that serves to introduce a co-ordinate clause. Typical co-ordinating conjunctions are *and, but, either, for, neither, nor. See also* **subordinating conjunction**.

defective question a question that is an elliptical or grammatically incomplete sentence; this is a term employed in this book but is not in general linguistic use. A typical defective question might be 'The gate? What gate?'

direct question a straightforward question ending in a question mark. The sentence 'Do you like oranges?' is a typical direct question.

direct speech the verbatim quotation of what someone said. Such a quotation is enclosed within quotation marks. For a full explanation of direct speech, *see* the chapter on Quotation Marks.

direct statement a straightforward sentence that is neither a question nor an exclamation and is therefore followed by a full point. *See* the chapter on Full Point.

elliptical connected with or resulting from ellipsis (of sentences, questions, etc.) and so condensed that the sentence is grammatically incomplete and the full meaning has to be supplied from the context.

finite verb a verb that appears in a form that has an ending showing the grammatical features by which it is linked to its subject in a sentence. These features include number (that is, whether the subject is singular or plural), person (that is, whether

Glossary

the subject is in the first, second or third person) and tense (that is, whether the action described by the verb is in the past, present or future tense).

gender any of up to three categories to which the nouns of a language may belong. In modern English, gender is generally correlated with sex, so that all male animate things (*man, boy, ram,* etc.) are classed as masculine, all female animate things (*woman, girl, ewe,* etc.) are said to be feminine, and all inanimate things (*chair, book, cup,* etc.) are considered to be neuter. Some English nouns, such as *car* and *ship*, are sometimes regarded as feminine and take the feminine pronoun *she*. In languages other than English, and in older stages of the English language itself, gender is a purely grammatical classification based on such criteria as the endings that different nouns have. German has three genders: masculine, feminine and neuter. But French and the Celtic languages (e.g. Welsh and Irish) have only two: masculine and feminine.

genitive case a form of pronouns and certain nouns that denotes possession, ownership or some other form of association usually indicated by the word *of*. In Old and Middle English, masculine and neuter nouns added the suffix *-es* to form their genitive cases, and this form survives as the *'s* still used today but now extended to feminine nouns too. *See* the chapter on Apostrophe.

gerund a verbal noun that indicates an action or state and ends in *-ing*. Although a noun, the gerund retains its verb's ability to take an object, as in the sentence 'Killing him will be easy; getting away from the scene will be virtually impossible.' It is easy to confuse the gerund with the present participle, which also ends in -ing but functions as an adjective. In the sentence 'Jane's walking down the street with Tony made me very angry', the word 'walking' is a gerund because it denotes an action performed by Jane. *See also* **participle**.

grammar the whole body of rules that seeks to account for the way in which a language works, classifying its linguistic forms (nouns, verbs, adjectives, etc.) and describing the ways in which they are used in sentences and the changes to which they may be subjected. Linguists also use the word grammar to mean the system of rules by which a person can get to know and speak his or her native language. In its most modern usage, the word grammar denotes an abstract system of rules that generate or produce all the sentences of a language that are recognized as being correct by the native speakers of that language.

grammatical of or concerning **grammar**; in accordance with the rules embodied in the grammar of a language. A grammatical sentence is one that is considered to be correct in its observance of such rules.

hyphenate to spell a word with a hyphen or to use a hyphen to divide a word at the end of a line when there is not enough room to get the whole word in.

hyphenation and justification the process of laying out typed or printed matter on a page so that the lines of text align with each other on both the left- and the right-hand sides and, if necessary, words are divided at the end of a line to ensure that the spaces between the words are as even as possible. Hyphenation and justification are usually carried out by means of a special computer program on word processors and typesetting machines, known colloquially as an H & J program.

idiom a phrase or group of words whose meaning as a whole is different from what one would expect as a result of considering the meanings of the words individually. Typical English idioms are the phrases 'rain cats and dogs' and 'be up the creek without a paddle'.

independent clause a clause that can stand alone and form a complete sentence. Pairs of independent clauses that are linked by a logical connection rather than a conjunction are normally set off from each other by a semicolon. *See* the chapters on Comma and Semicolon.

indirect question a question contained in a noun clause that is the object of a verb of asking and is cast in the form of a statement. A typical indirect question is the sentence 'She asked him who he was.' *See* the chapters on Full Point; and Question Mark and Exclamation Mark.

indirect speech the reporting of someone's words through a recasting or paraphrase of them rather than by means of direct verbatim quotation. Also called **indirect discourse** or **reported speech**. *See* the chapter on Quotation marks.

interjection any of a class of words that are used to express an exclamation or a sudden outburst of emotion. Interjections are normally thought of as being outside the main pattern or structure of the sentence and often used to render a loud noise of any kind. *See* the chapter on Question Mark and Exclamation Mark.

intransitive verb a verb that is not usually followed by an object. Typical intransitive verbs are *come*, *go*, and *struggle* in their straightforward meanings. *See* **transitive verb**.

linguistic form any word, clause or sentence, or any part of these, that can be isolated for grammatical analysis or for the study or learning of a language.

linguistic unit a word or group of words that denote a single concept. The term covers such locutions as 'old man' or 'young woman'. This is a non-technical term not generally used by linguists.

main clause the principal clause of a sentence, which can in fact stand on its own. In 'I saw a man who said his name was Jim', the words 'I saw a man' represent the main clause and form a grammatically complete sentence.

masculine one of the genders of nouns, usually correlated in modern English with male animate things. *See* **gender**.

modify to alter or limit the effect of (a sentence, noun, verb, adjective or adverb). In the sentence 'He fights bravely', the adverb 'bravely' modifies the verb 'fights'.

Glossary 234

neuter one of the genders of nouns, usually correlated in modern English with inanimate things. *See* **gender**.

non-specifying relative clause a type of relative clause that does not define the noun to which it refers but serves to add extra information about it. Non-specifying clauses are set off from the rest of the sentence by one or two commas. In this sentence, the commas mark off a non-specifying relative clause: 'The polar bear, which can weigh up to 450 kilograms, is ferocious.'

noun any of a class of words that denote people, places, living and non-living things, and abstract concepts. In English, nouns can be subdivided into countable nouns, such as *cat, bicycle, door*, etc.; uncountable, or mass, nouns, such as *sugar, disbelief, absent-mindedness*, etc.; and proper nouns, denoting people and places, such as *Suzanne, Fred Smith, London*, etc. Nouns are often preceded by a linguistic form called a determiner, which includes the definite article *the*, the indefinite article *a* (not used with uncountable nouns and rarely with proper nouns), and the possessive forms *my, your, his, her, its, our* and *their*. Nouns and their respective determiners are referred to by modern linguists as noun phrases and can be the subject (or agent) of a verb as well as the object of a transitive verb.

noun clause a subordinate clause that functions within a sentence like a noun and can be either the subject or object of a verb. A subordinate clause introduced by *that* after a verb of saying is typical of the modern noun clause.

onomatopoeic words words such as *crash, splash, bang*, etc., which are conceived of as imitating a sound.

open punctuation a relatively sparse use of punctuation marks, especially commas. The tendency in late 20th-century English has been to use open punctuation and to reduce the number of marks even more.

parenthesis a word, phrase, or clause that interrupts but does not belong to the structure and logic of a sentence. *See* the chapters on Comma, Dash and Parentheses.

parenthetical characteristic of, concerning, contained within, or representing a **parenthesis**.

participial phrase a phrase containing a present or past participle The phrase may or may not be part of an **absolute construction**. In the following sentences, the italicized portions are participial phrases: 'I saw Jane *lying on my bed*'; '*Jim having resigned*, the task of running the company was given to Tom.'

participle an adjective formed from a verb. Participles can show tense in modern English but not person or number. Past participles usually end in *-ed*, but there are many old irregular forms, such as *spoken*, from the verb. *speak*. An example of a past participle is *smashed* in the sentence 'He found the vase smashed to pieces on the floor.' Present participles end in -*ing* and can be confused with a gerund. In the sentence 'The sight of Jane walking down the street with Tony made me very angry', *walking* is a present participle because it is an adjective modifying the noun 'Jane'. *See also* **gerund**.

period fault excessive use of the full point where other lighter punctuation marks would be more appropriate. This is an error recognized chiefly by United States writers. *See* the chapter on Full Point.

phrase any group of words lacking a finite verb. Phrases often lie outside the main sentence structure and are consequently parenthetical word-groups set off by commas.

points of suspension another name for an ellipsis. *See* the chapter on Ellipsis.

possessive case another name for the **genitive case**.

preposition any of a class of words that are placed in front of a noun or noun phrase in order to establish a link between the noun phrase and some other part of the sentence. In 'The book is on the desk', the word 'on' is a preposition that links the words 'desk' and 'book' and in so doing specifies the whereabouts of the book.

prefix *see* **affix**.

punctuation mark any of the symbols used to denote pauses or break points in a sentence. Punctuation marks include the comma, semicolon, colon, full point, and dash. Exclamation and question marks are technically not pause marks, but tones of voice written down.

quotation a phrase or passage from a book, play, speech or piece of conversation or dialogue that is presented word-for-word within quotation marks. *See* **direct speech** and the chapter on Quotation Marks.

relative clause an adjectival clause, introduced by *who*, *which* or *that*, which serves to modify a noun, known as the antecedent. Relative clauses can be either **specifying** or **non-specifying**.

reported speech another name for **indirect speech**. *See also* **direct speech** and the chapter on Quotation Marks.

reporting clause a clause such as 'he said', 'she asserted', as used with direct **quotation** or **indirect speech**.

restrictive comma a comma (often one of a pair) that adds information by which a preceding word is restricted, specified or narrowed down, as in this sentence: 'He went to university at Cambridge, Massachusetts.'

rhetorical of or concerning rhetoric as an art form, the use of language or discourse to persuade, elucidate, influence or entertain. The word is used in grammar to describe a kind of punctuation that is designed to achieve a certain rhetorical effect.

Glossary

The use of the term rhetorical has been extended to cover dramatic and stylistic effects in punctuation. Modern punctuation has moved away from such devices, which often lead to the overuse of punctuation marks.

salutation the phrase used to address the recipient at the beginning of a letter, as in 'Dear John', 'Dear Sir', 'Sir', etc.

sentence a series of words that can stand alone to make a declaration, issue a statement or command or to ask a question. It usually consists of a subject, a predicate and a finite verb. A typical sentence begins with a capital letter and ends with a full point, question mark or exclamation mark. *See also* the chapter on Full Point.

sentence modifier an adverb or adverbial phrase that modifies a whole sentence. An example of a sentence modifier is the word 'admittedly', as in 'Admittedly, he was confused at the time.'

specifying relative clause an adjectival relative clause that defines or specifies its antecedent. Specifying relative clauses are not set off by commas. The words in italics in the following sentence form a specifying relative clause: 'The cows *that are good producers of milk* are not sent to the abattoir; the rest are slaughtered for their meat.'

stop any of the punctuation marks that were used to mark a pause. Traditionally, they include the full point, colon, semicolon and the comma. Some people also include the question mark and the exclamation mark, but strictly these are not stops but tones.

subordinate clause a clause that cannot stand on its own but serves as an adjective, noun or adverb relating to parts of the main clause. The subordinate clause in italics in the following sentence is an adverbial clause telling us when the action of the main clause took place: '*While I was getting an ice cream*, a gang of boys stole my bicycle.'

subordinating conjunction a conjunction that introduces a subordinate clause. Examples are *because, if, until, while*.

suffix *See* **affix**.

syntactical of or concerning syntax. In relation to punctuation, the term refers to the use of punctuation marks to set off one syntactical element from another inside a sentence.

syntax the grammatical arrangement of the words in any given sentence of a language, or the rules or system that governs such an arrangement.

tag question a short question added onto the end of a sentence to confirm the truth of the sentence by requiring an expected answer. Thus *isn't she?* in 'She's Welsh, isn't she?' is a tag question that invites the answer 'yes', thereby confirming the truth of the assertion.

transitive verb a verb that usually takes a noun, noun phrase or noun clause as an object, as in 'He bought a blue car', in which bought is the past tense of *buy*, a transitive verb. Other such verbs are, for example, *take, spread, throw, make, prove*, and many more. *See* **intransitive verb**.

verb any of a large category of words that denote the occurrence or performance of an action or the existence of a state or condition. Typical verbs are *sit, jump, throw*, etc. In modern linguistics, a verb phrase is the whole of the sentence following the subject noun phrase.

vocative comma another name for a **comma of address**.